# GRAMPIAN

# GRAMPIAN

*A country in miniature*

**ROSS LECKIE**

**CANONGATE**

# JORDANHILL COLLEGE LIBRARY

First published in Great Britain 1991 by Canongate Press Plc, 14 Fredrick Street, Edinburgh.

ISBN 0 86241 343 5

Designed by Dorothy Steedman, Almond Design
Map of Grampian by Andras Bereznay

The Publishers gratefully acknowledge copyright permission granted from the following sources for
the right to reproduce photographs in *Grampian a Country in Miniature*

*Jonathan Basan*, **colour**: 10, 14/15, 15 top and foot, 19, 22, 23, 26 left and right, 27, 28 top, foot, 29,
32, 35, 58, 62, 63, 75, 79, 102, 103, 111, 114, 115; **monochrome**: 20 top, foot 21, 24, 25 top, foot,
30, 48, 49, 53, 69, 76, 97 top 101, 104, 105 top, foot. *Bill Marshall*, **colour**: 2/3, 11, 18, 54/5, 78,
82, 91, 95, 99, 106, 123, foot; **monochrome** 80 top. *Old Scotland in Pictures*, **monochrome**: 12, 13,
40, 57, 74, 80 foot, 92, 93, 97 right, 98 top and foot. *Phil Banks*, **colour**: front cover, 47, 67, 70,
122. *Alan Gawthorpe*, **colour**: 50, 83, 86, 99. *Douglas Shirran*, **colour**: 38, 71, 79, 126. *Royal Botanic
Garden Edinburgh*, **colour**: 118, 123, top; **monochrome**: 121. *Still Moving Picture Company*, **colour**:
126, 127; **monochrome**: 61. *John MacPherson*, **colour** backcover, 94. *Jim Inglis*, **colour**: 39:
**monochrome**: 36; *Grampian Region Council*, **monochrome**: 31, 72. *Aberdeen Journals*, **monochrome**:
135. *Aberdeen Art Gallery and Museums*, **colour**: 131. *City of Aberdeen*, **monochrome**: 100. *Ross Leckie*,
**colour**: 87. *National Galleries of Scotland*, **colour**: 134. *National Library of Scotland*, **monochrome**:
128. *Cordelia Oliver*, **colour**: 130.

Front cover photograph: the River Spey in spate near Grantown, by Phil Banks
Title page photograph: Glen Dee by Bill Marshall
Back cover photograph: Heather and pines, Cairngorm Mountains, by John MacPherson

Typesetting and black and white origination by Almond Design, Edinburgh
Colour Origination by Gorenjski Tisk, Kranj, Slovenia
Printed and bound in Great Britain by Eagle Colour Books, Blantyre

*for my children,*
*Douglas, Xenia and Patrick*

# ACKNOWLEDGMENTS

This book, more one of synthesis than originality, has been long in gestation. I acknowledge with thanks many midwives: my friend and agent, Charles MacLean; Elizabeth Langlands, lately of Drumtochty Castle, Auchenblae; the book's editor, Ghillie Basan and her husband Jonathan for his photographs; Stephanie Wolfe Murray and Neville Moir of Canongate who know about vicissitudes; my employer, Willis Coroon plc, and especially Roy Matthews, Frank McCarron and Susan Morgan; the much enduring Alistair Findlater; then, some amongst many, those who encouraged, inspired or criticised: Anna Bisewska, Ian Shepherd, Ian Cameron, Paddy and Catherine Imhof, Geordie Burnett-Stuart, Ian MacNab, Marion Nagahiro, Jim Inglis, Robbie Shepherd, Christopher Cox. The librarians and museum staff of Grampian were unfailingly helpful. But, above all and always, I thank the people of Grampian whose lives remain an inspiration. Any mistakes in this book are mine; any good is theirs.

ROSS LECKIE
*Monymusk, Summer Solstice 1991*

# CONTENTS

# GRAMPIAN
*A country in miniature*

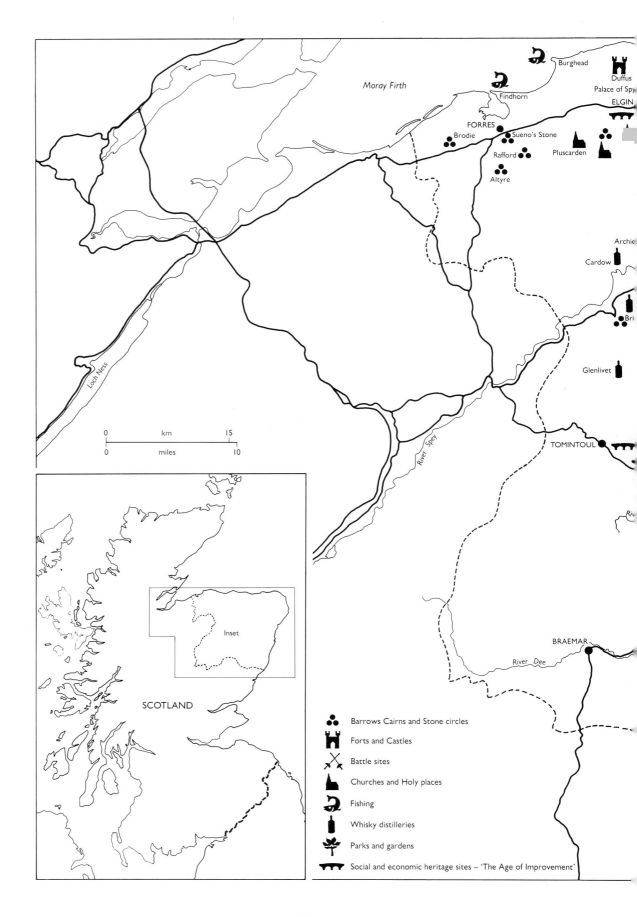

Moray Firth

Burghead

Duffus
Palace of Spy

ELGIN

Findhorn

FORRES

Brodie · Sueno's Stone

Rafford

Pluscarden

Altyre

Archie

Cardow

Bri

Glenlivet

Loch Ness

km        15

miles      10

River Spey

TOMINTOUL

Riv

Inset

BRAEMAR

River Dee

SCOTLAND

Barrows Cairns and Stone circles

Forts and Castles

Battle sites

Churches and Holy places

Fishing

Whisky distilleries

Parks and gardens

Social and economic heritage sites – 'The Age of Improvement'

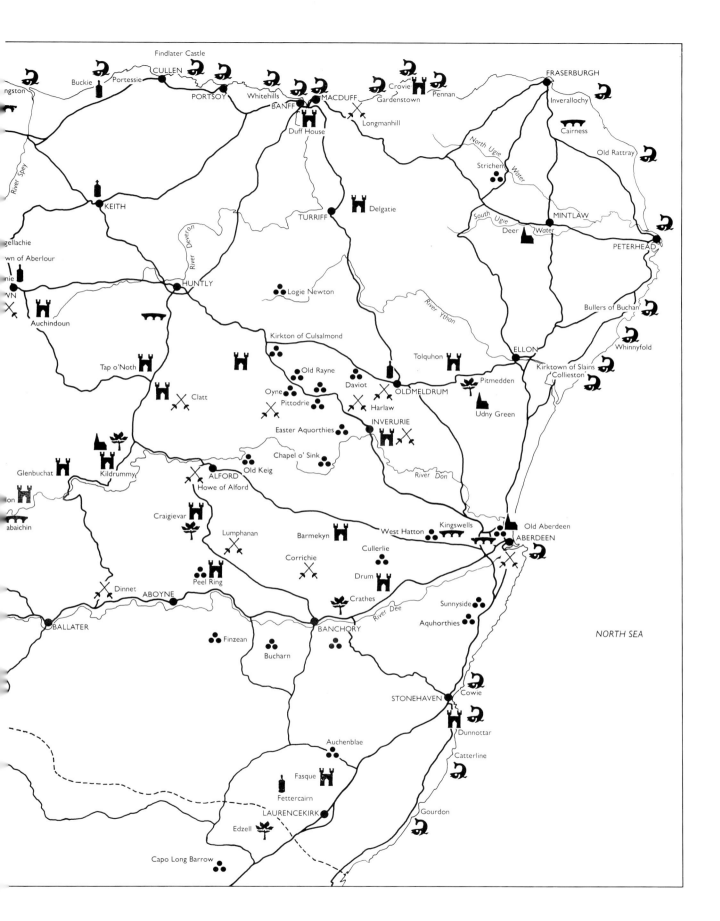

# GRAMPIAN: AN INTRODUCTION

*Sed transgressis immensum et enorme spatium procurrentium extremo iam litore terrarum... But when you go further north you find a huge and shapeless tract of country, jutting out towards the land's end...*
*– The Roman historian Tacitus (c. 55–120 AD), describing Grampian. (Agricola, chapter 10.)*

Grampian is, in a sense, an artificiality: the region came into being as a political entity only with Edward Heath's "regionalisation" of 1975. But if that process was laboured elsewhere in Britain, in Grampian it served merely to formalise that which was already the case. For this arrow-shaped land, jutting out into the grey North Sea and naturally bounded to the south and west by mountains, to the north by great firths and rivers, has always been both physically and culturally distinct from the rest of Scotland, "on the way to no-where but itself, its people quietly, sometimes dourly self-sufficient... a country in more than miniature." (IAG Shepherd.)

These characteristics were recognised by Tacitus, the first to write about Grampian: his character Calgacus, chief of the "Caledonii", says before the battle of *Mons Graupius*: "Nos terrarum ac libertatis extremos recessus ipse ac sinus famae in hunc diem defendit; atque omne ignotum pro magnifico est. We, the last men on earth, the last of the free, have been shielded till today by the very remoteness and seclusion for which we are famed. Unknown, we have been regarded as formidable." (*Agricola*, chapter 30.)

Grampian takes its name from the great spine of mountains, the *Grampians*, which define both its natural and its regional boundary to the west: Tacitus' "Graupius" was mis-spelt as "Grampius" by Hector Boece (pronounced *bo-ees*), colleague of Erasmus and first principal of Aberdeen University, in his 1527 Latin *Historia Gentis Scotorum* (*History of the Scots Race*). The mistake has never been rectified.

In physical terms alone, Grampian is formidable: composed of the four former counties of Kincardine, Aberdeen, Banff and Moray, its 3,400 square miles (8,800 square kilometres)

form 11.3 per cent of the Scottish landmass and rise in stepped plateaux from the coast to the high Cairngorm mountains. The land itself is of great antiquity, combining with the region's many pre-historic remains to produce a sense of the past that is unrivalled by any other Scottish region. For unlike the rest of Scotland, Grampian's bedrock has remained largely unchanged for over 10 million years. The great ice-sheets that so changed the Western Highlands had relatively little impact on Grampian, leaving only such thin surface deposits as survive around Elgin, between Rosehearty and Peterhead, between Cruden Bay and Aberdeen and which coat the valleys and hill-sides of the Cairngorms.

*The high Cairngorms*

Five distinct areas make up the region. Beginning in the south, the rich red sandstone soil of the Mearns reaches up to the steep hills of the Mounth which form an older and more natural southern boundary for Grampian than its present one, the river North Esk. Next, Deeside defines the long land through which the river Dee passes from its source high above *Braemar* to its mouth at Aberdeen. It has been immortalised as "Royal Deeside" in the wake of Prince Albert and

# GRAMPIAN
*A country in miniature*

*Balmoral Castle,
circa 1920*

Queen Victoria's love for the area, continued since by the House of Windsor whose attachment to *Balmoral* and Grampian is well-attested. Rolling and fertile, Grampian's heartland is the Garioch (pronounced *Gee-ree*, possibly from the Gaelic *garbhthach* for "rough ground") which embraces the rivers Don and Ugie and extends westwards to encompass Insch and Rhynie. Fourthly, Buchan pushes into the North Sea to the north of the river Ythan and reaches west into the valley of the river Deveron. Finally, Moray is the area enclosed by the great rivers Spey and Findhorn. In contemporary terms, the region consists of five districts, (Kincardine and Deeside, Aberdeen, Gordon, Banff and Buchan, Moray) each distinguished by much more than district boundaries on a map.

The region's climate is as varied as its topography: the lowest temperature and the highest windspeed ever recorded in Britain have been recorded in Grampian. The rivers of the Laich of Moray flood often and ferociously; the Cockbridge to Tomintoul road is infamous for being so quickly and regularly blocked by snow. Yet Moray has more hours of winter sunshine than London;

the region's rainfall is well below the national average and her lowlands regularly record Britain's highest daily temperatures. Her farmlands and her gardens are amongst the best in the land.

Matching such diversity, Grampian contains a great range of industries. This has long been the case: a deputation from the Scots Parliament visited Grampian in 1694 and marvelled at the "range of commerce so much pursued and so ably effected". Agriculture, fishing and boat and ship building have gone on here for centuries. Aberdeen's Hall Russell shipyard may have closed; agriculture and fishing may live in troubled times, but all are still at the root of Grampian's economic vibrancy. Despite quotas and "set-aside", agriculture still accounts for 8 per cent of Grampian's economic activity, compared with 4 per cent for Scotland and 2 per cent for the UK, whilst Grampian's fishermen now catch and land over 80 per cent of the total Scottish catch.

As it always has been, Grampian is the heart of Scotland's thriving whisky industry, more and more of her fine single malts sold as such to a growing market. Another industry long-established in Grampian and now fully adapted to the international market-place is paper-making. The Grampian mill that made the paper for the penny edition of the *Doomsday Book* is the same mill that today produces the world-famous Conqueror paper. As it has for centuries, weaving and cloth-making thrive in Grampian: the company whose gloves kept Confederate soldiers' hands warm in the American Civil War is now the largest producer of knitted gloves in the western hemisphere. As they have done for years, such members of Russia's Politburo as survive still wear Crombie coats, made in Grampian.

Further afield in the region, forestry is a major force and affords some check on rural depopulation. Some 15 per cent of Grampian, 120,000 hectares, is now under commercial forests: a staggering 10.7 million cubic metres of conifers and 2 million cubic metres of broadleaved trees represent 22 per cent of Scotland's conifers and 15 per cent of her broadleaves. Not all, mercifully, stand in bleak and regimented rows. The mixed planting on the braes of Glenlivet is exemplary; the Scots and Corsican pine forests at Culbin and Roseisle in Moray not only afford pleasant walks but check the blowing of Moray's light soils. The many gorges of the river Findhorn are much enhanced by mixed ash, beech and oak.

Tourism has become a major part of Grampian's economy. The region's tourist boards have been innovative, establishing Scotland's only Whisky, Victorian Heritage and Castle Trails, soon to be followed by a unique Stones and Archaeological Heritage Trail. Two of Scotland's four skiing centres are in Grampian, whilst the region has long been a mecca for hillwalkers and climbers. As for golf courses, Robert Price is clear: "there can be nowhere else in the world where the basic simplicity of the game has been retained amidst such delightful landscapes." (*Scotland's Golf Courses.*) There is one golf course in Grampian for each week of the year, and more being built, to satisfy every taste and ability. As for other sports, Grampian is equally happy welcoming the fisherman and the wind-surfer, the hang-glider and the water-skier, the balloonist, the ornithologist and the sailor.

Cultural life is vigorous: Aberdeen's His Majesty's Theatre, built in 1904–8, is a "banquet of Edwardian exuberance" (WA Brogden) and universally regarded as the finest small theatre in Britain. Scottish Opera are regular and welcome visitors to His Majesty's. Aberdeen's Music Hall hosts many concerts, whilst there is a profusion of small but interesting arts centres throughout the region, complementing its many local museums.

But if all this variety in an adaptive and innovative region has been the product of evolution, the discovery in 1969 of oil off Grampian's coast brought a revolution. The "black gold" soon dominated the region's economy and changed the physical appearance of, at least, the coastward land. A remote and self-regarding region, always rightly proud of itself and its peculiarities, had almost overnight to absorb the economic, social, physical and cultural ramifications.

The capacity of Grampian's response has yet adequately to be chronicled. Little of what has been done had been done before; oil was drilled for and then piped ashore in one of the harshest environments ever known to man, from depths that had hitherto been regarded as impossible, with technology that marked new bounds. From having no oil, in 1980 Britain became a net exporter and by 1984 was ranked as the world's fifth largest oil producer. In 1974, 13,500

*The market square, Huntley, circa 1905*

*The Ladder Hills in snow*

Scottish jobs were related to North Sea oil: by 1985, there were 52,000 oil-related jobs in Grampian alone. A remarkable £90 billion in oil revenues since 1979 has been used or abused, depending on your point of view, by Her Majesty's grateful governments.

There have been setbacks: the dramatic fall in the world oil price in 1986 saw exploration cease and production fall. Perhaps as many as 15,000 jobs were lost as companies economised desperately. Then on 6 July 1988 the gas compression unit on the platform Piper Alpha exploded. The world was scarred by pictures of an ineluctable holocaust and traumatised by the terrible deaths of 167 trapped and burning men.

Grampian drew on her old resilience. As the oil price rallied and then stabilised, the industry went back to work. Estimates of recoverable reserves of oil are constantly being revised upwards. With many of the North Sea's oil fields viable at even $4.50 a barrel, the oil industry will dominate Britain's and Grampian's economy for

*Left: Scots Pine, Moray.
Below:The Cabrach road
in winter*

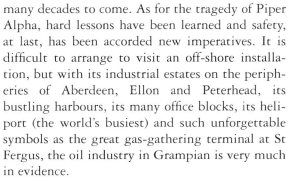

many decades to come. As for the tragedy of Piper Alpha, hard lessons have been learned and safety, at last, has been accorded new imperatives. It is difficult to arrange to visit an off-shore installation, but with its industrial estates on the peripheries of Aberdeen, Ellon and Peterhead, its bustling harbours, its many office blocks, its heliport (the world's busiest) and such unforgettable symbols as the great gas-gathering terminal at St Fergus, the oil industry in Grampian is very much in evidence.

## GRAMPIAN
*A country in miniature*

New or old, Grampian's industries have in common one of the region's enduring strengths: her people. Travelling through Grampian in 1764, the antiquarian Alexander Carlyle noted that "the people here are more acute and livelier than in other parts of Scotland." In 1967, one of Grampian's most distinguished Members of Parliament, Bob (Lord) Boothby, echoed Carlyle, observing that "though proud of their tradition of independence, the people of the north-east are justly famed for their interest in and openness to the wider world."

The virtues of innovation, initiative and energy that have characterised Grampian's response to the challenge of oil have long been the marks of her people. RW Thomson (1822–73), the son of a Stonehaven merchant, invented amongst other things the pneumatic tyre, the fountain pen and the portable steam crane. When a Strathdon postman of the 19th century wanted to speed up his rounds, he simply added a motor to his bicycle. Known as the "Craigievar Express", it is preserved in the Alford Transport Museum. The marriage of Janet Anderson to an Aberdeenshire minister, John Gregory, early in the 17th century founded a family which was to produce 16 professors and was cited by Francis Galton in his classic work *Hereditary Genius* as an example of the inheritance of scientific gifts. The family included Professor James Gregory, inventor of the reflecting telescope and another James who created the mainstay of the 19th-century plant nursery, Gregory's Mixture.

As is appropriate for a region whose university founded, in 1523, the first Chair of Medicine in the English-speaking world, Grampian's doctors have been and remain distinguished. Sir James McGrigor was schooled at Aberdeen Grammar School and read medicine at King's College. He then bought a post as an army surgeon, serving under Wellington in the Peninsular War and earning the Iron Duke's commendation as "one of the most industrious, able and successful public servants I have met". He went on to found the Army Medical Corps. Another "local loon" knighted for his services to medicine was the "Father of Tropical Medicine", Patrick Manson, born at Old Meldrum in 1845. A third was Sir Alexander Ogston, Professor of Surgery at Aberdeen University, who in 1881 discovered the pus organism. JJR Macleod, Professor of Physiology at Aberdeen from 1928 to 1935, is a name well known to diabetics for his pioneering work on insulin.

Other men and women distinguished Grampian abroad. John Strachan (pronounced *Strawn*), Bishop of Toronto, was born and educated in Aberdeen. In 1826 he founded a university in his diocese, calling it "King's College" after his *Alma Mater.* Of the hundreds of Christian missionaries that Grampian sent forth, Mary Slessor (1848–1915) is perhaps best known. In 1908, Thomas Blake Glover of Aberdeen was the first non-Japanese to be awarded the Order of the Rising Sun for his services to Japanese industry. The mansion he built himself still stands over Nagasaki harbour. India owes its first tea plantations to Hugh Falconer of Forres (1808–65), latterly Professor of Botany at Calcutta. Mary Garden was born in Aberdeen in 1874 and died at Inverurie in 1967. Between times, she was a distinguished singer and actress, paid $125,000 by Sam Goldwyn for ten days' filming in 1916. The village of Peille near Monte Carlo has a square and an avenue named after her. Modest and self-effacing, she declared in her autobiography: "I began my career at the top, I stayed at the top and I left at the top."

It is a particular charm of Grampian that her people now are as vibrant as they have always been. There is a strong sense of common identity, reflected for example in the region's devotion to its media: if the region's newspaper, the *Press and Journal*, is parodied abroad it is almost universally read at home. Sixty per cent of Grampian's inhabitants are regular listeners to the region's local radio station, North Sound. Aberdeen's *Evening Express* is Britain's most popular evening newspaper: 78 per cent of Grampian's households buy a copy.

There survives in the region an intangible spirit of independence, an attitude of mind that even the many "incomers" brought by oil have responded to. Much of this must come from Grampian's tongue, the *Doric*, a dialect of Lowland Scots that is pervasive in a way unmatched by any other British region. The language of Grampian's poets and novelists – Charles Murray, Lewis Grassic Gibbon (JL Mitchell), George MacDonald, William Alexander, Jessie Kesson – is one which began in 1375 with John Barbour's great epic poem *The Bruce* and which lives on today not only in the Doric poetry competitions of Grampian's schools but in her fish and cattle markets, her lawyers' offices and oil citadels.

Secondly, perhaps, the character and ability of Grampian's people is maintained by the region's long-standing commitment to education. A Headmistress or Headmaster is still, in Grampian, a "domine", even if the National Curriculum and the demise of Latin recognise neither the language nor the vocative case. Despite the traumatic effects of massive cuts in the funding of Aberdeen University, Grampian retains a sense of the worth of education epitomised by the Papal Bull of 1494 which established King's College: "Among the blessings which mortal man is able to obtain, not least is that he may win the pearl of knowledge which shows the way to living well and happily."

This spirit lives on in a remarkable range of educational and research institutes: the Institute for Terrestrial Ecology, the Torry Marine Laboratory, the Rowett Institute, Craibstane Agricultural College, the Robert Gordon Institute of Technology, Grey's School of Art, the world's first and only Hyperbaric Centre and, surviving despite draconian reforms, Aberdeen University. Reflecting the changes brought by oil, Grampian has an American School, a Dutch School, a French School. All contribute to Grampian's having the highest graduate workforce in the United Kingdom.

The quintessence of the "north-east folk" lies in self-deprecation. There is no better articulation of the nature of Grampian's people than her own contemporary comedians, the "Scotland the What?" team, successors to a long tradition of north-east comedians like 19th century's Harry Gordon, the "Laird of Inversnecky". Buff Hardie, Steve Robertson, George Donald and Jimmy Logan epitomise with their outrageous humour the Grampian spirit that would never call a spade an agricultural implement. They repudiate years of tartan bathos – Sir Harry Lauder, Donald Stewart, banks and braes and model "Hieland Coos", sold in gift shops and made in Taiwan – this perversion of a people destroyed at Culloden and "tartanised" by Sir Walter Scott. "Scotland the What?"'s version of *The Highland Soldier*, for example, is a refreshing antidote: "There was a

plumber, a Scottish plumber, no finer plumber than he, to mend your WC..." Their Sandy Thomson, from "Auchterturra", may be trying to ring his brother-in-law in Clatt, but gets Ronald Reagan on a crossed line when he isn't ringing Buckingham Palace with the greeting, "Is that you, Beldy?"

Such humour is a fitting tribute to the remarkable people of an unforgettable region. This book seeks to chronicle some of the vast variety of a region of great contrasts that is, nonetheless, always a whole and, somehow, always the sum of its parts. Each chapter concludes with a suggested itinerary: one of Grampian's many pleasures is that many of the sites in these itineraries are not easily found. Thus Ordnance Survey co-ordinates are given for each site. Grampian region is covered by OS maps 27, 28, 29, 30, 36, 37, 38, 43, 44 and 45, all readily available from newsagents and bookshops. Each OS reference in this book has three parts: the first two letters give the 100,000 square metres in which the site lies; of the three numbers that follow the letters, the first two give the nearest vertical line on the map to the left of the site. The third number estimates the distance in tenths from that line to the site. Of the next group of three numbers, the first two identify the horizontal line below the site. The third number once more estimates that line's distance in tenths from the site.

Visiting these sites can only reinforce the spirit of Grampian that has been reflected, most recently, in the endeavours of "Aberdeen Beyond 2000" and "The Grampian Initiative". Both groups are devoted to ensuring that Grampian's virtues are better known, virtues epitomised in a shepherd I met in Ellon. He had come there from the Cabrach, that moorland between Rhynie and God, to shop and to visit his sister. When I expressed the hope that he was enjoying himself, he paused, drew himself up, looked four-square at me and replied: "Laddie, a day awa frae the Cabrach's a day wastit." During the harsh winter of 1985, I asked a Strathdon farmer how he was getting on. "In a good year," he said, "we warstle thro' somehow. And a bad year doesna mak the warstle mickel waur." It is for such as these that this book is humbly written.

*Deeside, the land of the stones*

# BARROWS, CAIRNS, STONES AND CIRCLES OF THE MOON

*Grey recumbent stones of the*
*dead in desert places,*
*Standing stones on the vacant*
*wine-red moor*
*Hills of sheep and the homes*
*of the silent vanished races,*
*And winds, austere and pure.*
                    —RL Stevenson (1850–94)

The earliest known inhabitants of Grampian were hunter-gatherers who had followed the retreating ice-cap north into the region perhaps as much as 8,000 years ago. Theirs was a nomadic life, based on the cycles of the plants in the forests and the fish in the rivers. Grampian's first settled people, around 4000 BC, were farmers who may have come to the region by crossing the sea from mainland Europe and passing easily into this isolated land by way of its rivers, the Esks, Dee, Don, Ythan, Deveron and Spey. Growing wheat and barley, raising sheep and cattle, these were peaceful people, drawn to a rich and fertile land. The many barrows and cairns that they have left us bear witness to their social cohesion, their perception of themselves as groups, rather than as individuals, as do the remains of their timber halls such as Balridie on Deeside (approx. 3500 BC), a substantial house or barn for an extended family of farmers.

Around the middle of the third millennium BC these mesolithic peoples of Grampian built henges (ceremonial enclosures surrounded by a circular earth bank and then a ditch). The best surviving example is Broomend of Crichie, 2 kilometres south of Inverurie beside the A96. The size of this site and the finds of urns, axes and bones point to its having been a major and complex ceremonial centre. A particular tragedy of Broomend has been the destruction of its great avenue of standing stones, running south from a now destroyed stone circle to the henge and on for 400 metres to the river Don. The avenue would have been some 18 metres wide with 36 stones on each side. Three remain. Another fine henge is Wormy Hillock in the Clashindarroch Forest at NJ 449 307.

An equally impressive communal monument of Grampian's third millennium is the stone circle and, in particular, the unique "recumbent stone circle", found nowhere else in the world. In these, a large recumbent stone lies horizontally between two, flanking uprights. The rest of the circle is formed, usually, by 10 graded standing stones.

Although often containing sites of burial, these henges and circles had more complex uses than their cousins, the barrows and cairns. Like a village hall and church rolled into one, they were the focus of their communities' religious and ritual life. A Gaelic speaker, asking a neighbour if he is going to church, might still say, *"Am bheil thu dol do'n clachan* – Are you going to the stones?"

In western Grampian, the dominant monument was not the recumbent stone circle but the Clava cairn circle, so called from the complex of these circles at Clava, near Inverness. Although these circles seem to have been used strictly for burial, they do share the distinctive attributes of the recumbent stone circles, such as their use of quartz or their orientation towards the south-west. They represent, as it were, the marriage of the earlier tradition of cairns to that of recumbent stone circles. Once again, they are quite unique – chambered tombs set inside stone circles are found only in Grampian. Given the marked similarities of the Clava cairns to Irish monuments such as New Grange, it is probable that the Clava circles combine two traditions: that of mesolithic man from the West, sailing up

*Logie Elphinstone*
*Pictish symbol*
*stones*

# GRAMPIAN

*A country in miniature*

*Newton Pictish stones: the undeciphered Ogham script*

Loch Linnhe from the Irish Sea and following the Lochy valley to settle on the Inverness plain, and that of the builders of recumbent stone circles from the East.

In the second millennium, a new wave of farmers came to Grampian, the Beaker People, men of the early Bronze Age from the mouth of the Rhine. They are so named because of the characteristic pottery they brought with them. They continued to build circles of stone, although theirs were smaller and often without a recumbent stone, as well as being less regular in shape. Similarly, although the Beaker People also buried their dead in cairns, theirs were smaller than those of their neolithic predecessors, reduced in size to the "kerb cairn". Beaker Man was buried singly, in a crouched position, the "beaker" from which he takes his name beside him. (An outstanding example of a beaker-burial and cist from Catterline, Aberdeenshire, now lies in the Marischal Museum, Aberdeen.) Tall, square-jawed and broad-faced, he is still thought by some to be the antecedent of the native Grampian stock. Others think that "Beaker Man" is something of a mirage: that no actual "Beaker People" came to Grampian: the Beaker tradition was a religious cult of mainland Europe that was adopted by the indigenous people of Grampian.

By about 1200 BC, this society of the stones was supplanted by the coming of the Celts, able warriors and assiduous farmers of a strongly hierarchical society. Whether they came from the south of Britain, or whether, like their predecessors, they came from mainland Europe, remains unknown. There is certainly evidence that at least some north European Celtic-speakers came to Grampian in the last millennium BC. The Roman historian Tacitus, for example, records that the Caledonii encountered by the Romans differed but little from the rest of the Britons or Gauls in language, religion or ritual. These Celts left behind them great forts and defended settlements (see chapter 4) before the emergence of Pictish society towards the beginning of the first millennium AD. Pictish civilisation, caught between the Viking raids that began around 900 AD and the absorption of the Pictish kingdoms by the Scottish kings of Dalriada in Argyll, passed away in its turn, but not before it had ensured the enduring curiosity of men by way of the many sculpted stones that are its unique and poignant memorial.

The relationship, if any, that exists between the many stones and cairns of Grampian and those of mainland Europe or, indeed, the rest of the

*Standing stones, Insch, Aberdeenshire*

world, remains a matter of conjecture. Megaliths (from the Greek, meaning "big stones") like those in Grampian are found across the world, from Japan to India to Scandinavia. Their greatest concentration – some 50,000 separate constructions – lies in a broad swathe from Scandinavia to Italy and includes the British Isles. The "hyperdiffusionists" believe that all these monuments are related, from the great, conical burial grounds of the North and Central American Indians to the cairns of Grampian, from the avenues of Carnac to those of Callanish, from the megalithic "graph paper" of Mid Clyth, Caithness to the solar calendars of the Incas and the Aztecs.

Many theories have attempted to explain these strange testaments to the genius of man. Dr William Stukely, an 18th-century clergyman and historian, was the first to recognise their importance and object to the ritual mutilation of the stones that the Church, in those days, was encouraging. Men like "Stone Killer Robinson", a Methodist lay preacher, believed stone circles to be the works of the Devil and devoted his life to their "utter extirpation". In Grampian, men of the cloth were more moderate and many were fair antiquarians, recording the destruction of stones. Of the Haerstanes Circle near Lhanbryde in Moray (NJ 274 607), the Rev James Morrison wrote: "These stones were unfortunately found to lie in the line of a road then formed, and were ignominiously tumbled down the slope on which for ages they had rested, and buried in a gravel pit by the side of the road." A Rev A Chalmers recorded the 1872 destruction of the circle at Gaval in Buchan: "The recumbent stone was of enormous dimensions and the destroyers shattered it with gunpowder."

It was hardly surprising that when, in the early 1900s, FR Coles travelled the length and breadth of Grampian at the behest of the Society of Antiquaries of Scotland to record such stones as had survived, his account was often chilling: "Throughout this once so richly stored district [Buchan], scarcely one object now remains tangible to the archaeologist." As recently as 1976, such destruction continued: the earthen long barrow at Roseisle in Moray (NJ 149 670), 49 metres long and 20 metres wide, was removed in order to grow even more barley for EEC food mountains. It is a bitter irony that the field in which the barrow stood has now been taken out of production

and is in "set aside". A 6,000-year-old barrow was destroyed for 12 years of unwanted grain.

Yet it is to Grampian's credit that, on occasion, stones were spared. The fine circle in the graveyard of Midmar Church (NJ 699 064) is an example: far from being destroyed, it was "Christianised" and incorporated within the 1914 graveyard.

The well-known theory that these prehistoric sites are all linked by "ley lines" was first advanced in 1921 by a sucessful beer salesman and amateur historian, Alfred Watkins, who "saw a web of lines linking the holy places and sites of antiquity. Mounds, old stones...stood in exact alignment." Anyone who has stood at a Grampian circle such as Daviot or Old Keig and marvelled at the situation will be sympathetic to Mr

*Stones at Candlehill, Old Rayne*

*A ley road?
Many roads in
Grampian follow
ley lines*

Watkins, even if many of his critics thought that his profession had impaired his judgment. There are many plausible ley lines in Grampian; even the most cursory examination of the Ordnance maps of the region is revealing. Many of the stones stand on clear lines, such as that running absolutely straight from the Sunhoney circle (NJ 715 056) east to the mouth of the Dee.

Another explanation is that of the "astro-archaeologists". Again, Dr Stukely began the idea by observing that the axis of Stonehenge was aligned precisely towards the north-east sky, where the sun rose at summer solstice. Then, in the 1930s, a Scotsman called Alexander Thom, Professor of Engineering at Oxford University, began a meticulous study of Britain's megaliths that was to be his life's work. He argued that all the stones and circles were aligned to facilitate the study of the moon, sun and stars and advanced the idea that the stone circles were constructed using the "megalithic yard", a standard unit of 2.72 feet. Going even further, Thom believed that these "primitive" men had worked out the Pythagorean theorem, hundreds of years before the Egyptians.

Insufficient research has been done on Grampian's stones for any one interpretation to be absolute. Yet the knowledge of the sun, moon and stars that we know other early peoples to have possessed makes Thom's theories eminently plausible. His studies of Grampian's stone circles remain seminal, even if some find his approach too exclusive of others and inadequate to explain some of the more mysterious qualities of such stones as the Iron Stone at Cairnie (NJ 531 456) which rings when hit by a hammer.

What is certain is that Meso and Neolithic man in Grampian and throughout Europe made good use of the sun, moon and stars. For the early farmers of Grampian, only the moon provided a fixed measure of time, apart from the very short measures of day and night. So they developed a means of measuring time – the stone circle – to assist them in foretelling the seasons, in knowing when to plant their crops. When Julius Caesar recognised that the Druids in Gaul had "much knowledge of the stars and their motion, of the size of the world and of the earth, of natural philosophy", he was commenting on a science that was already, in Grampian, thousands of years old.

There can be little doubt that, whatever other purposes these circles served, they were indeed Circles of the Moon, ingenious lunar observatories. Several sites have "cup marks" on one or more of their stones, possibly to mark particular phases of the moon's cycle. Again a link to the moon, the milky-white stone quartzite is often in great evidence at Grampian's stone circles, either as a complete block (memorably at Balquhain, NJ 735 242) or in seams or, in flakes, scattered over the site.

As for barrows and cairns, these early tombs survive as mounds of earth or cairns of stone, usually wedge or oval in shape. The word "barrow" is from the Aryan *bhergh*, meaning a mound of earth over a grave; "cairn" comes from the Celtic *carn* or the Gaulish *karnen*, meaning a heap of stones. What barrows and cairns hold in striking common is their location – on a hilltop or skyline, or on the edge of an elevated terrace. So situated, they must have been symbols of common pride and identity. Perhaps, too, they served as territorial markers, visible to neighbouring communities and to those approaching by land or sea.

What remains most extraordinary is the effort, the skill and co-operation that the construction of these monuments must have required, especially given the short life of Neolithic man – perhaps only thirty years. The labour, then, must have spanned several generations and occupied a great part of each society's time and resources. The Dalladies barrow, for example, is estimated to have required 0.73 hectares of turf and 600 man-hours: so great that we must assume it and others like it to mark the graves of chiefs or holy men.

Less mystery surrounds the function of the Pictish standing stones, though little is known of the Picts (called *Picti*, or "painted ones" by the Romans) and even less of the strange symbols – combs and discs, mirrors and animals – that they carved so painstakingly. Most of the stones they have left behind them were erected as commemorative monuments, either for the dead, or for victory in battle or for a marriage and clan alliance. Why many of these stones stand on sites of earlier ritual importance remains an enigma, whilst the ogham script (a 4th-century Irish alphabet) that can be seen on several of Grampian's Pictish stones (eg Newton House, NJ 662 297 and Auquhollie, NO 823 908) remains undeciphered.

Grampian's Pictish stones fall into three, distinct groups: the first, from approximately 400–600 AD, contains rough boulders or rudely dressed stones, incised with crude but striking animals or abstract patterns. Those of the second period, 600–800 AD, are carved with much greater sophistication, in relief. Those of the third period from 800 onwards show, in addition to the pagan symbols, the Christian Cross, often interlaced with intricate Celtic patterns. These crosses illustrate the increasing influence of Christianity in Grampian after the famous meeting between the Pictish King Bridei and Saint Columba around 560 (see chapter 2).

At its simplest, then, the history of the many stones of Grampian lies within the following approximate framework:

4000–3000 BC  Barrows and Cairns (Mesolithic Man)
3500–2000 BC  Henges and Circles, Clava Cairns (Neolithic)
2000–1200 BC  Stone Settings, Kerb Cairns (Beaker People)
1200–200 AD  Celts- Forts (Iron Age).
200–1000 AD  Pictish Symbol Stones.

Grampian, then, provides a microcosm of the pre- and early history of Scotland and of Europe. Whether or not one agrees with Daniel Defoe (1660–1731): "All that can be learned of them is, that there they are," the sheer number and quality of Grampian's stone relics make the region a place of primary importance and afford the visitor an unparalleled opportunity, a window to the past.

## BARROWS AND CAIRNS

**Bucharn Round Cairn**, Strachan, Kincardine and Deeside

NO 659 929, Map 38 or 45. 5km SW of Banchory. 1.5km W of village of Strachan, turn N off B976 and onto single track road. After 1km, park at road fork (for Glendye Sewage works) and walk E for

*The hills of the Mounth from Bucharn Round Cairn*

0.6km along farm road, through Bucharn farm steading, along field edge to cairn.

The setting of this great, gaunt cairn is spectacular, with its massive, open views to S, E and W over the vastness of the Mounth, its curves blending with those of the great hills beyond it. The cairn of bare stones is 27m in diameter and 4.5m high. Since it has never been excavated, no-one knows whether or not it contains a chambered tomb or cist. Standing conspicuously on the edge of a hill terrace, here would have been a fitting resting-place for a man great in his lifetime. One km to the NE, at NO 668 933, stands another cairn of similar size. Such groupings are common, both to cairns and to stone circles.

Rejoining the B976, note the Motte of Castlehill of Strachan, just to the SE of the road junction. This was used as a hunting lodge between 1250 and 1350 by the Giffards, an Anglo-Norman family.

## Capo Long Barrow, Stracathro, Kincardine and Deeside

NO 633 664, Map 45. 9km NNE of Brechin. Turn W off A94 at bridge over the North Esk (sign-posted Fettercairn and Edzell) and then immedi-ately left (sign-posted Gannochy and Edzell). After 1.6km, turn left along track. Park after 300m. Barrow to N of track, on forest edge.

This fine barrow is one of several ancient burial sites in the vicinity (NO 615 633; 611 651; 644 673). A similar barrow at Dalladies, 1.1km NNE, was excavated in 1971 before it was destroyed by gravel quarrying. Composed of earth and turf, Capo Long Barrow is 80m long, 28m wide at the ENE and 2.5m high. On its low terrace above the river North Esk, it might well have marked a territorial boundary or a burial place.

## Finzean Long Cairn (pronounced *Fing – en*), Marywell, Kincardine and Deeside

NO 591 937, Map 37. 13km NW of Banchory, off B976 from Banchory to Aboyne. Park in layby at War Memorial to the Men of Birse and walk W along clear track. After 160m, turn SW along smaller track (second on your left). Follow this main track along the brow of the hill for approx. 300m to cairn.

This is the best preserved of the hundreds of mesolithic cairns in Grampian even though it only received official recognition as recently as February 1989 by being scheduled and protected as an ancient monument. It is an astonishing construction, both for its remarkably steep profile and memorable setting, on a hill crest between the rivers Feugh and Dee, despite the regiments of conifers that surround it and block the view. Its dominating position makes it easy to interpret this wedge-shaped cairn as both a funeral site and some kind of boundary marker. The cairn, 3.5m high and 33m long, varies in width from 26m at the ENE to 9m at the WNW. There are smaller cairns and tumuli on the adjacent hill at NO 614 945.

## Logie Newton Kerb Cairns, Kirktown of Auchterless, Banff and Buchan.

NJ 659 391, Map 29. 13km E of Huntly, between B9001 and Ythanwells. Park at old quarry, 0.5km west of junction for "Wells of Ythan" at Logie Newton farm. Walk up track past old quarry to ruined house and then NNE along field edge for 1km to cairns, eminently visible throughout.

On even the darkest of days, the milky quartzite of these cairns shines out from the southern side of Kirk Hill and draws the eye towards them. The commanding view from these cairns, S to Bennachie and the Mounth, over the

*Cullerlie stone circle, Echt*

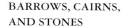

*Easter Aquorthies
stone circle, Inverurie*

rich farmland of Buchan to the E, is alone sufficient reward for the brisk walk to them. Three cairns, 27, 24 and 17.5m in circumference, survive in a line of some 40m and stand in harmony with the graceful curve of the hill behind them. Their survival, in a landscape of agricultural improvement, is remarkable.

Just as stone settings and "four-poster" stone circles (rough circles formed by 4 standing stones) are the later descendants of the recumbent stone circles, kerb cairns like these represent the end of the tradition of cairn burial. Instead of a great ring cairn, like Loanhead of Daviot, the size has diminished; the tradition has been refined. The use of quartzite points to the relationship between such kerb cairns and the earlier recumbent stone circles and Clava cairns.

The Logie Newton cairns have never been excavated. It is likely, though, that they contain cists or cremation pits. There is no sign of actual cairns within the kerbed circles; rather, the interiors are flat. Perhaps the cists or ashes were simply buried and covered with earth, the quartzite circle around them sufficient testimonial. A menhir stands in the field to the SE below the cairns. According to FR Cole's sources in 1902, the menhir was "removed from one of these circles and set up...to mark at that spot the discovery of an urn containing human bones". The cairns afford a marvellous view of the site of the Roman marching camp of Ythan Wells on the hill to the S (NJ 655 382).

**West Hatton Long Cairn**, Kingswells, Gordon.

NJ 851 070, Map 38. 10km W of Aberdeen. Turn N off A944 just after Five Mile Garage, sign-posted "Blackburn". After 1.2km, park at track entrance at top of hill and walk 100m across field to cairn.

Overlooked by pylons and itself overlooking the dormitory of Westhill, this despoiled cairn remains a formidable monument, turning its side away to the far hills as if unconcerned by the ravages of modernity. The fine stone dykes in the nearby fields explain its present low height of 1.8m, but it was originally 54m long with a maximum width of 17m. Its northern edge is still well-kerbed. Although unexcavated, locals main-

tain that a cist was once found within it. Coles records that "many years ago, a cist was found in the cairn and the slabs removed to make a roadside water-trough, subsequently moved to Wester Hatton where they cannot now be located."

*Easter Aquorthies
recumbent and
flankers, Inverurie*

# CIRCLES OF THE MOON

*In the times of King Mainus...huge stones were erected in a ring, the biggest of them...on the south side to serve for an altar...Who so sees them will assuredly marvel by what mechanical craft or by what bodily strength stones of such bulk have been collected to one spot.*

–Hector Boece,
*History of Scotland*, 1527.

**Auchquhorthies**, Portlethen, Kincardine and Deeside

NO 902 963, Map 45. 1km S of Portlethen, turn NW onto side road sign-posted "Cairnwell". After 1.3km, turn S down farm track, sign-posted Aquhorthies. Park just after bend in track and walk 200m E across field to circle.

Like its near neighbour, Old Bourtree Bush, 400m to the SE, this recumbent stone circle is memorably situated with wide, open views to the sea. The name comes from the Gaelic for "stone circle in a field". Including the recumbent stone and one surviving flanker, 13 stones make up the circle's 82m circumference and are graded in height with the northern stones much smaller. Most are of reddish, but now very weathered, local porphyritic granite, whilst the recumbent stone and its flanker on the W are of a coarse-grained,

blue-grey granite, again locally quarried. As often, these dominant stones have seams of white quartz, associated with the moon. The recumbent stone is relatively small, weighing 10 tonnes, but stands exactly on the circle's SW.

Two features of this circle are unusual: the recumbent stone stands well within the circumference of the standing stones rather than forming part of the circumference; it seems, then, to have been part of the inner platform. This is a peculiarity of Kincardineshire circles, a deviation from the "norm" of the circles of central Aberdeenshire. Secondly, the mound on which the circle stands extends for some 14m beyond the recumbent stone. These and other factors point to Auchquhorthies' being late in the tradition of recumbent stone circles, built around 1700 BC and developing from the older "prototype" circles of Aberdeenshire.

Although the interior of the circle is badly damaged, the inner circle of stones is clearly seen and delineates a kerb cairn. Excavations of the inner circle in the 1850s and 60s produced a cist containing ashes, an urn and "half calcined bones".

**Candlehill**, Broombrae, Old Rayne, Gordon

NJ 679 280, Map 38. 1km SE of village of Old

*Esslie the Greater stone circle, Banchory*

Rayne, 13km NW of Inverurie off A96. Turn off A96 into Old Rayne and take the first road to the SE after 500m. The circle lies beside this road, to the north, after 800m. A more spectacular, if less easy, approach is to cross the ford of the river Urie from the A96 S of Old Rayne and approach the circle from the S along a road remarkable for its straightness.

*Hatton of Ardoyne stone circle*

Ruined, but still recognisable as a recumbent stone circle, Candlehill is worth visiting for its views to the peaks of Bennachie and over the fertile Garioch. The circle was excavated by Dalrymple in 1856. Before then, there were 12 standing stones with three cup-marks on the recumbent stone.

Only one gaunt, fang-like flanker, 3.2m high and 1.4m broad, has defied the march of agricultural progress to remain proud and standing, part of a circle that was perhaps 26m in diameter. Excavations in the circle's central pit revealed a "reddish urn" and a fragment of an archer's wristguard.

Locals relate that the circle, formerly known as Tap o' Mast, was used as a seat of justice – Henry

II is known to have held Assizes here, continuing a long tradition for this place of power. Prior to 1856, the recumbent stone, together with two pillars and a fourth slab had been arranged to form two sides of a parallelogram, whose two other sides were dry-stone walls, forming a medieval courthouse.

### Chapel o' Sink, Blairdaff, Gordon

NJ 706 189, Map 38. 4.5km NW of Kemnay. Turn E off minor road from Blairdaff to Chapel of Garioch along track just N of Blairdaff. Follow track for 1km and park at Westerton farm. Walk N up hill along field, then forest edge for approx. 850m. Circle stands 200m to E of forest edge. Alternatively, park at Newton farm on east of forest and force your way due NW through dense larch and birch and brashings!

This gentle little circle is ample reward for those determined enough to find it. Lying low, half-hidden and forgotten in the dim reaches of a dark wood, it is easily missed but, once found, always remembered. It catches the breath and quickens the heart, a place for sprites and fairies.

The diminutive stones form a circle 15m in diameter. Three, side by side, in the SW quadrant perhaps perpetuate the tradition of a recumbent and flankers and are orientated towards the Mither Tap of Bennachie. Now darkened and cowering under moss, they are carefully matched in their small size and, rectangular in shape, different to the circle's other jumbled stones. A vague lump in the centre of the circle may mark the remains of a ring cairn.

Obvious similarities to the smaller and later stone settings of Kincardineshire and to the smaller, non-recumbent circles of Buchan and Morayshire probably identify this circle as late in the stone circle tradition, perhaps around 1500 BC. Like Backhill of Drachlaw (NJ 672 463) or Image Wood, Aboyne (NO 524 990), it may mark the transition between the recumbent stone circles of the third millennium and the stone settings of the second.

### Craighead, Hillside, Kincardine and Deeside

NO 912 977, Map 45. 2km NW of Portlethen. Take minor road W off A92, sign-posted "Maryculter". After 1.6km and opposite turning to N for Banchory Devenick, park at chicken farm on S of road. Walk S down track past chicken farm for 300m. Circle in field to W.

# GRAMPIAN
*A country in miniature*

*Loanhead of Daviot stone circle and ring cairn, Inverurie*

*Loanhead of Daviot stone circle and ring cairn, Inverurie*

Open to the wonder of all on its hill above the sea, this is an enigmatic circle, some 8m in diameter, of four standing stones on a dyked mound. The stones stand almost N, S, E and W on the compass, implying a possible 18th-century reconstruction. The circle once boasted a flagpole. The iron rings to which guy ropes for the pole were attached are still on the stones.

The stones are all of local, reddish granite, with veins of quartzite in the N and W stones. They reduce in height from 2.3m in the S to 1.2m in the E in a way typical of the later tradition of "Four Poster" circles. Perhaps Craighead was nearer in time and ancestry to such eight-stone circles as Cullerlie. Others prefer to see an influence from further S in Scotland, remarking on the similarities between the smaller circles of Grampian, like Craighead, and those even smaller four-posters of Perthshire. Yet it would seem more probable that the tradition moved from N to S, the size of the circles and the tenacity of their SW orientation diminishing as it went.

## Cullerlie, Garlogie, Kincardine and Deeside

NJ 785 043, Map 38. 15km W of Aberdeen. Turn S off B119 at Garlogie and, after 250m, fork SE. Circle on E side of road after 1km.

Now in the care of the Secretary of State for Scotland, this gem of a site is the result of sensitive restoration and proof of what a little maintenance can do. It exemplifies the tradition of stone circle building after the "golden age" of recumbent stone circles. Its eight stones form a ring 10.2m in diameter, within which are eight small kerb cairns. The largest of these, in the centre, is 3.4m in diameter and has a double kerb. Like six of the other cairns, it has 11 kerbstones.

The site was thoroughly excavated in 1934 by the archaeologist H Kilbride-Jones. His findings shed valuable light on the construction and use of the circle. First, the site had been levelled; the eight stones and the cairns' kerbstones set in place; willow branches were placed within the circle and burnt, their ash settling at the base of the stones and around the kerbs; cremated bone was deposited in seven of the cairns and the stones of the cairns placed on top to complete the work. The cairn to the W of the central cairn contained a fire-pit covered by a capstone.

A late development of the tradition of recumbent stone circles, Cullerlie's primary function seems to have been funereal. Its situation, on a ridge of gravel in the low plain of Leuchar Moss, is unusual.

### Easter Aquhorthies, Inverurie, Gordon

NJ 732 207, Map 38. 3km W of Inverurie. Turn W along Blackhall Road at roundabout at N of town. After 2km, drive straight on at junction up minor road (sign-posted). Park at top and walk SE up track for 100m then turn W for circle.

Beautifully restored and maintained by the Scottish Development Department, like its near neighbour Loanhead of Daviot, this recumbent stone circle is a classic of its type and, probably, an early one. Easter Aquhorthies is almost perfectly circular; as the tradition of circle-building declined, circles became egg-shaped or eliptical. Like its Portlethen namesake in the older spelling "Auchquhorthies", the name is from the Gaelic for "stone circle in the field".

Although its setting is now marred by a plantation on the SW, the circle stands in a dominating position on its hill crest, its views characteristically wide and open. The circle, 19.5m in diameter, is composed of nine standing stones which reduce in height from the 2.25m tall flankers on the SW to the smallest in the NE. The recumbent stone is 3.8m long; two large, throne-like blocks are set at right angles to it. The stones stand irregularly along the length of a low bank, showing the circle, perhaps, to be a development of the henge. A lump under the thick turf is all that remains of the circle's central cairn. Excavation in 1934 uncovered a cist within the cairn.

The most fascinating and unexplained aspect of this circle is the variety of stone it displays. Why were different types of stone used? The recumbent stone is of a reddish granite veined with quartz and quarried near Bennachie. The stone's outer face has been carefully and laboriously smoothed. The two flankers shine in the light as if made of quartz. The stone next to the eastern flanker is a glowing red jasper and the others of a pinkish porphyry, blue-grey granite and the greenish-black colouring of whinstone.

Professor Alexander Thom attributed particular astronomical functions to these stones. If you stand in the centre of the circle, the stone two stones W of the recumbent has the same shape as that of the Mither Tap of Bennachie, clearly seen to the NW.

### Esslie the Greater, Banchory Ternan, Kincardine and Deeside

NO 717 915, Map 45. 4km S of Banchory. Leave Banchory on B976, cross the Dee and take first turning E to cross the river Feugh. Turn S at fork after bridge and fork SW (right) after 300m. After 1.8km fork SE (left) and then turn right at T junction after 2km. Circle in field to W after 500m.

When FR Coles surveyed this circle in 1900, he found seven standing stones, two flankers and a recumbent stone. There are now five, plus the recumbent group, forming this elliptical circle, 26.5m by 23.2m, and varying in height from 1.5 to 0.8m with the smallest, as normal, opposite a recumbent stone which is 2.9m long and weighs 8.5 tons. Like other Deeside recumbent stones, this one lies slightly E of S. From stones he found

*Recumbent and flankers, Old Keig stone circle, Aberdeenshire*

# GRAMPIAN
*A country in miniature*

*Logie Elphinstone Pictish stones, Pitcaple*

lying near the circle, Coles deduced that the original circle had at least 10 standing stones, plus the recumbent group. Ian Shepherd, the Archaeolo-gist for Grampian Regional Council, believes that the original circle was built, like Cullerlie, with eight standing stones.

The circle encloses a ring cairn of 18m in diameter. A report on the 1873 excavation of the circle recorded: "a stone kist was found, if we may call it one, built of common boulder-stones little more than half a foot, i.e. from 8 to 10 inches in diameter...In the grave were found black marks and pieces of bone, but no more."

On a shoulder 20m higher, 0.8km to the NE, stands another recumbent stone circle, Esslie the Lesser. It has been mangled, used as a tip for stones cleared from the fields and much dug into. In memorable language, FR Coles deplored "those ineffective, half-hearted diggings, productive of nothing but hallucination and hearsay, that have occurred here also plentifully". Yet Esslie the Lesser remains impressive, sharing with the Greater wonderful views to S and W.

## Hatton of Ardoyne, Oyne, Gordon

NJ 659 268, Map 38. 15km NW of Inverurie. Fork W off A96 onto B9002, 10km NW of Inverurie. Go through village of Oyne and, in 2km, turn N onto minor road. After 400m, park and walk E up track for 300m to farm, Hatton of Ardoyne. Circle to E of steading, 300m across field.

Standing on the hill known locally and appropriately as the Hill of Parnassus (the mountain home of the Greek gods), this recumbent stone circle seems to sit on the top of the world, far removed from the frenzy of the 20th century. It is a place to rejoice in nature, open and free on all sides. The best way to appreciate its situation is laborious but worthwhile: 1km W of Oyne, turn N onto the minor road opposite the turning to "Back o' Bennachie". Park and walk along the track under the railway bridge, past the farm and then NW uphill along the field edges. En route, an astonishing menhir, the Petmathen Stone, stands squarely hewn, some 2m tall and orientated to the SW.

Of the circle, only one flanker, the recumbent

stone and two standing stones are left relatively unscarred by agriculture and ignorance. The outline of the circle, 24.4m in diameter, is clear. The recumbent stone forms a platform within the circumference of the stones and the remains of an inner ring cairn are still obvious. Excavations in 1856 revealed a beaker urn and cremated bones. The reddened stones attest the intense heat of funeral pyres within the circle.

### Lagmore West Clava Cairn, Ballindalloch, Moray

NJ 176 358, Map 28. 11km SW of Abelour. Turn S off A95 just before its junction with the B9137, sign-posted Kilnmachie, Shenval and Chapel-town. Park in layby 400m on left. Walk S up hill through field for 130m to circle.

This is the only known passage grave of the Clava type in Grampian and worth visiting for this reason alone, quite apart from its dramatic situation high above the meeting of the Avon and the Spey. The cairn is 12m in diameter and 1.2m high, with its entrance passage on the south formed by two stones which project beyond the kerb. The internal burial chamber, now blocked, is 3.3m in diameter.

Of the stones that form the circle, 16.5m in diameter, round the cairn, only four still stand, the tallest at 2.3m on the W. In his book, *The Stone Circles of the British Isles*, Aubrey Burl argues that this circle may have been aligned to the planet Venus, rather than orientated to midwinter sunset or midsummer setting of the moon.
Beside the main road below, 300m to the E, stand what little is left of the Lower Lagmore standing stones, encircling what was very possibly another passage grave.

### Loanhead of Daviot, Inverurie, Gordon

NJ 747 288, Map 38. 7km NW of Inverurie. Just N of Inverurie, turn N off A96 onto B9001, sign-posted Rothienorman. After 5km, turn E for Daviot. Go N through village. Circle to E after 500m.

Like Easter Aquhorthies this site, described by FR Coles in 1902 as "this sequestered and umbrageous nook", has been well restored and is beautifully kept by Historic Buildings and Monuments, marred only by a tree plantation which blocks the view to the SW. A leaflet by Ian Shepherd, Grampian Region's Archaeologist, describes this important site in exemplary detail and is readily available at Tourist Information Offices.

Eight standing stones, graded in height in the normal way, join two flankers and the 12-tonne recumbent stone to make up this circle. The second stone to the E of the recumbent bears five cup-marks. Most of the circle's interior is taken up with a well-kerbed ring cairn which was found to contain cremated bone and flakes of flint.

Immediately SE of the stone circle is a later, bronze age cremation cemetery, similar to those found in the Scottish Borders. Excavations in 1934 uncovered the cremated bones of 31 people, eight of whom were children, in the enclosure. The remains of the New Craig recumbent stone circle, 800m to the NW at NJ 745 296, its recumbent and flanking stones incorporated into a dyke, are well worth visiting.

### Old Keig, Keig, Gordon

NJ 596 193, Map 37. 4km NNE of Alford. Turn NW off B992 Whitehouse-Insch road, sign-posted Lethenty, at Keig crossroads. After 2km at top of hill park at old quarry on E side of road and walk S down through field alongside shelter belt of beech trees for 300m to circle.

*The Rhynie Man, Pictish symbol stone, now in the foyer of Grampian Regional Council, Aberdeen*

# GRAMPIAN
*A country in miniature*

Standing hidden and mysterious, as if guarding some great secret, this circle lies in perfect accord with the beauty of the Howe of Alford and the magic of the Coreen and Ladder hills beyond. Two flankers, the recumbent stone and one other bear witness to a circle that was 20m in diameter and contained an eccentric ring cairn. The recumbent stone, a vast hewn block of sillimanite gneiss that was quarried near Kemnay, 10km away, is the largest known. It weighs 53 tonnes and measures 4.9m x 2.1m x 2.0m. We can only marvel at the labour entailed in installing this megalith, rolling it for the last km up a gradient of 1:14, just as we can only wonder at what was so special about this stone as to justify so monumental an endeavour.

Old Keig was first dug into before 1692 and continued to be much disturbed. In 1932 and 1933, the archaeologist Professor VG Childe carried out a scientific excavation, finding sherds of pottery, a piece of an armlet and flint-scrapers. His work, expanded by Kilbride-Jones and recorded in the Proceedings of the Society of Antiquaries of Scotland, sheds valuable light on

*Pictish symbol stone, Newton, Insch*

the way these vast stones were erected: sockets were dug for each stone and packing stones slipped under the stone after each levered lift until the stone slid into its hole. The stones were carefully shaped and trimmed to make their erection easier, for example, by making their bases pointed.

## Strichen House, Banff and Buchan

NJ 936 544, Map 30. 15km NW of Peterhead. 1.3km S of Strichen, turn W off A981 onto unmarked road and bear Rt. Park at steading and walk past E side of house, up through field for 400m to circle.

The poignancy of this abandoned circle, approached by way of the vast and sombre shell of Strichen House, is unforgettable, as are the views it affords over Buchan, clear to all points of the compass. Yet Dr Samuel Johnson, that great man of letters, was not impressed. In his *Journey to the Western Islands of Scotland* (1773), he records: "We dined this day at the house of Mr Frazer of Streichton, who shewed us in his grounds some stones yet standing of a druidical circle, and what I began to think more worthy of notice, some forest trees of full growth." Nonetheless, the story of this circle and its survival is extraordinary.

In 1810, the tenant farmer pulled all the stones down; forced to re-erect them by the laird, Lord Lovat, he botched the job, re-creating the circle to the S of its original site and placing the recumbent stone on the northern arc. The estate was then sold and a timber contractor knocked the stones down again. What remained was bulldozed away in 1965.

Blessedly, the circle was restored and excavated in 1979–83, assisted by glass slides taken in the early 1900s and found on a local rubbish tip. The excavation showed that the whole site had been covered with chips of quartzite, broken on site on an anvil stone, whilst the veins of quartzite in the standing stones are still clearly visible. The recumbent stone is orientated to the extreme southern moon, under whose light the whole site must have glowed with an unearthly beauty.

## Templestone, Rafford, Moray

NJ 068 569, Map 27. 3.5km SE of Forres. Turn E off B9010, sign-posted Blervie, 2.8km SE of Forres. Park after 800m opposite houses to S and walk up hill 50m to circle.

This charming little four-poster is lovingly protected and shown off to visitors by Mr Smith, on whose land it stands and whose goats like to lie in the rectangular circle. Its diameter is 3.4 x 2.7m. Within the circumference are the remnants of a ring cairn. Members of the nearby Findhorn Foundation believe Templestone to stand on an especially strong ley line.

Like North Burreldales, Alvah (NJ 675 549, Map 29), Doune of Dalmore (NJ 185 308) and Raich (NJ 618 436), it represents the end of the tradition of stone circle building in Grampian. The great megalith-raisers were no more, although the practice of encircling a grave with stones persisted. The tradition of the stone circle seems to have passed south and lived on at such sites as Croft Moraig in Pethshire (NN 797 472) before it disappeared for ever.

# PICTISH STONES

*The sculptured stone monuments of Scotland may be considered the earliest existing expression of the ideas, and the most genuine records of the skill in art, of the early inhabitants of Scotland; but they have been so long neglected, that now...we find them diminished in number and...mutilated in their form.*

– John Stuart,
*Sculptured Stones of Scotland*, 1856

*If you take the trouble to look closely and penetrate with your eyes to the secrets of the artistry, you will notice such intricacies...that you will...declare that...these things must have been...the work, not of men, but of angels.*

– Gerald the Welshman,
late 12th century

## Altyre Slab, Altyre, Forres, Moray

NJ 039 554, Map 27. 4km S of Forres. Go S out of Forres on A940 Grantown road. Take first fork to left, sign-posted for distillery. After 1km, turn right down drive at lodge house, immediately right again and, after 300m, left at T junction in drive. Stone 30m S in field.

It is, above all, the austerity of this great dressed slab of stone that is so arresting. Its only ornament is the linear Ogham script that runs up its N edge (Oghams should be read from the bottom up). Faint and weathered signs of a cross are just discernible on the W side of the stone that is 3.35m tall, 84cm across (though tapering to a broken top) and 17cm thick. Almost nothing is known of this stone. In his 1839 *Sketches of Moray*, Rhind is uncharacteristically brief: "The Altyre Stone was found, it is said, about Duffus, and was transferred to the position which it now occupies. There appear to be faint marks of Runic knots on this stone, or other carvings. Its height is fifteen feet."

## Logie Elphinstone Stones, Inverurie, Gordon

NJ 7012 259, Map 38 (Not marked on Ordnance). 9km NW of Inverurie. Turn N off A96 up drive to ruined Logie House, 800m before fork off A96 for B9002. Stones on left (N) off drive after 300m.

Little is known of these three perplexing stones, greened by moss and largely ignored for many centuries. Their triangular circle is most akin to that of Monymusk, (NJ 683 156). Because there is no precedent for carved Pictish stones in a circle, it is believed that these were separate stones, brought together to form a circle long after the time of the Picts. Two of the stones show the remains of broken iron stanchions. Yet we know so little of the Picts that we should be cautious in maintaining that these three strange stones were never meant to form a circle, each gazing upon the symbols of the other. John Stuart's evidence (*op. cit.*) is particularly interesting: "They were originally placed on the adjoining Moor of Carden, having been...disposed horizontally, at a little distance apart, but more probably members of a circle...A fourth [stone], which was used by the tenant as a hearthstone in his kiln, was split by the heat and destroyed."

The first stone shows a crescent and V-rod and double disc symbol, the second a Pictish "beast" (mammoth? elephant?) above a crescent and V-rod and the third, the most interesting, a double disc and Z-rod, a crescent and V-rod and then, quite uniquely, a circular Ogham. Unusually, these symbols have been inscribed over the now-faint traces of an earlier double disc and Z-rod.

## Rhynie Man, Woodhill House, Westburn Road, Aberdeen

In the foyer of Grampian Regional Council's HQ, just off North Anderson Drive. Viewing during office hours, Mon-Friday, 8.30 a.m.–5.30 p.m.

# GRAMPIAN

*A country in miniature*

This menacing figure, 1.03m tall, was unearthed by the plough in 1978 on the farm of Barflatt, Rhynie, one more in a series of Pictish stones found in the vicinity. Such a large-scale depiction of a single figure is almost without parallel in Pictish art and the powerful, confident, detailed carving of this figure is unmatched. The man is depicted in profile, wearing a sleeved tunic, walking forward and carrying an axe over his shoulder. His nose is hooked, his teeth bared — who is he? Perhaps a Pictish warrior, or a figure from Pictish mythology; another suggestion, made on the assumption that the stone was carved as late as the 9th century, is that the Rhynie Man is the Christian symbol representing St Matthew. A cast of the stone is displayed in the Royal Scottish Museum, Edinburgh.

## Fordoun Stone, Auchenblae, Kincardine and Deeside

NO 726 784, Map 45. 9km N of Laurencekirk, in towered church at S end of Auchenblae. Key at manse.

This was originally the Chapel of St Palladius; the stone was found here in 1872. On its upper left corner survives the faint inscription "PIDARNOIN", written in an early Christian script. The base of the stone's cross is flanked by hunting horsemen; below them is an elaborate and fine double disc and Z-rod. The bottom arm of the cross depicts a horseman carrying a spear, whilst the lower part of a fish monster stands in the top arm of the cross. This merging of carvings with the cross is unusual; typically, the cross is on one side of the stone, the symbols or figures on the other.

## Upper Manbeen, Miltonduff, Moray

NJ 187 576, Map 28. 6km SSW of Elgin. Follow B9010 from town. After 4km, turn right then first left and first left again, sign-posted to Upper Manbeen farm. Park at steading. Stone in field, 50m W.

This small stone, much rubbed by cattle, stands rather forlornly in the flatness of the Laigh of Moray. It boasts three fine symbols, etched in the hard mica slate: on the bottom left, an unusual tripartite rectangle; then a mirror and above them a fish-monster, now half-obliterated. More recently, initials have been carved on both sides, a reminder of how such stones have long been abused. Almost nothing is known of this stone: Stuart (*Sculptured Stones of Scotland*) merely informs us that "there is no tradition of its even having been on another site, nor is there any local history attached to it." The stone has the shape of a throne and recalls the long tradition of stones as, literally, seats of power.

## Newton Stones, Insch, Gordon

NJ 662 297, Map 38. 10km NW of Inverurie off A96; 1km N of turning to Old Rayne, turn N (right) at lodge and up drive to Newton House. Park discreetly and ask at house for further directions.

One of the stones is incised with a double disc and serpent (note the vivid scales) and Z-rod. It is, however, the second stone that has intrigued and baffled scholars for centuries: in 1855, Lord Aberdeen maintained that "this monument is probably the most interesting of the sculptured stones...in Scotland." Inscribed upon its blue granite is not only a long Ogham, but also an unknown, cursive script that has remained untranslated and engendered many theories — it has even been considered to be a form of the ancient Buddhist Lat alphabet. A fascinating book, *Ancient Pillar Stones of Scotland* (Edinburgh, 1865), by George Moore, ranges far and wide over possible translations.

Neither stone is in its original position: the inscribed pillar came from Shevoch, 1.6km to the SE; graves were found in the gravel on which it stood. The other stone stood 1km W of Shevoch.

## Sueno's Stone, Forres, Moray

NJ 046 595, Map 27. Turn into Forres off A96; stone sign-posted to right after 300m.

This breathtaking monument is arguably the finest piece of Dark Age sculpture in Britain. It is certainly the tallest (over 6.5m) and most complex. The western side bears a great ring-headed cross; the eastern a battle scene, divided into four panels: rows of horsemen at the top, then foot soldiers with swords and spears, piles of decapitated bodies and ranks of soldiers, archers and horsemen surrounding what may be a broch in the third panel and, finally, a battle scene.

Eight human skeletons were found in 1813 in a mound close to the stone, substantiating the belief that Sueno's Stone records the defeat of a great army in battle — perhaps the final defeat of the Picts by the Dalriadan Scots under Kenneth MacAlpine around 850? The name "Sueno" is an

*Esslie the Greater stone circle, Banchory*

anachronism: he was an 11th-century Danish king.

The stone is badly weathered. Controversy rages about its preservation: if it is left much longer exposed to the elements, the carvings will soon disappear altogether. It was thought best to place it in Forres Museum, but experts thought that the stone would break if moved. The idea of protecting it with a perspex case introduced fears that condensation within the dome would damage the stone even more. The debate continues.

### Rodney's Stone, Brodie, Moray

NH 984 576, Map 27. 5km W of Forres, turn N off A96, following sign-posts to Brodie Castle. Stone in castle grounds.

This is a fine, elaborate, well-worked stone, carved in relief and very different to the earlier incised Pictish stones. The whole stone has been carefully dressed and bears a cross flanked by intertwined serpents on the front, two fish-monsters, a Pictish beast and double disc and Z-rod on the back. Near the base, on the side angles, are the vestiges of an Ogham inscription.

Discovered during the digging of foundations for the church of Dyke and Moy, the stone was first put up in the village to commemorate the victory of Rodney over the Count de Grasse at the Battle of the Saints in 1782. It was moved to the castle grounds around 1850, but kept its name.

### Raven Stone, Tyrie, Banff and Buchan

NJ 930 631, Map 30. 9km SW of Fraserburgh, on A98, in church to S of road. Key at manse.

Of blue mica schist, this stone was used as a foundation stone for the north-eastern corner of the old church, where it was found, according to the 1843 *Statistical Account of Aberdeenshire*. It was then built into the walls of the new church. Its incised carvings are of a bird (an eagle?) above a notched rectangle (a chariot?) and Z-rod with floriated ends.

### The Maiden Stone, Gordon

NJ 7103 247, Map 38. 9km NW of Inverurie. Sign-posted up minor road off A96. Park in layby 20m W of stone.

A cross on one side, symbols on the other, these 3ms of red granite are justly famed. The stone is, for Grampian, a rare example of a "class II" Pictish monument, showing the transition from incision of the symbols to carving in full relief. The word "Maiden" is common in Scottish topography and may come from the Gaelic *maoid-hean* for prayer or supplication or *meadhon* for midst or centre. Gordon district prefers a more fanciful explanation: a maid of Balquhain was baking a bannock on her wedding day when she accepted a stranger's wager that, if he could build a road to the top of Bennachie before her bannock was baked, he could have his evil way with her. Alas, the stranger was the Devil himself: the road was made before the bannock was baked. Fleeing her fate, the maiden ran towards Pittodrie. Just as Auld Nick was seizing her, she turned into the Maiden Stone, the broken V in its side the result of the Devil's grasp.

Like Sueno's stone, the Maiden Stone is sadly weathered. Once more, proposals to move it to a museum and install a cast in its place are countered by plans to cover it with a perspex dome.

*Effigy of Sir Gilbert de Greenlaw, a hero of the battle of Harlaw, Kinkell Churchyard, Inverurie.*

# 2

# BATTLES and BLOODSHED

*The Scots spend all their time in wars, and when there is no war they fight with one another.*

— Don Pedro de Ayala

Isolated for many centuries from the rest of Scotland, protected and determined by her great natural barriers, Grampian has nonetheless been of great importance in Scottish history. Matters of great moment to Scotland have been decided in the hills and straths of Grampian, amongst her fast and strange retreats.

It was in Grampian that those who became Scots first found a common cause in opposing the invading Romans at Mons Graupius in 84 AD; it was in Grampian that Scotland's autonomy was assured at the battle of Nechtansmere in 658 AD and here, too, at Lumphanan that the claims of Scotland's indigenous Gaels were finally overwhelmed by Norman feudalism. It was on Grampian's soil that Robert the Bruce, his cause seemingly in ruins, once more raised his standard and gave a fledgling Scotland hope. And it was in Grampian that the struggle of Scottish Catholic against Protestant was resumed at the battle of Corrichie for all that the Reformation was assured; that the great drama of the Covenant unfolded, that the Jacobite cause first flourished and died.

If they were of little moment to the nation, the many feuds and bloodsheds of Grampian are no less interesting. This chapter describes, in chronological order, some of both the major and minor battles and bloodshed that enliven Grampian's history. Much has now changed at these places of blood, with conifers at Harlaw and grouse moor at Glenlivet. Yet many sites, like Culblean and Corrichie, are worth visiting for their vistas and beauty alone. Grampian's battlefields give the persevering visitor something rare in the 20th century, the opportunity to stop, to contemplate the past in peace and then to ponder on the future.

Scant, written records begin only in the late 1st millennium AD. There is, then, no written reference to battles or bloodshed in the preceding two millennia of Grampian's history. For our interpretation of the war-like peoples of the region's Bronze Age, we must rely on the archaeological record. We know of no belligerence on the part of the earlier Stone Age peoples of Grampian who were first hunter-gatherers and then farmers. If there were disputes between different groups of families, nothing is known of them.

The early forts of the Bronze Age are ample testament to the wars and conflicts that characterised these times. We have further evidence in the form of armaments found throughout the region, such as the seven flat axes found in a pot at Colleonard, Banff and more at Fingelly, Rhynie and the Pass of Ballater. The bronze war-trumpet from Deskford in Moray is a relic of a sophisticated military power, as are rein-rings (probably for use on war-chariots) and such massive armlets as those found at Castle Newe, Strathdon and Belhelvie, Aberdeenshire.

We know, then, that the Bronze and Iron Age peoples of Grampian possessed the accoutrements of war. We surmise that competition for and control over the new technologies gave ample cause for conflict. We must wait, however, for the description by the Roman historian Tacitus of the battle of Mons Graupius in 84 AD for any idea of the large-scale battles these people fought, imagining, meanwhile, the raids, pillaging and tribal conflicts of those shadowy times.

The Roman presence in Scotland seems never to have extended as a permanent force beyond Strathmore in Angus; the most northerly permanent fortification of the Empire was at Stracathro. In the mid-80s AD, however, perhaps impelled by raids on his northern march by Celts and Picts from Grampian, the governor Agricola began a punitive campaign by land and sea into Scotland's north-east. Retreating before him, the indigenous peoples brought their forces together under the leadership of Calgacus and made their stand in pitched battle at Mons Graupius.

The next known class of battles and bloodshed in Grampian is that of the Picts, fighting either the Dalriadan Scots from Argyll or fighting amongst themselves. Again, hard historical evi-

# GRAMPIAN

*A country in miniature*

dence is rare, but we can glean something of the bloody wars of the Picts or "Cruinthe" (as the Scots called them) from various written sources of the period.

By 501 AD, Fergus mac Erc had moved the centre of Scottish power from Ulster to Argyll. Hungry for land and power, the Scots looked to the Pictish kingdoms of the south and east. The *Annals of Tigernach* for 559 record the result: "Death of Gabran, Domnagart's son, King of Scots. Flight of the Scots before Brude, Maelchon's son, King of the Picts." There is also evidence of a great battle between Scots and Picts at Circhenn (the Mearns) around 598. The interpretation of Sueno's Stone at Forres is notoriously contentious. Its decapitated heads and bound prisoners seem to support the idea that the stone was erected to mark a great battle: could this have been the final, crushing victory of the Scots over the Picts, their last stronghold Moray, early in the 9th century? Kenneth McAlpin had certainly unified Picts and Scots by 843; by 899 the *Annals of Ulster* refer, for the first time, to "Ri Alba", King of Alba or Scotland.

Meanwhile, the Picts had not been free of internal conflicts. Pictland was never a homogenous entity but a series of semi or totally independent provinces. Terrain alone would have made unification difficult. The 12th-century *De Situ Albanie* tells us that Pictland "was divided anciently by seven brothers into seven parts. Of

*Kildrummy Castle*

these, the principal is Angus with Mearns...the second part is Athole and Gowrie. The third part is Strathearn with Monteith. The fourth of the parts is Fife with Fothreff; and the fifth part is Mar, with Buchan. The sixth is Moray and Ross. The seventh part is Caithness..."

Such order presumes bloodshed we can only guess at. There was regicide and murder, attested by the *Annals of Tigernach* for 726: "Drust was cast from the Kingdom of the Picts and Alpin reigned in his stead." Alpin, however, lost two battles of internal feud in 728. The *Annals of Tigernach* again: "Battle of Moin-Craibe amongst the Picts themselves. Angus and Alpin were they that fought this battle. And the rout was before Angus and the son of Alpin was slain there; and Angus took authority." Within a year, Oengus (Angus) reinforced his High Kingship with a victory over other Picts at Monith-Carno, probably Cairn o' Mount (NO 649 806).

The independent kingdoms of the Picts were at an end by the middle or late 9th century. Yet Pictish authority, *mormaers* and *toiseachs*, lived on, indicating a degree of autonomy for the Picts within Scotland. That the Picts of Grampian were far from content under the new, Scottish control is suggested by the number of Scottish Kings who met their death in Grampian.

Donald I was killed in Moray in 900. In battle against a band of Picts from Moray, Malcolm I was killed in 954, probably on Malcolm's Mount near Stonehaven. King Dubh was murdered at Forres in 966 and Kenneth II at Fettercairn in 995. In 1040, Macbeth, of Pictish descent, killed Duncan I in battle near Elgin and took the crown of Scotland before himself being killed at Lumphanan (NJ 584 043). (Macbeth's Cairn at NJ 578 053 is not his burial place, but a prehistoric cairn. Macbeth was buried on Iona.) The long struggle of Pict against Scot only came to an end with the killing by William I of Donald MacWilliam, last Pictish claimant to the Scottish throne, near Inverness in 1187.

The next distinct phase of battles and bloodshed in Grampian was occasioned by the Vikings, who raided and looted along the coast of Grampian from around 800–1150 AD. By the late 9th century, the pirate Viking had become the coloniser and farmer, establishing formal Viking earldoms in Orkney, Caithness and Sutherland and the Western Isles. The Picts of

Grampian were assaulted without mercy. We learn from the *Annals of Ulster* that in 866, for example, Olaf, Viking King of Dublin, defeated the Picts at Fortrenn and then "plundered all the territories of the Picts and took hostages". Grampian was caught between the anvil of the Vikings and the hammer of the waxing Scots. The days of the Picts were numbered.

Of many Viking raids on Grampian, one of the best known was at Longmanhill, near MacDuff, around 1000. More determined Viking invasions were repelled in pitched battle by Malcolm II, who defeated the invaders at Mortlach in 1010 and Cruden Bay (NK 095 365) in 1012. King Eystein's raid on Aberdeen in 1151 is of interest as not only one of the last Viking assaults on Grampian but also as one of Aberdeen's first appearances in recorded Scottish history.

It is with the next catalogue of battles and bloodshed, those of the long Wars of Independence, that Grampian enters the documented domain of national history. It would be no exaggeration to claim that the Scottish succession was settled in Grampian. The region certainly saw troubled times after the death of Alexander III in 1286 and the death of his heir, Margaret, en route from Norway. Scotland had neither a monarch nor an obvious successor and no less than 13 claimants to the throne. Both of the leading contenders, Robert Bruce (grandfather of King Robert) and John Balliol, had their supporters in Grampian – the burgh of Aberdeen and the Earl of Mar for Bruce and the Earl of Buchan for Balliol. The consequences were bloody indeed.

Scotland's guardians were unable to settle the question of the succession, known as Scotland's

*The "Sair Field o' Reid Harlaw"*

# GRAMPIAN
*A country in miniature*

*Dunnottar Castle, Stonehaven, circa 1895*

"Great Cause". They asked Edward I of England to arbitrate. He decided, eventually, on Balliol, treating him as a vassal and obtaining the surrender of the royal Scottish castles. Edward's demand that a Scottish army should support him in France proved too much even for Balliol who, in 1295, revolted. But Edward crushed the Scots at Dunbar and then advanced through Scotland, strengthening such royal castles as Kildrummy, before returning south with both John Balliol and the Stone of Destiny in his baggage.

It was the son of an obscure Clydesdale knight, William Wallace, who resurrected hopes of Scottish independence. In May of 1297, he killed one of Edward's many placemen, the Sheriff of Lanark. Scottish humiliations ignited; a revolt in Moray spread throughout Grampian, the English Sheriff of Aberdeen joining the rebel cause. A combined Scottish force defeated the English at Stirling Bridge in September. The Scots proceeded to capture English-occupied castles, such as Grampian's Dunnottar (see chapter 4).

With Wallace defeated at Falkirk in 1298 and then hung, drawn and quartered in 1305, Robert the Bruce took up Scotland's struggle. By murdering his rival, John "Red Comyn", Lord of Badenoch and nephew of John Balliol, he secured the enmity of the Comyns of Buchan; Grampian, once more, was inextricably involved in Scotland's destiny. Losing the battle of Methven in 1306, Bruce fled to Ireland. Returning, he defeated the English at the battle of Loudoun in 1307 and then marched north to Grampian, where the Comyns awaited him.

Bruce's campaign in the north-east was vital to his eventual and final victory over the English at Bannockburn in 1314. His victories at Slioch (NJ 554 391), Barra, Aikey Brae and Inverurie, between 1307 and 1308, transformed a hopeless refugee and criminal into a great King of Scotland. Barbour's great epic poem "Brus" tells us of Bruce when first he reached Grampian, seeking succour there after his defeat at the battle of Methven:

*Thus in the hills livit he*
*Quhill the mast part of his menyhe*
*Was rivin and rent: na schone tha had*
*Bot as tha tham of hidis mad:*
*Tharfor tha went till Abirdene.*

At first, things went ill for Bruce in Grampian. According to Barbour once more:

*Thar him tuk sic ane seknes*
*That put him to full hard distress;*
*He forbar bath drink and met.*

Yet two years later, this same man was able to convene, in St Andrews, the first Parliament of his reign. From victories in Grampian, King Robert sat securely on his throne.

Grampian's peace, was to be short-lived. Bruce had rewarded his supporters – Hay, Leslie, Irvine, Seton – with the Grampian lands of the dispossessed Comyns and Strathbogies. Many other Scottish knights and barons had been exiled, their lands forfeit. With Bruce's death in 1329, Scotland was placed once more under weak guardianship in the name of the boy King, David II. The Disinherited, as they were known, saw their chance.

An English invasion in 1335 and the Peace of Perth secured another English puppet, Edward Balliol, to the Scottish throne. One of his supporters, David of Strathbogie, had lost much in Grampian under Bruce. Named the King's Lieutenant in the north, Strathbogie set out with a strong army to regain his patrimony and restore the Balliol cause in Grampian.

Strathbogie chose his time, arriving at harvest-time and wreaking a terrible revenge. As Andrew de Wyntoun recorded:

*His hart fra Scottis all turnyd was;*
*And Inglis man became agayne*
*And gert his folk wyth mekill mayne*
*Ryot halyly {ravage wholly} the cwntre*
*And lete, that all hys awyne suld be.*

But to gain an effective grip on Grampian, Strathbogie had to capture the castles which still held faith with David II as their true King. The strongest of these was Kildrummy where Lady Christian Bruce, King David's aunt, was living. Lady Christian was the wife of Scotland's new Guardian, Sir Andrew Moray, Lord of Garioch, who came in haste to relieve Strathbogie's siege.

His force defeated Strathbogie and his Athollmen at the battle of Culblean on 30 November 1335. The tide of the war was turned in Scotland's favour. Although Grampian continued to suffer – Aberdeen was sacked by the English in 1336 – Edward III, like his grandfather, could not subdue Scotland. The English gave up and, in 1341, David II returned to claim a throne that had, once more, been secured in Grampian.

The next major battle in Grampian's history, that of Harlaw in 1411, was a more parochial affair, a conflict between Highlander and Lowlander. Yet, as always, national politics played their part: Harlaw, the result of a feudal dispute, might not have been fought had the Scottish King James I not been in an English prison at the time and unable to adjudicate. Nonetheless, it is with the battles of the Reformation and those of Corrichie in 1562 and Glenlivet (NJ 248 295) in 1594 that Grampian once more enters the national stage. Corrichie ended any hopes of a Catholic Counter-Reformation; Glenlivet was Catholicism's last fling.

All over 16th-century Europe, the winds of the Reformation were blowing. In miniature, with the battles of Tillyangus and Craibstane and the burning of Corgarff, the storm blew on in Grampian. Simmering feuds between two of the region's great families, the Gordons and the Forbes, became part of and confused with the greater issue that Luther and 95 Theses had begun in 1519.

*The Aberlemno Pictish stone probably depicting scenes form the battle of Nechtansmere.*

# GRAMPIAN
*A country in miniature*

Civil war became inevitable after Mary, Queen of Scots' enforced abdication in 1567: many, including the Catholic fifth Earl of Huntly, took up arms for her cause. If the war in Grampian was brief, it was bitter and cruel – Montrose took no prisoners. It was also complex and confusing for at least three reasons. Firstly, traditional rivalries re-emerged: the Gordons and their allies supported King Charles I and episcopacy, the Forbes and theirs the National Covenant of 1638 and presbyterianism. Secondly, Montrose's army in his Grampian campaign of 1644–6 was composed of Catholic Irishmen and Highlanders. The memory of Harlaw was exacerbated. If ordinary people in Grampian knew little of the Covenant and cared less, they did know that they disliked Highlanders. The schism in Scotland between Scottish Highlander and Lowlander became unbridgeable: the great tragedy of Culloden was assured. And finally, Montrose changed sides: in 1639, he was leading the Covenanting forces in Grampian. In 1644 he was back, but this time for the King.

Thus is the history of the Civil War in Grampian a complex one. It saw many skirmishes, most famously the "Trot of Turriff" and the struggle at the Brig o' Dee (NJ 929 035), both in 1639, but only three battles, Justice Mills, Fyvie (NJ 774 392) and Alford. Grampian was once more prominent with the submission of Dunnottar Castle to Cromwell in 1655.

Thereafter, the region knew a brief but relative peace until the two Jacobite rebellions, despite such gestures of support for King James as that of James Fraser of Castle Fraser at Fraserburgh, in the year of the massacre at Glencoe. The planned landing of a French army in Buchan in 1707 never took place but did draw wide support in Grampian. The standard of the Old Pretender's 1715 rebellion was raised at Braemar; when the Stewart King did eventually arrive, it was to Peterhead that he came, before travelling south through Aberdeen en route to his ill-fated army in Perth. The many ports of Grampian were much in demand from fugitives when the rebellion collapsed.

When Prince Charles Stewart raised his standard at Glenfinnan on 19 August 1745, there was little rejoicing in Grampian. If the ordinary people of the north-east favoured Jacobinism because they wished rid of the hated Malt Tax, most of Grampian's aristocracy sat firmly on the fence throughout the '45. With the exception of the skirmish of Inverurie, the second rebellion passed Grampian by. Too many of her younger men fell to Cumberland's cannon at Culloden; those lairds who had fought and survived, like Old Gordon of Glenbuchat, never returned to Grampian.

Like the rest of Scotland, Grampian was to be "pacified" after Culloden. Redcoats and roads epitomised the ethos of the new verse in the national anthem:

*God grant that Marshall Wade*
*May by Thy mighty aid*
*Victory Bring. May he sedition hush*
*And, like a torrent, rush,*
*Rebellious Scots to crush,*
*God save the King.*

At last, the region knew a settled peace and the Age of Improvement (see chapter 5) began. The history of battles and bloodshed was over, save one, small postscript.

Recalling Harlaw and the harrying of Grampian by Montrose's wild Highlanders, blood flowed once more in Grampian in 1874 with the "Highlanders' Great Riot". Fraserburgh was by then a thriving fishing port, its growth fuelled by immigrant, Highland labour at the herring. The evening of 1 August saw some 2,000 of these men, even their Gaelic speech foreign to their Grampian employers, riot through the town until 1.30 on Sunday morning, when a great downpour of rain dampened their spirits. When a detachment of Gordon Highlanders at last arrived from Aberdeen, there was little for them to do but arrest the ringleaders.

The riot ended. But old grievances were renewed; the Highlanders did not come again. Grampian's isolation from the rest of Scotland was renewed, until the coming of oil.

## Mons Graupius (84 AD)

NJ 68? 25?. Turn W off A96, 9km NW of Inverurie, onto B9002, sign-posted "Insch". 0.5 km after Oyne, turn S up road sign-posted "Back o' Bennachie" to Forestry Commission carpark.

*The fiery cross sped throu' the lan*
*By Don an' Dee an' Deveron fair,*
*An' seen wiz mustert on Bennachie*
*Thretty thoosan' men or mair.*

– Duncan Mennie, *The Battle o' Bennachie*

Vexed indeed has been the question of the site of Grampian's first recorded battle. Kempstone Hill, Stonehaven (NO 879 897) was long favoured, but many sites have entered the lists since the battle was first placed in Ardoch, Perthshire by an 18th-century antiquarian. Since then, Mons Graupius has flitted about with all the felicity of a swallow.

Recent consensus places it on the northern slopes of Bennachie. There are several large Roman camps in the vicinity – Kintore, Ythan Wells and Durno. Our only source for the battle, chapters 29–38 of the *Agricola* of the Roman historian Tacitus, refers to the *summa collium*, the top of several hills. Bennachie consists of "several hills".

Only time, money and archaeology will clinch the argument, for Tacitus is infuriatingly vague about the site of the battle. He gives us, nonetheless, an enthralling account of what happened.

The ranks of some 30,000 "Caledonians", their vanguard and chariots on lower ground, rose "as it were in tiers up the gentle slope", facing Agricola's army of, perhaps, two legions and their auxiliaries, some 12–15,000 men. The Caledonians, says Tacitus, welcomed the choice between revenge or enslavement (*ultionem aut servitium*).

The Roman army had two centuries of experience of battle with the Celtic tribes of western Europe. The Caledonians, with their long swords and small shields, were unequal to the disciplined fighting at close quarters that Agricola imposed on them. Tacitus is clear: "Arms, bodies, severed limbs lay all around and the earth reeked of blood." The following dawn showed 10,000 of Grampian's warriors lying where they had fallen, the rest routed, and 340 Roman dead. On all sides, says Tacitus, there reigned a profound and dismal silence (*vastum ubique silentium*).

Despite his sweeping victory, Agricola did not consolidate his position but withdrew to winter quarters at Ardoch. Grampian was to remain outwith the boundaries of the Roman Empire, preserving her proud and lonely isolation for at least another seven centuries.

**Longmanhill** Sometimes referred to as the battle of the Bloody Pits (*c.*1000 AD)

NJ 786 648. Follow coastal footpath off B9031, 2km by road W of Gardenstown, past ruins of St John's Church, to series of grassy hollows. Alternative site: NJ 727 634 at Bloodmyre Farm, 2km SE of Macduff off A98.

Only excavation will reveal whether the grassy hollows were the "bloody pits" or whether they are a natural feature. This site's claim to be the battlefield, however, is supported by the local tradition that the heads of three of the slain Vikings were built into the walls of a church, founded on the battlefield. Yet although there was a medieval church at Gamrie Bay, the ruins of St John's Church date from the 16th century (despite the date on the gable of 1004).

The site of Bloodmyre Farm is equally strong in local tradition. Local grandparents can recall the farm recorded on old maps as "The Bloody Pits". But wherever fought, the story of the battle is consistent.

A party of raiding Vikings was intercepted by locals led by Mernane, Thane of Buchan. They had been alerted to the marauders by warning beacons, lit on high mounds like the Longman cairn at NJ 738 620, and forced the Vikings to take refuge on the Castle Hill of Findon, near Gardenstown (NJ 794 643). Although joined by reinforcements who had landed at Oldhaven of Cullen (NJ 733 646), the Vikings were driven inland and slaughtered to a man in a place appropriately known thereafter as the Bloody Pits. Pratt's book *Buchan* quotes Geddes' poem *The Old Church of Gamerie* on the subject:

*The war I ween had a speedy close*
*And the Bloody Pits to this day can tell*
*How the ravens were glutted with gore...*

**Mortlach (c.1010 AD)**

NJ 325 393. The church marks the approximate site of the battle, just S of Dufftown and clearly sign-posted from the village square.

One of our best sources for information on the Vikings is the *Orkneyinga Saga*, written down around 1200. Yet it accords the battle of Mortlach no mention, perhaps because the Vikings were defeated. This was an important victory for the newly founded nation of Scotland under a king longer-lived and more successful than any of his predecessors, Malcolm II.

Our earliest and longest account of the battle comes from Hector Boece and his 1527 *History of Scotland*, itself dependent upon earlier chronicles such as John of Fordun's *Scotichronicon*. We know of the background to the battle from the *Orkneyinga Saga*: the claim of Findlay, Mormaer of Moray, to his lands was being disputed by the Viking Earl of Orkney, Sigurd the Stout. Findlay appealed to Malcolm II for help; via Glen Fiddich he came upon the Viking army from the E, finding them camped in the glen of the Dullan Water by the monastery of Mortlach. The Scots attacked impetuously, only to be driven back, three of their leaders slain. Malcolm fell to his knees in prayer to God and St Moluag for victory, in return for which, he promised, he would build a cathedral church on the site of the chapel. Other versions of the story have Malcolm promise to build as long an addition to the chapel as he could throw his spear.

Malcolm won his battle and built (or extended) his church. On that, the various versions of the battle are agreed. Whether or not he won by flooding the Viking camp with the dammed Dullan Water, as one local tradition insists, is less certain. What is absolutely clear is that the site of Mortlach, with its footpath up the Dullan Water to the Giant's Chair, is one of Grampian's most beautiful and memorable. Two Pictish stones enhance the visit – the Battle Stone in the churchyard is said to commemorate the battle but is almost certainly much earlier. Although sadly eroded, it still shows a Celtic cross on one side and Pictish symbols – a bull's head, a snake, a mounted hunter – on the other. A smaller Pictish stone is preserved in the church's porch.

### Lumphanan (1076)

NJ 57? 05?. The precise site of the battle is unknown. The proximity of Macbeth's Cairn and the discovery of sword-blades and battle-axes on the slopes of Perkhill make this as likely a site as any.

Scottish history groans under the burden and the pain of centuries of conflict with the English. The roots of Culloden and Flodden and Bannockburn arose, once more, in Grampian. Macbeth, of Pictish descent, seized the Scottish throne by killing Duncan in 1040. The Shakespearean version of him as a usurper is unfair – the early Scots Kings succeeded under the Gaelic custom of tanistry and Macbeth was a legitimate tanist.

Duncan's two sons had been brought up at the English court of Edward the Confessor who saw them, perhaps, as a means to his ambitions on Scotland. In 1054 the elder son, Malcolm, crossed the border with a strong Anglo-Danish army led by Siward, Danish Earl of Northumbria, and forced Macbeth to retreat after an inconclusive but bloody battle at Dunsinane.

From his base as King of Cumbria, Malcolm launched a second campaign in 1057, attacking Macbeth's palace at Scone. Wounded, Macbeth fled N, aiming to reach his native and loyal soil in Moray. But Malcolm intercepted him near Lumphanan. Macbeth, at the head of his small force, charged into Malcolm's soldiers and was killed. According to Andrew de Wyntoun:

*Thus Makbeth slew thai thun*
*In-to the Wode of Lunfanan*
*And his Hewyd thai stak off thare*
*And that wyth thame fra thine thai bare*
*Til Kynkardyne.*

By 25 April 1058, Malcolm had disposed of Macbeth's son and heir, Lulach, and was crowned King at Scone. The Normanisation of Scotland had begun; the time of the Picts, their stronghold in Grampian, was past.

### Barra (1308)

NJ 797 268. 1km W of Old Meldrum between A920 and B9170. Battlefield (and Bruce's approach to it from Inverurie) best viewed from iron-age hill-fort on the top of Hill of Barra (NJ 802 258). Local tradition maintains that Bruce's opponent, John Comyn, camped here before the battle.

Repulsed once more in his assault on Elgin Castle in the spring of 1308, Bruce, desperately ill in body and spirit, retreated S to Inverurie and the safety of its great Bass. If he had any clear plans, we know nought of them although it was obvious that he had to impose one crushing defeat on his arch-enemy, Comyn of Buchan.

His hand was forced by a sudden attack on Inverurie by a detachment of Comyn's cavalry. According to Barbour's *Brus*, the King leapt from his sick-bed, roaring that Comyn's attack had cured him better than any medicine could. He found the Comyn army waiting for him on the level ground between the Hill of Barra and the Lochter Burn. What might have been a battle was, in fact, a rout. Comyn's men, according to Barbour, had been told that Bruce was sick and bed-bound. Seeing him advance upon them in person, they simply turned and ran away, soon to be followed by Comyn's mounted knights.

Many were caught and slaughtered in "Bruce's Field", a marshy hollow by the Lochter burn (NJ 791 269). Bruce's hold on the Scottish crown was assured.

He wreaked a terrible revenge on the earldom of Buchan, reducing it to a desert by burning crops and farms, razing to the ground such Comyn castles as Dundarg and Rattray. Barbour is clear: Bruce:

*Gert his men brin all Bouchane*
*Fra end till end, and sparit nane,*
*And heryit tham on sic maner*
*That eftir that wele fifty yher*
*Men menit the herschip {harrying} of Bouchane.*

Those who survived the battle of Barra and continued to espouse the Comyn cause were killed in great numbers at the battle of Aikey Brae (NJ 959 471), near the great monastery of Old Deer, later that year.

### Culblean (1335)

NO 429 996. There is a monument to the battle beside the A97, 1.6km N of the café at the Muir of Dinnet Nature Reserve within which the battlefield lies. Following the geological trail round the reserve will give as good a view of the battlefield as any.

Once more, it is to Wyntoun that we owe most of our knowledge of this battle which, though small in scale, nonetheless marked a turning-point in the Scottish Wars of Independence. Sir Andrew Moray, Guardian of Scotland, had marched N from Bathgate with 800 men to relieve the siege of Kildrummy Castle. When he heard of this, the besieger Strathbogie came S to Culblean to meet Moray, taking up his position on the hill of Culblean "at the est end, rycht in the way" as Wyntoun puts it.

On the evening of 29 November, the armies faced each other across the waters of Loch Davan. Splitting his force in two, Moray decided to approach Strathbogie under cover of darkness, ready for a surprise attack at dawn. But his main force, under Sir William Douglas, was detected by Strathbogie's sentries whose men, aroused, formed ranks facing S towards the Burn o' Vat. Douglas was reluctant to climb towards the enemy up a ridge which is still bush and boulder-strewn. Strathbogie made a fatal mistake. Thinking that those he saw were the whole of the Moray force, he cried, "Hey, apone thame tyte, for thai ar welle nere dyscumfyte!" and rushed with his men down towards the burn and the ranks of Douglas. As the fighting proceeded without order or discipline, Moray attacked Strathbogie's rear and the battle was all but over. Tradition asserts that the Tarland burn to the N of Aboyne castle (10km to the E!) ran red for 24 hours with the blood of the slain.

As his men deserted him, Strathbogie set his back to an oak tree and fought courageously on: "there by an aik deyd Erle Davy and sundry of his company." Although the war of which Culblean was a part dragged on, English hopes of conquering Scotland died with David Strathbogie.

### Harlaw (1411)

NJ 752 242. 3km NW of Inverurie. Follow B9001 from town centre and take first minor road W (signposted) to monument.

The "Sair Field o' Reid Harlaw" is still remarkably "weel kent" in Grampian. This is puzzling, for it was not a battle of national significance or momentous event. Yet at Harlaw north-easterners found again a common cause, as they had at Mons Graupius; at Harlaw they were as one and so the battle has assumed great importance in Grampian's lore. Equally, the battle was an engagingly simple one between Lowlander and Highlander; it has, then, something of the attractive simplicity of cowboys and Indians.

Yet there is a sadness to the memory of Harlaw, that of the division between Lowland and Highland Scot that has not healed and, some say, never will. Harlaw is wrongly portrayed as a racial conflict, for there were Gaelic speakers on both sides. It was, rather, a conflict of cultures and one errs to dismiss the Highlanders as the barbarians. Alexander Stewart of Mar, whose actions in part provoked the battle, had a criminal past to match the most bloodthirsty Highlander. It is ironic that a battle which brought the feuding families of Grampian together saw Scotland divided.

Donald, second Lord of the Isles, had a rightful claim to the earldom of Ross which had been granted by Scotland's Stewart regent the Duke of

# GRAMPIAN
*A country in miniature*

Albany to another Stewart, the Earl of Buchan. Denied, as he saw it, justice, Donald mustered an army of 6,000 on the Sound of Mull and set off to claim his earldom "or else be graithed in his graif". By defeating the clan Mackay en route at Inverness, he found others flocking to his cause and he marched towards Aberdeen with an expanded army of some 10,000.

Late in 1410, Mar assembled the leading lairds of Grampian at Kildrummy in order to plan Grampian's resistance to the "fifty thousand Heilan' men a-marching to Harlaw" and, of course, to defend the Stewart earldom. Aberdeen's interests were represented by its Provost, Robert Davidson, who was able to muster the princely number of 36 Aberdonians to "go forth against the cateran".

As the Highlanders approached, Mar raised his standard at Inverurie, guarding the road to Aberdeen. His plan was simple: a dawn attack on Donald of the Isles who had chosen well his camp for the night of 23 July, the plateau of Harlaw. According to the 1548 poem the *Battel of Hayrlaw*, the Highlanders were taken by surprise. If so, it mattered little as the Highland vanguard charged upon Mar's, near the summit of the Harlaw ridge. All accounts agree that the day was one of bloody carnage and hand-to-hand fighting, devoid of strategem or generalship. By evening, neither Highlander nor Lowlander could claim victory: the only losers were the many, many dead. Not even the issue of the earldom was settled.

Sadly, cairns which marked episodes of the battle have fallen victim to 20th-century "progress". Drum's Cairn at NJ 752 241 marked the place where Irvine of Drum slew Red Hector, Donald's chief lieutenant and Davidson's Cairn at NJ 755 238 the demise of the only Provost of Aberdeen ever to die in defence of his city.

Two memorials, however, do survive. Within the walls of the ruined chapel of Kinkell (NJ 786 191) is the grave slab of Sir Gilbert de Greenlaw, one of many of Grampian's chivalry to fall at Harlaw. Near Auchronie, Skene (NJ 802 101) stands the Drum Stone, its inscription still just legible: "Drum Stone – 1411– Harlaw". It was here, both Harlaw and Drum Castle visible (although a stand of conifers now blocks much of the view to the S), that Sir Alexander Irvine, on his way to the battle, paused to give instructions for his family to follow should he be killed fighting the Hielandman.

## Corrichie (1562)

NJ 697 025. Turn E off the A980 from Banchory along the B977, past Raemoir House Hotel. After 1km, park and walk up track through Green farm. A stiff 5km walk uphill to the battlefield, though along a discernible footpath. The monument to the battle stands well wide of the mark, by the roadside at 733 014 and surrounded on three sides by trees.

*Mourn ye Highlands and mourn ye Lowlands,*
*I trow ye hae meikle need*
*For the bonny burn o' Corrichie*
*Has run this day wi' bluid.*
— From a contemporary threnody

It is at best a pity that a place so important to Grampian's and Scotland's history should be both so inaccessible and so much changed, in this case overwhelmed by conifers. The walk is reward in itself, but imagination is required to see Huntly's clansmen where now there are trees.

The Catholic fourth Earl of Huntly, a major force in Grampian, took exception to Mary, Queen of Scots' wooing of the Protestants and was outlawed for his pains. Mary had accepted the reformed religion, however reluctantly; advised by her Protestant half-brother, James Stewart (soon to be elevated to Earl of Moray), she decided to bring the rebellious Huntly, "Cock o' North", to heel: "she will do something that will be a terror to others. She trusts to put the country in good quietness", as a contemporary letter records. The new Earl of Moray was given command of a royal army of 2,000, whilst Huntly, despite his boast that he could raise an army of 20,000, mustered only 800.

He camped on 27 October near Garlogie on a moor still called "Gordon's Moss". The next morning, Moray's vanguard advanced. So clearly outnumbered, Huntly decided to retreat to higher ground where Moray's cavalry would lose their advantage. His choice was obvious: 5km to the W, "ane place callit Bank-a-fair, utherwayis callit Coruchie", a hill-top. But he was driven from his position by the gun-fire of Moray's arquebusiers and forced back and off the hill-top to the boggy ground to the W. Cornered, extermination awaited Huntly and his men at the hands of Moray's Lothian pikemen. According to the *Diurnal of Occurents*, the Gordons were "put upoun their bakkis with speiris and thairefter fled".

The great Cock o' North surrendered – 200 of his men were dead; 120 were taken prisoner. But as for Huntly himself, having been placed upon a horse "withowte ether blowe or stroke…he sodenlie fawlethe from his horse starke dedde." The earl had died of a heart attack. His son, Sir John Gordon, was beheaded in Aberdeen's Castlegate on 2 November. The blade of the "Maiden" which beheaded him is on display at Provost Skene's House in Aberdeen. Other leading Gordon lairds were hung. The fall of the house of Gordon was complete; with them, at Corrichie, fell the Catholic cause in Scotland.

## Tillyangus (1571)

NJ 525 245. 1.5km SW of village of Clatt, 14km S of Huntly. Turn off Clatt-Rhynie road at first track S to Mains of Tillyangus and Gordonstown farm. A drove road leads from there to Smallburn, the approximate site of the battle.

In the late 16th century, life in Grampian was complicated; in addition to feuds between the great families of the region, the Counter-Reformation raised tempers even higher. For the Catholic cause and the deposed Queen of Scots were the Gordons, earls of Huntly; for the Protestants, the house of Forbes and, in particular, Black Arthur Forbes of Putachie who, according to Holinshed, "mortallie hated the Gordouns". Sir Adam Gordon of Achindoun felt much the same about the Forbes.

Late in 1571, Black Arthur summoned "the whole surname of Forbes" to the family seat at Drumminor to "plot something against the Gordouns". Hearing of this, Adam Gordon marched against the Forbes who, by then, had taken up a well-defended position on the Mar road across the Coreen Hills at Tillyangus. But the Gordons were numerically superior, perhaps 1,000 to the Forbes 300, and overwhelmed the Forbes. In one account, Black Arthur was killed in the mêlée; in another, he fought with his retreating rearguard until, stopping to drink from a burn, he was stabbed through a chink in his armour by William Gordon of Terpersie.

The Reformation proceeded; for the time being, at least, the Gordons, sacking Drumminor and capturing Lord Forbes' second son, were victorious. The feud continued.

## Corgarff

NJ 255 087. Near Cock Bridge, sign-posted from A939, 75km from Aberdeen.

This gaunt and imposing castle was last used by Hanoverian troops in the wake of the failed

*Corgarff Castle, Strathdon*

*Corgarff Castle, Strathdon*

*I winnae gie up my house, my dear*
*To nae sik traitor as he;*
*Cum weil, cum wae, my jewels fair,*
*Ye maun tak share wi' me.*

Not all her daughters did so, however. One escaped from the burning castle on a rope of knotted sheets. She was caught and killed by the Gordons.

## Craibstane (1571)

NJ 936 056. Just off the W end of Union Street, Aberdeen, near the junction of Hardgate and Justice Mills Lane. A plaque in the wall above the Craibstane commemorates both this battle and that of Justice Mills.

Not only blood feuds but once more religion were the cause of the Craibstane. After Tillyangus, the master of Forbes had gone S to seek troops from the Protestant government. On 16 November, his forces mustered at Brechin and marched N for vengeance on the Gordons and Papistry. At a ford of the Dee, the army separated: one half pressed N to ravage Gordon lands. The other, under Forbes, marched on Aberdeen.

Arriving tired and hungry, Forbes' force was met near what is now Union Glen by a determined muster of Gordons. According to Holinshed, "a sharp conflict was committed between them...cruelly fochten for the space of ane hour." In the end, the Forbes, hungry, tired and outnumbered, "were put to fearfull flight by the bowmen of the Gordons who persued them eagerlie and continued the battell until night".

If the Gordons, proverbially, had won the battle, they had lost the war. Although Grampian, after Craibstane, was secure for Queen Mary and Catholicism, the Catholic cause and the fortunes of the Gordons perished after the Protestant pacification in February 1573. Craibstane was a glorious but vain victory.

## Alford (1645)

NJ 562 164. 40km W of Aberdeen. The crossroads of the A944 and A980 mark the probable battlefield.

With victories over the Covenanters at Fyvie and Auldearn, by the summer of 1645 Montrose had transformed the Royalist cause in Grampian. But before he could strike S, he had to deal with one more covenanting army, that led by Major General Baillie, a professional soldier.

1745 Jacobite rebellion. It dominates strategic passes to the W and N and is now in the care of Historic Buildings and Monuments. In 1571, however, it was the scene of one of the grislier episodes of the Gordon/Forbes feud.

The Gordons made the most of their victory at Tillyangus, looting and burning at will through Forbes' land. Adam Gordon sent one Captain Ker to one of the Forbes' seats, Corgarff, commanding its surrender in the Queen's name. The laird himself was away but his doughty wife, Margaret Campbell, refused to yield the castle. On Gordon's orders, Corgarff was set alight; the lady of the house, her daughters and servants, some 27 people in all, were burned alive. The ballad *Edom o' Gordon* records Margaret's courage:

Always a brilliant strategist, Montrose chose his ground well. Concealing most of his men behind the ridge of Gallows Hill, he waited on the S side of the Don to draw Baillie across the river. His cavalry crossed first and were met by Montrose's Gordon horsemen. Then Montrose unleashed a Highland charge upon Baillie's Lowland levies, whilst his cavalry reserve attacked the covenant infantry from the rear. The covenanters broke and ran.

They might have been better to die where they stood. Angered by the death of their laird and Montrose's friend, Lord George Gordon, the Gordon horsemen pursued the fleeing covenanters E. At Feight Faulds, the western end of Alford, and then again at Blaudy Faulds near Tough, the Gordons caught and killed the covenanters without mercy. Some 1,600 of them were killed in one of the bloodiest battles ever fought in Grampian. Yet its only memorial, the Gordon Stone, lies under Alford's rubbish dump.

## Inverurie (1745)

NJ 780 203. The battlefield surrounds the Bass of Inverurie. Take the B993 at the S end of Inverurie. The Bass is on your left, just after the railway bridge. The Aberdeen/Inverness railway passes straight through the battlefield.

By September 1745, Aberdeen was under Jacobite control. A government force, mostly of MacLeods from Skye, was despatched from Inverness to relieve the town and reached Inverurie on 20 December. Three days later, the Jacobites marched out of Aberdeen to meet them in the last pitched battle to be fought in Grampian.

Half the Jacobite force of 1,200 approached by the main road through Kintore; the other crossed the Don and came upon Inverurie from the E. Astonishingly, both forces went largely undetected and caught the government troops both unprepared and spread out in billets throughout the town.

As dusk fell a brave band of Jacobites forded the Urie to the E of the Bass; another, under the command of Gordon of Avochie, forded the Don and approached the Bass from the W. The detachments formed up and advanced on such of the MacLeods as had been mustered in the confusion. Quite simply, the MacLeods turned and ran away into the night, offering little if any resistance to the concerted fire of the Jacobites. Inverurie and the counties of Aberdeen and Banff remained in Jacobite hands until the Jacobites marched S in January 1746 to join their ill-fated Prince in Stirling.

*Graveyard below the Bass of Inverurie*

# 3

# CHURCHES, CLERICS AND CATECHISMS

Because of her geographical isolation, Christianity came later to Grampian than to much of Scotland. By the mid-9th century, however, the new religion was well established in the region, as the many Christian crosses on Pictish stones of the period attest. If the year 807 saw St Columba's community on Iona disbanded and western Celtic Christianity retreating to its origins in Ireland, in Grampian the faith flourished and grew strong; the region and its Christianity were still relatively unscathed by the marauding Vikings who were such a scourge of Christianity on the west coast of Scotland and who sacked Lindisfarne in 793.

Great bishoprics and buildings arose; the Middle Ages saw the Church in Grampian add secular to its religious power. The Reformation in Grampian was marked by few of the excesses that characterise it elsewhere and the "Aberdeen Doctors" consistently upheld the doctrine of a moderate Reformation. Catholicism survived in the region. If blood was spilled during the Covenant, it was not from indigenous but imported passion. Tolerance was Grampian's hallmark: Lord Forbes of Pitsligo (1648–1717) was an admirer of the French mystic Antoinette Bourignon, who "shared some of the principles of the Quakers and Pietists". Quakerism lives on in Grampian today. Lord Deskford (c. 1640–98), son of the Earl of Findlater, had the works of Kempis, Scougal and Pascal in his library. George Garden (1649–1733), a professor at Aberdeen University, studied Pascal's *Thoughts* and wrote in support of Madame Bourignon, in whom he found "the doctrines of the love of God and charity represented as the essentials of Christianity".

Such broadmindedness was and is typical of the Church in Grampian; it is appropriate that the most dramatic incident in Grampian's long Christian history was not inquisition or prejudice but the great Disruption of 1843 when Grampian's ministers to all but a man supported the principle of the Church's spiritual independence from the state. In many manifestations, and even if it is much in retreat elsewhere, the best of

Christianity lives on in Grampian today.

In the year of our Lord 313, the Roman emperor Constantine promulgated his Milan Edict of Toleration: no longer was Christianity to be persecuted and the new religion that had become established in Britain by the middle of the 3rd century was assured. There are references to Christianity in Britain in the writings of Tertullian (c. 200) and Origen (c. 240). In 381, the emperor Theodosius went further, declaring Christianity the official religion of the Roman empire. Although the Western empire went down before the barbarians in 476, the invaders were converted to the laws of Christ.

Meanwhile, in any case, the Christian Church in Britain had been founded formally by St Ninian at Whithorn in 397. Centuries were to pass before it came to Grampian and, when it did, it came not from the south but from the west, along the traditional access to the region, the Great Glen. The Christian missionaries who came to convert the Picts of Grampian were the forerunners of those who eventually destroyed Pictish autonomy, the Dalriadan Scots of Argyll. They, in turn, had taken their Christianity not from the south but from Ireland.

How and when Christianity came to Ireland is unknown. But in 431, according to the *Chronicle* of Prosper of Aquitaine, a man named Palladius, deacon of the church at Auxerre in what was then known as Gaul, was sent to Ireland as first bishop to the nascent Christian community there. A little later, St Patrick was despatched by the British Church. The Christianity that was to come to Grampian was one which retained the early influences of both Britain and Gaul.

Initially, the Irish faith was organised along Roman lines, with ecclesiastical hierarchies and territorial dioceses based on the old Roman military regions. Although many luminaries of the early Irish Church like Columbanus (c. 600: evangelist of Merovingian Gaul) and Cummianus (c. 633) appear to have retained their allegiance to Rome, a Roman Church was doomed for at least three reasons: the Roman army had finally with-

*Opposite:*
*Crathie Kirk, Deeside*

## GRAMPIAN
*A country in miniature*

drawn from Britain in 407. By the 7th century, Roman civil influence on Ireland was vestigial and decayed as the once-great Roman roads and walls on the mainland. Secondly, the practice of territorial dioceses centred on large towns was inappropriate to a rural agrarian Ireland that had never, in any case, been Romanised. Finally, the great plagues of the mid to late 6th century depopulated large tracts of the countryside. Celtic monasticism, free of territorial restrictions, was born and it was this form of Christianity that was to come to Grampian with the greatest of the early missionaries, St Columba (Colum Cille, the Dove of the Church).

Columba was born a warrior aristocrat, a member of the royal house of Tir Connail in Donegal. This was to prove telling when he began his mission to convert the Picts of Grampian to Christianity. Columba's father was Fedelmid mac Fergusa, son of Cenel Conaill, son of the semi-legendary Niall of the Nine Hostages and he could address any Scottish or Pictish King as his peer. As a child, he must have passed to the shores of the Atlantic by way of Loch Swilly and looked from there at Iona, Tiree and the Outer Hebrides where he was to begin the process that made him the holy man of Scotland.

His biography by Adamnan tells us little of his first 40 years, although we learn that he studied under the Bishop Finian in Leinster, the heart of Irish ecclesiastical scholarship. But then, we are told, "after many years had passed, when on a charge of offences...St Columba was excommunicated by a certain synod...in those days the saint sailed over to Britain with 12 disciples as his fellow soldiers." Christianity, then, came to the west coast of Scotland and thence to Grampian as the result of the voyage of a penance, either voluntary or enforced, that Columba began in 563.

By 574, Columba's foundation on Iona was sufficiently advanced for him to make it his permanent residence; there were Columban monasteries too on the (unidentified) island of Hinba and at Mag Luinge on Tiree, where Columba's foster-son, Baithene, was Prior.

But from the perspective of Iona, Scotland was clearly divided into an eastern and a western part. As his monasteries spread in the west, Columba's thoughts turned east, across the country's spine, the Grampian mountains, to the land of Bridei, King of Picts. In search of converts, round about 585 Columba began his "first tiring expedition" to the kingdom north of the Mounth and west of the Grampians.

Passing along the Great Glen, the saint sought out the Pictish King in his hillfort at Craig Phadraig, near where the river Ness joins the Moray Firth, or possibly near what is now the village of Urquhart. Although Adamnan's account is rather garbled, it is clear that Columba found converting the Picts hard work. At first, Bridei refused to meet the saint and remained locked in his fortress. To gain access, Columba the magician had to out-perform the Pictish Druids: he forced Broichan, Bridei's prime Druid, to release a slave-girl by having an angel shatter a glass in Broichan's hand. He vied with the Picts, much as Elijah vies with the priests of Baal in I Kings 18. According to Adamnan, when Columba wished to leave Pictdom by sailing along Loch Ness, Broichan raised a terrible wind against him: "Our Columba, seeing the furious elements stirred up against him, calls upon Christ the Lord...and orders the sails to be rigged against the wind. Which being done, the whole crowd looking on meanwhile, the boat is borne along against contrary winds with amazing velocity."

Similarly, we are told, Columba made stones float, defeated the Loch Ness monster, turned water into wine, raised the dead and opened the locked gates of Inverness. It is unlikely that Columba discussed theology with the Pictish druids: his intention was to show the pagan Picts that Christianity had practical advantages. In Dalriada to the west, Columba the warrior-priest was already accepted as a bringer of victory. Adamnan shows us Aedan, King of Scots, securing victory in battle against the Pictish Miathi by means of the intercession of Columba's prayers. By the 650s, Cummene the White believed that Dalriada could only sustain its military success by keeping faith with Columba. Oswald of Northumbria's victory over the Welsh invader Cadwallon was secured by the saint who said, "The Lord has granted to me that your enemies shall be turned to flight and your adversary Cadwallon shall be delivered into your hands."

The Monymusk Reliquary is one of the relics of Columba the warrior-priest. Another was the "Battler", the Cathach, a metal case containing Columba's psalter. If carried three times around an army by a hereditary warden who was free from mortal sin, victory was assured. In the 10th century, Columba's crozier was carried before Scottish armies to win them victory against the Vikings.

It was, then, with magic and power that Columba sought to woo the pagan warlike Picts, offering them a new victory God. How successful he was is unknown. When he died in 597, Grampian was still pagan. It was his successors who eventually and courageously won the day, even if some of the Picts were not just agnostic but patently hostile: the *Annals of Ulster* record, for example, the "burning of Donnan of Eigg with 150 martyrs" by a party of Picts on 17 April 617.

There may have been a chapel of the same unfortunate Donnan at Auchterless in Aberdeenshire. If he had such a foundation in Grampian, it was remarkably early and far removed from his principal area of activity in the Western Isles. It is only with Adamnan that we can begin to trace the certain development of Christianity in the region.

Like all of his acolytes, Columba's biographer followed the saint's example of mission. The "Breviary of Aberdeen" mentions Adamnan's church at Furvie, near the Ythan estuary, in Aberdeenshire. Further north, at Forglen in north-east Banffshire, he established another church which once housed what became known as the Monymusk Reliquary. Aboyne on the Dee had a church of Adamnan and the phenomena of what seem to have been a cult – a holy well and a tree sacred to the saint.

But it is still difficult to maintain that Grampian had been "Christianised". In 697 Adamnan admittedly made a great step forward, persuading the Pictish King of Grampian, Bridei son of Derile, to accept his Law of Innocents, under which "innocents" (women, children and clergy) were protected from the horrors of Dark Age warfare. Yet this probably tells us more about Adamnan's remarkable skills as a diplomat than it does about the pervasiveness of Christianity in Grampian.

Leaving Scotland for Ireland in 692, Adamnan died in 704. But many carried on in Grampian that which Columba had begun and Adamnan advanced, even if, lacking biographers, their successors are shadows and their actions more the stuff of legend than of history.

We know of St Drostan, a converted Pict, who founded the monastery of Old Deer early in the

8th century. Monasteries spread in both number and vigour throughout the region. Yet the story of St Monire shows that the old ways lived on. Early in the 9th century, Monire sought converts on Deeside. Convinced by the local Druid that he was an evil spirit, the villagers of Auchendryne assaulted him, leaving him for dead.

The saint crawled away, however, up the slopes of Cairn o' Mount. As he lay dying, a miraculous stream sprang from the hillside and revived him. The pagan priest appeared and blocked the stream. Monire prayed to his Lord and the stream was unblocked. So impressed was the pagan that he and his flock were converted to Christianity.

*Tombstones, Strathdon*

# GRAMPIAN

*A country in miniature*

Before his death in 824, St Monire had established churches at Crathie, on Deeside and Balvenie, near Dufftown, where for many centuries the fair of St Monire was celebrated on 18 December each year.

But even in remote Grampian, the force of the Roman church began to be felt. At the Synod of Whitby in 664, Northumbria had chosen the diocesan Christianity of mainland Europe as opposed to the Celtic monasticism of the Scottish west coast and Ireland. It too sent its missionaries forth into Grampian. They came at a time when Viking raids on the west coast were weakening the vigour of the Columban foundations. Kenneth McAlpin's union of the Scots and Picts in 843 began the end of Celtic Christianity in Grampian: Dunkeld in Perthshire became the ecclesiastical centre of the unified kingdom, in turn organising such churches in Grampian as Kinkell. *Caenn Cill* in Gaelic means Head Church. Kinkell was the ecclesiastical superior of a number of subordinate churches that included Dyce, Kintore and Skene. Tullich on Deeside appears to have been another important centre: although the first documented church dates from the 13th century, the site is associated with a large number of earlier Christian crosses and gravemarkers which relate to a church founded there by St Nathalan in the late 9th or early 10th century. At Brechin, Mortlach and Monymusk communities of Culdees (from the Irish *Cele-de*, servant of God) were established by the 10th century, whilst there was a bishop's seat at Mortlach prior to 1131.

By the early 12th century, then, the Church in Grampian had become thoroughly Roman. Celtic monasticism was vestigial, surviving only in such relics as the Monymusk Reliquary. Although the region was still removed from the mainstream of Scottish political life, its Church was in full accord with Scottish and indeed European practice, writing in Latin and even sending its bishops to Rome.

As the Church grew in stature, it absorbed the superstitions and practices of the old ways: throughout Grampian are wells named after saints – St Muchriehan's Well at NO 503 998, St Finian's at NJ 471 350, St Carol's at NJ 510 469. Well-worship was an important part of Celtic religion. By re-naming such wells, the Church brought the old within the new. The patron saint of Kemnay was St Anne: this was an effective

*Catechism of fire*

attempt by the Church to take within itself the Pictish *Santann* or magic fire. At Midmar and at Marnoch, the churches showed their superiority over the old ways by having the stone circles within their kirkyards. At Culsalmond, they simply buried them: 12 stones, once a stone circle, lie under Culsalmond's graveyard.

The middle ages saw the Church in Grampian flourish as it did throughout Scotland. Seeking more than spiritual benefit, Scotland's medieval Kings invested heavily in the Church. An ecclesiastical structure did much for the kingdom's stability, whilst the men of the Church did much for its economy with their trade in fish and in wool.

A crucial development, however, was not the founding of more abbeys and monastic houses but of the parochial system. In 1100, there were a few parish churches in Grampian, entrusted to parish priests who were secular clergy and not members of a religious order. By 1200, nearly all of the region's medieval parishes had been formed. The parish church, its tower a symbol of strength and the only public building, became the vehicle of the Church's advancement – only one major monastery was founded in Scotland after 1273.

As the medieval centuries advanced, the faith grew stronger, spreading by new institutions and methods. The three universities founded in Scotland in the 15th century combined the religious with the secular. King's College, Aberdeen was founded not only for "the praise of the Divine Name, the exaltation of the Catholic faith, the salvation of souls", but also for "the good order, profit and advancement of the region and the nation".

When Luther protested in 1517, Grampian was not marred by the gross use of indulgences that so angered Luther. And so as the Reformation approached, the region displayed the moderation that has remained its religious hallmark. In the 1540s and 1550s, John Watson, canon of Aberdeen, advocated a compromise between traditional Catholicism and the zeal of the reformers: on the Protestant claim that only the "elect" are saved, he argued that "God desires the salvation of all, and offers grace to all; He also gave us free will. The elect are those who serve God for love."

After the Reformation of 1560, the "Aberdeen Doctors" continued Grampian's tradition of moderation, consistently propounding a view that was more moderate than that of the zealous Calvinists for whom determinism was absolute. Their views are well expressed in the Confession of Faith and Catechisms produced by the Westminster Assembly of Divines and adopted by the General Assembly of the Church of Scotland in the 1640s: "By the decree of God...some men and angels are predestinated unto everlasting life and others foreordained to everlasting death... Their number... cannot be increased or diminished..." But amongst the "Aberdeen Doctors", Robert Baron argued that Christ died for all men. Both he and another of the group, John Forbes, maintained that whilst God does indeed predestine the wicked to hell, he does so only in the sense that He foresees their evil deeds.

Naturally, in this context of a moderate Reformation, Catholicism fared much better in Grampian than elsewhere in Scotland. For alone in the land, both the Reformation and the Covenant of 1638 had to be imposed on Grampian by force. In 1677 an envoy from Rome reported that of the 12,000 Romanists left in Scotland, most were to be found in the Highlands of Aberdeen and Banff. The Catholic seminary at Scanlan in Glenlivet (NJ 246 194) survived until the aftermath of the 1745 Jacobite rebellion saw it burned. The great Catholic family of the Gordons, earls of Huntly, maintained their faith in the fastness of the region. Indeed it was in Gordon country on the Braes of Enzie that the first Vicar Apostolic, Thomas Nicholson, found sanctuary in 1697. Despite the Reformation, the last Catholic Bishop of Aberdeen remained in his palace until his death in 1577.

Catholicism lives on in Grampian, its expressions not only the cathedral in Aberdeen but fine churches in Huntly, Buckie and Keith. It is fitting that the first building for Roman Catholic worship to be erected in Scotland after the Reformation should be in Grampian. Built in 1755 when, after Culloden, Catholics were execrated elsewhere in Scotland, St Ninian's Church at Tynet in Moray (NJ 378 612) is a fine symbol of Grampian's religious tolerance.

This was reflected not only in Catholicism. Quakerism too found fertile ground in Grampian and lives on amongst the "Bretheren", both "Closed" and "Open", of the fishing villages of Buchan and Moray. Their creed was given one of its most definitive expositions by a Grampian man, Robert Barclay of Urie (1648–90), in his classic *An Apology for the true Christian Divinity.*

*King's College,
Aberdeen, circa
1894*

Quakerism, with its emphasis on "inner light, that of God which is in man", emerged as an antidote to the schisms and conflicts that were already beginning to plague the reformed religion and that were to dominate its history in the 18th and 19th centuries.

Such schisms were almost inevitable in an Age of Reason: in 1690, the Scottish Parliament had replaced episcopal government in the established Church with presbyterian. Two-thirds of Scotland's ministers were so opposed to this decision that they were deprived of their parishes. Once more, however, Grampian was tolerant. The Episcopalian Church lived and lives on in the region, despite such incidents as the "Rabbling of Deer".

On 22 March 1711, the Presbyterian Church attempted to replace Old Deer's deceased episcopalian minister with the presbyterian Reverend John Gordon. Accompanying Revd Gordon to his new charge, the presbyters were met by a "great rabble armed with guns, swords, battons and great stones" (Pratt, *Buchan*) and withdrew. But Episcopalianism's triumph was short-lived. In 1719, the fiercely presbyterian Revd John Forbes took up the charge of Deer. His success may not have been hindered by the fact that he preached his sermons with a sword on his pulpit's cushion.

Meanwhile, the General Assembly complained that "there hath been in some a dreadful atheistical boldness against God, some have disputed the being of God and His providence, the divine authority of the Scriptures, the life to come and the immortality of the soul." Newton, Boyle, Locke and Hobbes may have been breaking new ground in physics, chemistry and philosophy, but in 1697 a youth of 18 was still hanged for blasphemy. This juxtaposition of reason and religion gave rise to great ferment in the Church.

Much took the form of heresies: the 18th-century Scottish Church was riven by controversy about Arminianism (the denial of predestination) and Arianism (the denial of Christ's divinity). The Auchterarder Creed of 1717 declared: "it is not sound and orthodox to teach that we must forsake sin in order to our coming to Christ." Christianity, then, the Creed maintained, is a religion not for saints but for sinners. But the established Church did not agree. These were the "Enthusiasts", distinct from the "Moderates".

Such challenges to orthodoxy led to the First or Original Secession of the 1730s, when conser-

vative ministers broke away from the Church of Scotland. This was but the first of many secessions which explain why most of Grampian's presbyterian churches are late in date. Each schism generated its own new buildings and, often, the abandonment of the old.

Secessions reached epidemic proportions. The presbyterian system lent itself to the disease, for any group of disgruntled ministers could simply form their own presbytery. The "New Lights" believed that the Church should be independent of the state, foreshadowing both the Great Disruption and bringing about the Second Secession or Relief Church of 1761.

Although few of these shenanigans had much impact on Grampian, no region of Scotland was more affected by the Scottish Church's greatest trauma since the Reformation, the Great Disruption of 1843. It is difficult to comprehend the passions that gave rise to the resignation from the Church of Scotland of 451 of her ministers and a third of her members. At issue was patronage: those who broke away and formed the Free Church of Scotland did so because they believed in the spiritual independence of the Church from the state and disputed the state's right to appoint ministers. Congregations, they thought, should be free to call their own. The secessionists were known as "Anti-Burghers" and the traditionalists as "Burghers" to reflect their attitudes as to whether or not the burghs or town councils could present a minister to a parish.

Even after the Disruption, controversy continued: within the Free Church, opinion polarised between the "Lifters" and the "Anti-Lifters". The first believed that the minister should lift the communion cup before the Act of Committal; the second believed that the cup should be left on the communion table. By such debates was the faith advanced.

If they were unsure about lifting, Grampian's ministers were in no doubt about patronage. To a man, the ministers of Aberdeen seceded. Revd David Simpson preached his last sermon in Aberdeen's Trinity Parish Church on an appropriate text: "Arise, let us go hence." They did, abandoning their church in the Shiprow. It was soon "transformed into a dilapidated structure, as if to remind the Establishment of the grievous wrong they had committed". In Aberdeen's fishing village, Footdee, the parishioners of St Clement's

Parish Church built themselves a new place of worship whilst their minister was still at the General Assembly in Edinburgh debating patronage. Constructed between the date of the Disruption and the first Sunday afterwards, this new church in the north-west corner of Baltic Street was the Free Church's first building in Grampian.

In Woodside, the seceders at first held their services in the school playground and then in a wooden shack in the field behind the school. The Church of Scotland church they had left was eventually put up for sale, only to be bought by the Free Churchers. Thus did those who had left return, whilst those few "Burghers" who had stayed departed. Much the same thing happened with the Union and Bon Accord Free Churches.

Within 10 years, the Free Church had built or bought 859 churches in Scotland. By 1870 it owned, at the formidable cost of £467,000, 719 manses. It is small wonder that a Church newspaper, the *Scottish Guardian*, reported in 1889 that "In some of our large towns the actual church building accommodation provided...is much in excess of any reasonable needs." The ferment of the Disruption left Grampian with an unusually large number of superfluous churches.

In the end, it all proved to have been unnecessary for the "Anti-Burghers" won the day. In 1929, the Church of Scotland repudiated patronage and accepted the United Free Church back into the fold. Especially in the Highlands, an independent Free Church (the "Wee Frees") lived and lives on, as it does to a lesser extent in Grampian. Vigorous and eclectic, tolerant and multi-faceted, the many churches, clerics and catechisms of modern Grampian are a natural reflection of its past.

**The Monymusk Reliquary**, now in the Royal Scottish Museum, Queen Street, Edinburgh

This remarkable relic, a house-shaped casket 10.8cm long, 9.8cm high and 5.1cm wide, dates from the 8th century and is arguably Scotland's finest early Christian artefact. For its breath-catching ornamentation is peculiarly Pictish and quite distinct from other early Christian house-shaped shrines. None of its embellishments are recognisably "Christian". Like the late Pictish Christian symbol stones, the Monymusk Reliquary demonstrates a vitality and energy that was indigenous

*Opposite:*
*Midmar Kirk stone circle*

and not merely imported with Irish Celtic Christianity. It shows that to some extent at least, captive Pictland took her captor captive.

What the casket contained is unknown. It may have held a physical relic of St Columba or his Eucharist or holy oils. What is beyond doubt is the veneration accorded such relics of saints. Throughout the early Christian Church they were believed to have healing powers and to ward off evil spirits. St Columba's Cathach or psalter and his crozier, known as Cath Bhuaith, were regularly carried in battle.

The reliquary's earliest association is with the church of St Adamnan at Forglen in Banffshire and it comes, therefore, from the very roots of the Christian Church in Grampian. Before 1211, King William I (the Lion) granted the church and lands of Forglen to the Abbot of Arbroath. This proved something of a barbed gift for with it the abbot received the reliquary which, for some reason which has never been explained, was also the *Brecbennoch,* the *vexillum* or sacred battle ensign, of St Columba. This entailed an obligation of military service, discharged by Bernard the Abbot with distinction at the battle of Bannockburn in 1314, carrying the reliquary before the Scottish army. The experience must have been salutary, for after the battle he passed the Brecbennoch, its military obligations and the church and lands of Forglen to Malcolm of Monymusk, who moved the reliquary from Forglen to the village from which the casket takes its name. There, by the river Don, it stayed until the Grants of Monymusk relinquished it to the then National Museum of Antiquities in 1933.

*The Monymusk Reliquary*

## Birnie Kirk, Elgin, Moray

NJ 206 587. 4km S of Elgin. Take B9010 out of Elgin from Gray's Hospital roundabout. First turning on left (E) crosses the river Lossie and leads to kirk after 500m. Unlocked.

Like Kildrummy raised on a mound, this church of St Brendan dates from 1140 and is the oldest surviving church in Grampian. The roughly circular site was almost certainly a place of earlier worship by the Culdee sect, whilst a simple incised Pictish stone stands in the churchyard beside the gate to the manse and adds to the sense of antiquity. Birnie was certainly one of the seats of the bishops of Moray before 1224.

Beautifully light within, a Romanesque arch divides the chancel from the nave in this pleasingly simple rectangle. The font and N and S doorways are original. Alterations were made in 1743 and again, by A Marshall MacKenzie, in 1891.

## Spynie Palace, Elgin, Moray

NJ 231 659. 3km N of Elgin, sign-posted off A941 Elgin/Lossiemouth road. HBM.

There is no better illustration in Grampian of the formidable power of the medieval Church than this majestic ruin, "one of the most splendid mediaeval monuments in Scotland" (McKean). Thankfully, a thorough programme of restoration is underway.

From 1200–24 Moray's cathedral was established here. When it moved to Elgin, the bishops kept their seat at Spynie, constructing a place of such strength as to rival any contemporary secular fortification, secure in their headland on Loch Spynie (drained by Thomas Telford 1808–12). The ruins consist of a late 14th-century curtain-walled castle with angle towers, protected to S and E by a moat. Over the main entrance are the arms of Bishop John Innes (1408–14). The walls are prodigious, 3.4m thick and rising 30m to the parapet walk and defended at basement level by enormous gunloops. Within the enclosure wall are the remains of a chapel and an indoor tennis court.

Yet what dominates the whole site is the huge David's Tower (*c.*1470–80), one of the largest tower houses in Scotland, 18m high and 18m long. It was built by a frightened Bishop David Stewart who had excommunicated the Earl of

*Elgin Cathedral*

Huntly; in retaliation, the earl threatened to "pull him from his pigeon hole". He never did. It was perhaps in one of the tower's five bedrooms that Mary Queen of Scots stayed in 1562 while conducting her campaign against a later Earl of Huntly and his Gordons.

### Elgin Cathedral, Elgin, Moray

NJ 221 630. Just N of Elgin town centre, signposted off A96. Open 9.30 a.m.–7.00 p.m. weekdays and 2–7 Sundays, April–September: 9.30–4.00 weekdays and 2–4 Sundays, October– March. HBM.

"My church was the ornament of the realm, the glory of the kingdom, the delight of foreigners and stranger quests: an object of praise in foreign realms." – Bishop Bur of Elgin, writing to King Robert III after the sacking of the cathedral by Alexander Stewart, the Wolf of Badenoch, in June 1390: Stewart had been excommunicated by Bur for deserting his wife.

This great triumph of medieval Scottish architecture simply wasted away after the Reformation. As Dr Samuel Johnson (*A Journey to the Western Islands of Scotland*) has it, the cathedral "was at last not destroyed by the tumultuous violence of Knox, but more shamefully suffered to dilapidate by deliberate robbery and frigid indifference". The lead was stripped from its roofs in 1567 to help pay for the Earl of Moray's army. In 1599, the Kirk Session of Elgin forbade the use of the ground. Thursday, 28 December 1640 saw one of the few acts of Reforming vandalism in Grampian: a party led by Revd Gilbert Ross, minister of Elgin, "came to the grand old cathedral of Elgin and destroyed every object in it...they tore down... medieval paintings, smashed the screen which was beautifully carved, probably gilded... The screen and the ornamental woodwork of pulpit, font lid and choir stalls they chopped up for firewood. All this they did to please God, who had since the foundation of the Christian Church, been plagued by the gaudy contrivances of man." (David Thomson, *Nairn in Darkness and Light.*)

The historian John Spalding, writing two years after this barbarism, records a fascinating post-script: "...this minister caused bring home the timber therof, and burn it for serving his kitchen...but each night the fire went out...and could not be held in to kindle the morning fire as use is; whereat the servants and others marvelled and...the minister...forebore to bring in or burn any more of that timber in his house."

In 1711 the middle tower collapsed. Only in 1807 did the government take over and begin to protect the ruins. This sorry history began, however, much earlier. Barely 20 years after the cathedral's consecration in 1224, it was badly damaged

*Midmar Kirk*

### Kildrummy Kirk, Kildrummy, Gordon

NJ 472 175. 11km W off Alford; clearly seen to E of A97 Huntly/Ballater road. Unlocked.

Although the present church dates from 1805, this is a site of great antiquity. The knoll on which the remains of the pre-Reformation church stand may have been a motte, possibly the precursor of Kildrummy Castle. By the door of the modern kirk lie grinding stones which were found amongst the "remains of prehistoric earth houses near Kildrummy".

The fine weathered sandstone font in the church dates to 1330. It was thrown out of the old church of St Bride after the Reformation and then given to Marischal College Museum by Alexander Reid, minister of Kildrummy, in 1812. Revd Reid's gravestone stands on the E side of the old graveyard. The font was returned to Kildrummy in 1967 by another Reid, David, whose Gaelic *New Testament* lies on the church's lectern. The pewter bowl in the font was once held as security for the year's stipend due to the widow of the minister of Kildrummy, who dedicated the standards of the Old Pretender (James VIII) in the 1715 Jacobite rebellion. For his pains, the minister was deposed and died in 1717.

Externally, the church is unusual, bow-fronted and rectangular; a finely worked bell is centrally placed; inside it is light and open, if austere. In typical Scottish presbyterian style, the interior is dominated by the pulpit in accordance with the Church of Scotland's emphasis on the Word. On the western wall is a corn dolly or "clyack" (a corruption of the Gaelic *cailliach* meaning "old women"). These are still made in parts of Grampian from the last corn to be cut from each harvest. The belief is that the spirit of the goddess of fertility lives on in the dolly until she is cast into the field at the spring sowing and set free once more. It is somehow appropriate that this "paganism" should live on within the Kirk of St Bride (from Bridei, King of Picts?) at Kildrummy.

### Deer Abbey, Old Deer, Banff and Buchan

NK 969 482. 3km W of Mintlaw on S side of A950 Peterhead-Fraserburgh road. Open April–September, Thursday–Saturday 9.30 a.m.–7.00 p.m. and Sunday 2–7 p.m.

by a fire. In 1390, it was so thoroughly burned by the Wolf of Badenoch that the Chapter decreed that all future bishops would have to devote one-third of their revenues to re-building the cathedral until the task was complete. In 1402, the Chanonry was sacked by MacDonald of the Isles and in 1506, the huge central tower collapsed. In 1555, the clans Innes and Dunbar fought the battle of the "Bloody Vespers" in the cathedral.

Despite these vicissitudes, the ruins remain compelling. The great processional W door, flanked by two identical towers, still speaks of the majesty of what is still a "glory of the kingdom".

Sadly little remains of this Cistercian abbey, founded around 1219 by William Comyn, Earl of Buchan. The antiquarian and aesthete Charles Cordiner drew substantial ruins in 1770 before Admiral Ferguson of nearby Pitfour (see *Temple of Theseus*) used the stones to build his mausoleum in 1854. The admiral's father had already turned the ruins into a walled garden in 1809. Some justice was done, however, when the Doric portico and pediment that now form the entrance to the abbey were brought here from Ferguson's mausoleum.

The area is an important one for early Christianity in Grampian. Nearby, on a bend of the Ugie Water, St Drostan founded a monastery in 719. It was here that the famous *Book of Deir* was written in the 9th century. The beautiful illuminated manuscript of 86 parchment folios contains the complete Gospel of St John and parts of the other three gospels, all in Latin. The manuscript's marginal *notitia* or jottings, written in Gaelic, hold particular interest. They tell, for example, of how Columba accompanied Drostan to Deer to see the foundation. As the saints parted, for Columba had to return to Iona, "their tears flowed" and Columba said, "Let this place be *Deara* [Gaelic "tears"] from henceforth." *The Book of Deer* is now in the Fitzwilliam Museum Library, Cambridge.

## St Machar's Cathedral, Old Aberdeen

NJ 939 087. In Chanonry, off St Machar's Drive.

This great cathedral, now only half of its medieval size, has the appearance more of a fortress than of a church. This is explained by its great western towers, which rise to cantilevered crenellated parapets, and by the use of unadornable granite. The see of Mortlach moved to Aberdeen in 1130; of its first cathedral on this memorable site, dedicated to St Mary and St Machar and built by 1170, nothing remains. A little of the nave's re-building in red sandstone around 1370 survives at the E end of the present nave, but it is to Bishop Henry Leighton's major refurbishments of 1422–40 that we owe the bulk of the present building. Between 1515 and 1531, Bishop Gavin Dunbar built the octagonal W spires and the glorious timber ceiling of the nave with its memorably fine heraldic shields. Of these, Ian Shepherd (*Exploring Scotland's Heritage:*

*The Kirk and the land, Buchan*

*Grampian*) especially notes the arms of the King of Scots "surmounted by an enclosed crown similar to that of the holy Roman emperor, signifying a monarch with full jurisdiction within his realm. The ceiling may thus be taken as a remarkable late medieval statement of Scotland's role as a distinct…part of Catholic Europe."

The cathedral was only just completed by the Reformation. In that year the "Barons of Mernes, accompanied with some of the townsmen of Aberdeen, having demolished the monasteries of the Black and Grey Friars, fell to rob the Cathedral, which they spoiled of all its costly ornaments". Yet the Aberdeen *Ecclesiastical Records* attest a measured benevolence in such religious vandalism: "That the organs, with all expedition be removed out of the kirk, made profit of to the use and support of the poor…" The roof's lead was removed in 1567. Roundhead soldiers demolished the choir, using the stone to fortify Castlehill. In 1688, the central tower collapsed, taking the transepts and the eastern nave with it. In the restorations that began in the 19th century and continue still (most recently with Professor Dunbar-Nasmith's work on the W towers), the eastern end of the cathedral was blocked off. The remains of the old choir and transepts are now kept up as a ruin.

## Pluscarden Abbey, Elgin, Moray

NJ 142 576. 8km SW of Elgin. Follow B9010 from roundabout at Gray's Hospital, Elgin, then bear right along minor road at first fork after 2km. Abbey sign-posted from there.

*Profound the peace of Pluscarden,*
*As if the pine-green closing hills*
*Shut in the grace*
*Of God and all His holy Saints.*

– RA Dick, 1950

There can be few finer religious experiences than Mass, sung in Latin by the Benedictine monks, in the church at Pluscarden (Sundays, 10 a.m.). It has long been a place of worship and contemplation. Although the abbey was founded in 1230 by Alexander II, there was a hermit's cell and a well dedicated to St Andrew there much earlier. That the community should be thriving today is all the more heartening, given Pluscarden's turbulent past.

Edward I of England ravaged Moray and damaged Pluscarden in 1303. When sacking Elgin Cathedral, the Wolf of Badenoch also burned the abbey. In 1454, the house of Pluscarden was merged with that of Urquhart Priory, 8km E of Elgin and an ancient dependency of Dunfermline Abbey. The founding monks, Valliscaulians, were replaced by Old Benedictines but the monastery declined after the Reformation and was finally abandoned around 1600.

It then passed through various lay hands. In 1680, its then owner Alexander Brodie of Lethen recorded: "We went thorou' that old ruined palace and did see the vestiges of a great old building and edifice." The Brodies sold it to the Duffs, later earls of Fife, before the distinguished Catholic antiquarian, the Marquess of Bute, bought it in 1897. His son donated the abbey and its grounds to the Benedictine community of Prinknash, Gloucestershire in 1943. Monks from Prinknash moved to Pluscarden in 1948 and began a programme of restoration that continues today. Pluscarden was granted independence from Prinknash in 1966 and raised to the status of an abbey in 1974. Thirty monks and novices now maintain their life of prayer there.

The beauty and peace of the abbey's church match the graceful calm of the building's exterior, reached through one of Scotland's best-preserved enclosure walls. The abbey's glass, especially in the E lancets of the restored chancel, is particularly fine and manufactured by Pluscarden's monks. One leaves Pluscarden with reluctance, full of the word which rightly graces the abbey gates, "Pax". For whilst many practical activites take place there, what stays with the visitor is an enrichening peace.

## St Gregory's Church, Presholme, Moray

NJ 409 614. 6km SW of Fochabers. Take minor road into Clochan off B9016 Buckie-Keith road. Church on left after 1km.

One little expects to find so grandiloquent and remarkable an Italian baroque façade on a hillside high above Buckie, but some ostentation was in order for the first overt Catholic church to be built in Scotland after the Reformation. The 33 years that separate St Gregory's (1788) from the self-effacement of St Ninian's Catholic church at Tynet (NJ 378 612) must have seen a considerable lessening of hostility towards Catholicism, for all the official tolerance expressed in the Catholic Relief Bill of 1783.

St Gregory's architect was her priest, Father John Reid. Ingeniously, his building is doubled in width by the staircase pavilions that flank the central door. It is a confident and compelling construction. It was once the headquarters of the Catholic Church in Scotland from 1697 to 1878.

### Udny Mort House, Udny Green, Gordon

NJ 880 262. 20km N of Aberdeen. Minor road sign-posted "Udny Green" off B999 Aberdeen-Tarves road. Mort house in graveyard on W side of green.

From the early 18th century, the growth of the study of medicine in general and anatomy, in particular, led to great demand for fresh corpses, despite the Anatomy (Scotland) Act of 1832 which provided for a legal supply of pristine cadavers. Body-snatchers, known as "resurrectionists", stalked the land; the churches had to guard their bodies destined for burial and those recently interred from the snatchers' predations. The buried were protected by watchmen; many of Grampian's churchyards have watchmen's houses, like the ones at St Fittick's Church at Nigg Bay, Aberdeen (NJ 964 049) and Dallas church, Moray (NJ 122 518). The corpses were kept safe in mort houses, such as Udny's, built in 1832 by Alexander Wallace and Thomas Smith. Those who had subscribed to the cost had free use of the mort house for themselves and their descendants; non-subscribers had to pay a fee.

Characteristic of such mort houses as that in Mortlach kirkyard (NJ 323 392), Udny is a formidable building, without windows and strongly doored – once by the outside door of oak and again by an inner sliding iron door. Udny mort house is unique, however, for its turntable, a revolving wooden platform attached to an irreversible ratchet, on which coffins lay for as long as three months before burial. By then the corpses would have been of little interest to even the most desperate of resurrectionists.

A simpler solution, often adopted, was the mortsafe, a capped iron cage covering the grave. There are four fine examples in Cluny Old Kirkyard (NJ 684 125) and an inverted mortsafe in Towie kirkyard, Strathdon (NJ 439 128).

# 4
# FORTS, CASTLES AND CIVILISATION

"The condition of man," wrote Hobbes, "is a condition of war." Wherever man has been, forts and castles and the works of war attest to his preoccupation with attack and defence. Paradoxically, such fortifications have brought peace as well as war, allowing security, affording structure, bestowing and permitting civilisation.

As a place in which to witness the pedigree or understand the development of the British castle over many centuries, Grampian is without equal. The region contains a complete and unique microcosm of the buildings of war, articulating centuries of consistent innovation in the architecture of fortification.

The earliest known fortifications of Grampian, the forts of the Celts, built from around 1200 BC, are as old as any in Europe. They point to the profound changes then taking place throughout the west, the emergence of a belligerent hierarchy of warriors and war-lords whose coming brought sweeping changes to Grampian. The pastoral, peaceful people of the stones (see chapter 1) were swept away and a highly organised, militaristic structure of Kings, sub-Kings and chiefs took their place.

The adoption of new technologies, first bronze around 1200 BC and then iron around 500 BC, must have intensified competition between the tribes and communities of Grampian as they vied for control or sought to retain that which they had. Such, perhaps, were the factors which led to the construction of such massive forts as the 21 hectares enclosed by the great walls that encircle Tap o' Noth. These forts could hardly be more different from the broch forts of Caithness, Orkney, Shetland and the Western Isles.

For the broch, a circular tower, was a place of temporary refuge: with its 6-metre-thick walls and single, low entrance, it is a passive, not an active structure, its purpose defence, not attack. Equally, brochs are found on arable land, not hilltops. They were, then, shelters in which a peaceful, pastoral people took temporary and impregnable refuge from sudden attack.

By complete contrast, the high and huge forts of Grampian point to a radically different, more aggressive society, one formed, perhaps, by an early wave of Celtic invaders from across the North Sea who came easily into Grampian, like earlier immigrants, by means of the region's rivers.

The passing of such great Celtic forts was as remarkable as their coming. The haunting, vitrified remains of such forts as Tap o' Noth, Dunideer, or Doune of Relugas (NJ 003 495) tell of a terrible vengeance. They were burnt by adversaries who first piled and then lit brushwood hard against the forts' stone and timber walls. Such was the heat that the very stone melted. The fate of the forts' inhabitants can hardly have been less dramatic, whilst the destruction and great burning of these awesome forts must have been long visible and salutary to those near and far.

By approximately the beginning of the first millennium AD, the Celtic society of Grampian was replaced by one we know as Pictish. Whether it was the Picts who so extirpated the Celts, we cannot tell. What we do know is that the Picts, too, were a hierarchical and military people who had also their forts and defended sites, notably Burghead. Of the duns (Gaelic *dun*: fort) which are found in other parts of Pictland, we know little in Grampian. Dunnottar is the only site generally accepted to have been such a place of Pictish strength.

It was almost certainly a Pictish Grampian that the Romans encountered during their first campaign here in 84 AD and, still, during their second, early in the 3rd century. Neither made much architectural impact, leaving none of the forts that are such impressive testament to Roman occupation elsewhere in Scotland. All that remains are the walls of temporary marching camps, such as at Raedykes (NO 841 902) or Logie Durno (NJ 698 271).

The early 9th century saw Pictland, like so much of Britain, under attack from marauding Vikings. Such fortifications as the timber-laced wall at Green Castle, Portknockie (NJ 488 687) attest to the response of Grampian.

*Opposite:*
*Crathes Castle*

# GRAMPIAN

*A country in miniature*

It was not until the Canmore dynasty of the first Kings of a newly united Scotland brought feudalism to Grampian that we encounter any significant development of the castle. Central, royal authority and control were extended by the granting of areas of land or knights' fees (feus) to faithful supporters who reciprocated by giving military service to their King.

The stark, crude, compelling mottes like those at Duffus, Inverurie, Strachan (NO 657 921) or Midmar (NJ 700 059) are vivid testament to the new, raw power of these first feudal barons of Grampian. In the heart of their fiefdoms they prepared a deep, circular ditch. The excavated earth was thrown into the centre, forming a high mound or motte. The top of the motte was then flattened and a fence or palisade of wood constructed around the top. Within the palisade stood a dwelling and, perhaps, a look-out tower.

At the base of the motte, an open space known as the bailey was encircled by some form of ditch. The excavated earth was used, this time, to build a defensive wall or rampart round the bailey. Such mottes and baileys are well depicted in the Bayeux Tapestry and described in the epic poem *Roman von Guillame le Clerc* (c.1209).

Norman feudalism, however, spread but slowly in Grampian. Large parts of it, certainly Moray, remained semi-autonomous under their sub-Kings, Mormaers and Toiseachs, Pictish relics in a Scottish age. Although it took time, six principal factors eventually ensured the supremacy of feudalism in Grampian.

First, the famous Picto-Scottish King, Macbeth, was to die at Lumphanan (not Dunsinane) in 1057. His successor, Malcolm Canmore, killed Lady Macbeth's son, Lulach (or Luath), in 1058, so beginning the end of the struggle of the Picts against the supremacy of the western Scots, for all that Lulach's son, Maelsnechtai, was still called "King of Moray" at his death in 1088. Then King David I, third son of Malcolm and his Saxon wife Margaret, defeated Macbeth's descendant, Angus of Moray, in battle in 1130 and accelerated the process of feudalism that his father had begun by planting royal burghs, 12th-century equivalents of 20th-century "new towns", and Norman churches throughout Grampian.

Next, the last Pictish pretender to the Scottish throne, Donald MacWilliam, was killed by William I in 1187. Finally, around 1200, the ancient and defiant Pictish mormaerdom of Buchan came to an end. Fergus, the last Mormaer, died without a male heir and his daughter Marjory married a Norman, feudal import, William Comyn.

Meanwhile, the indigenous Pictish overlords were not slow to copy the fortifications of the feudalism that first threatened and then destroyed them. Ruardhi, the Pictish Mormaer of Mar and Gartnait, built a motte for himself at Ruthrieston. Further mottes at Nigg, Banchory, Devenick and Tillydrone formed a watching, waiting ring around the new and foreign feudal royal burgh of infant Aberdeen. It took more royal burghs, such as Kintore, Inverurie, Banff and Cullen, the importation of more Norman "white settlers" – the de Lesselyns at Leslie, the Balliols at Dunideer – and, thirdly, the establishment of many new churches to complete the victory of the new over the old.

Although the next development, the stone castle, is the direct descendant of the feudal motte and bailey, in many ways the early stone castles mark not a continuation of but a break with tradition. The motte and bailey is clearly derivative of the prehistoric system of fortification by ditches and ramparts, surmounted by a palisade. The early stone castles are radically different.

As the power of the great feudal families of Grampian – the Irvines, the Bissetts, the Durwards, the Comyns – grew, these families required more telling expression of their status and, indeed, more space than could be provided by a grudging home on a motte. Some tried to build a true stone castle on an existing motte, but, as at Duffus, the result was catastrophic: the motte was unequal to the weight and the house came tumbling down.

Timber gave way to stone. The timber tower became the stone tower or keep, the timber palisade and earthern rampart the curtain wall of stone (the enceinte).

In Grampian, the Peel of Lumphanan and the Doune of Invernochty, both built around 1200, exemplify the earliest transition from motte and bailey to stone castle. Both are "shell-keeps", the simple re-fortification in stone of a motte and bailey castle.

The dating of the early stone castles, not only in Grampian but throughout Britain, is notoriously contentious. What is clear is that by the early 14th century, several important castles had been built in Grampian. Most, like Kildrummy or Balvenie (NJ 326 408) or Coull (NO 512 022) were castles of enclosure with curtain walls of stone, derivative of the great Edwardian castles of North Wales. Others, built late in the 13th century, exemplify another tradition, the tower castle. Such are Drum and Dunideer, followed around 1280 by the towers of Skene and Hallforest (NJ 777 154).

The heart of both types was the lord's hall and adjacent private chamber. Within castles of enclosure, these rooms were on a single level; in tower castles, on several. The logical extension to the tower castle was, simply, to add a wing at right angles to the keep. When, towards the end of the 14th century, Sir William Keith, Great Marischal of Scotland, did just this at Dunnottar, he built the first of the many L-plan tower castles in Grampian.

Simultaneously, the castle of enclosure was also evolving into the type known as the "palace house." Such a name is misleading if it implies any special grandeur, for it derives from the Latin *palatio*, meaning, simply, a hall-house. In this, hall and solar (lord's suite) are not confined to a perpendicular keep or tower, but adjoin each other on the same level with a staircase accommodated in an angle tower of its own.

The first of Grampian's "palace houses", Druminnor, was begun in 1440 by the first Lord Forbes. It was followed rapidly by the new castle of the first Earl of Huntly, built alongside his existing L-plan tower house.

A few years later, in 1457, a new castle was built at Pitcaple (NJ 727 260): its Z-plan design was a perfect synthesis of all that had preceded it. In a Z-plan castle, the central block of the building, whether tower or hall-house, has two flanking towers, either round or square, at diagonally opposite corners.

This was not only an aesthetic triumph; it was also a masterpiece of defensive architecture: each gunlooped tower could cover with its fire the main block, whilst the main block, in turn, could cover both towers. Although an innovation originating in Aberdeenshire, there were soon 170 Z-plan castles in Scotland.

From the remarkable Z-plan, the castle-builders of Grampian went on to achieve even greater feats. There developed, in the 16th and 17th centuries and particularly in Aberdeenshire, a school of castle-building that is, arguably, unsurpassed anywhere in the world. The *dramatis personae* were two extraordinary families of master masons, the Bells in Mar and the Leipers in Buchan.

With Midmar Castle, George Bell began the glory that is now known and envied as the Aberdeenshire School. Although based on Z-plan, the Bells' castles display an astonishing flowering of features and innovations: ogee (S-shaped in profile) roofs, crow-stepped gables, circular corbelled turrets, a breathtaking effusion of beauty and skill.

*Plaque to the Bell family, Midmar Kirkyard*

Over three-quarters of a century, from 1552 to 1626, George Bell and his two sons, John and David, built Midmar, Crathes (NO 734 968), Castle Fraser (NJ 722 125), Old Cluny, Pitfichie (NJ 677 166) and Craigievar.

In Buchan, meanwhile, Thomas Leiper and his son James were at work on such castles as Arnage, Tolquhon and the House of Schivas. They collaborated with John Bell in the building of Castle

*Balmoral Castle*

Fraser, whilst yet a third great but unknown practitioner of the Aberdeenshire School built Gight (NJ 827 393), Delgatie, Craig (NJ 471 248) and Towie Barclay (NJ 744 439) castles.

This remarkable and prolific period of castle-building in Grampian was, to some extent, the fruit of the 30 years of peace that followed the Union of the Crowns in 1603. The best of the medieval castle was married to the best of the Renaissance: painted ceilings, pillared balconies, timbered ceilings.

Perhaps castle-building in Grampian had reached its climax; the products of the late 17th century, such as Leslie Castle (NJ 599 248) in 1661, are more houses than fortifications. In any case, after the troubles of the Covenant came the Civil War; Grampian was to know no settled peace until the demise of the Jacobite rebellions in the middle of the 18th century. Although some castles were built, they lacked the perfection of the unparalleled products of the Aberdeenshire School.

The rest of the history of the castles of Grampian is a history of embellishment, alteration and refinement. From even the mid-17th century onwards, a few of the old families of the region and many new ones grew rich from trade and commerce. That much money was spent on re-fashioning the old is amply proved by Brodie Castle (NH 979 577), Leith Hall (NJ 540 297) or Fyvie Castle (NJ 763 393), to name but a few.

In simplistic essence, then, the development of the castle in Grampian is as follows:

| | |
|---|---|
| Celtic Forts | 1200 BC–200 BC |
| Pictish Forts and Duns | 200 BC–600 AD |
| Mottes and Baileys | 1150–1200 |
| Shell Keep | *c.* 1200 |
| Tower Castles | from *c.* 1260 |
| Enceinte Castles | from *c.* 1300 |
| L-Plan | from *c.* 1390 |
| Palace Houses | from *c.* 1440 |
| Z-Plan | from *c.* 1457 |
| Aberdeenshire School | from *c.* 1550 |

That Grampian should contain a wealth of examples of each of these types is one of her greatest riches. Their story, of course, is not merely one of earthworks and stoneworks, but of the people who lived and died within them. They help us to understand the people of our past and, therefore, the people of our present.

Too many of the great houses of Grampian were lost or ruined during the late 19th and the first part of the 20th century. The litany of the loss of Castle Newe, Lessendrum, Rothiemay, Blackhall, Gordon Castle and many, many more is chilling. Yet the tide, thankfully, has turned. Pitfichie, Leslie, Terpersie and Harthill are but four of Grampian's castles to have been restored privately, whilst the National Trust has saved many others. Historic Buildings and Monuments continue to care for those like Auchindoun or Balvenie which, though ruined, still have much to tell. Gordon District's Castle Trail is rightly lauded. By appointing, at last, a Field Monuments Warden in Grampian, HBM will be able to do much more to arrest the decay of the earlier fortifications in the region.

There survive in Scotland just under 1,000 castles of stone. At least a handsome tenth of these are in Grampian, whilst the region's concentration of castles built between 1200 and 1600 is even more disproportionate. As for earlier fortifications, no other Scottish region has so accessible a concentration. Grampian's unique and priceless heritage of the architecture of fortification is, at last, being accorded the respect and attention that it has long deserved.

The forts and castles in this section are described in approximate chronological order under their most common name. The selection attempts to blend the well-known with the relatively unknown.

## Tap o' Noth

NJ 484 293. 11km S of Huntly. Go W from Rhynie on A941 to Dufftown. 200m W of Scurdargue, turn N up track to carpark (Signposted). Path zig-zags to summit. Stout boots recommended. Unrestricted access.

The steep and strenuous walk (2–3 hrs return) to the spectacular summit is well worth the effort for the view alone. At 563m, this is the second highest hillfort in Scotland (after Ben Griam Beg, Sutherland). The site's 21 hectares are enclosed, first, by an outwork of a wall of stone on all but the steep SE side. The rectangle of the upper fort, the shape of a football pitch, is enclosed by a massive, now vitrified wall, thought to have been 6–8m wide at the base and 3.5m tall. When excavated, the cistern at the S end of the fort was found to be 2.2m deep.

As you climb steeply to the windy walls of this or any of the many other prehistoric hillforts of Grampian (eg Wheedlemount, NJ 472 260; Cairnmore, NJ 503 249; Cairnton of Balbegno, NO 633 722), you are bound to wonder how anyone could ever live in such places, especially in winter. The answer may be in two parts: up to the middle of the first millennium, the climate of Grampian was milder. Secondly, there is evidence to suggest

*Fyvie Castle*

*Duffus Castle,
motte and bailey,
Moray*

that these warlike Celts may have used adjacent but lower enclosures as well as their hill-top eyries — summer and winter residences, perhaps.

## Barmekyn of Echt

NJ 726 071. 2km NNW of village of Echt, 21 km W of Aberdeen. Turn right in Echt onto B977 signposted "Dunecht and Kintore". After 1 km, turn left up track to Upper Mains farm. After 1.5km, park in layby and walk E up track for 200m before striking N through thick heather to summit. Stout boots (45 minutes return walk).

The name "Barmekyn" is, possibly, a diminutive of the Old Norse *barmr*, the edge of a castle. Yet there is nothing diminutive about this great fort. The approach, via the great gateway in the fort's outer wall (on the SE side) is striking. Here was a place of great strength, one for a lord of all he surveyed. The fort commands unforgettable views to all sides over the rich land around it, rolling away to the hills that surround it and make it the centre of what was once, perhaps, a little Celtic kingdom. The Mither Tap of Bennachie and its great iron-age fort, perhaps a rival, stand clear in the N. To the SSW, best aided with binoculars, you can see the turrets of Midmar Castle rise from douce farmland on the lower slopes of the Hill of Fare.

The siting of such as the Barmekyn of Echt may be due to more than demonstrable reasons: it is interesting to note that the fort stands on a clear line that runs NE from the Sunhoney stone circle (NJ 716 057) bisecting not only the Barmekyn but the circle at New Wester Echt (NJ 738 084) and the standing stones at NJ 749 096 and 779 131.

More prosaically, the Barmekyn is of interest for the clear multivallation that surrounds its 500-odd-m circumference. There are three clear rows of bank and ditch, then a pair of (later?) stone walls. It was in their lee that Grampian's greatest novelist Lewis Grassic Gibbon completed *Grey Granite*, shortly before his death.

## Burghead Fort and Well

NJ 109 691. 11km SW of Elgin, at seaward end of modern village of Burghead. Unrestricted access.

Imagination is required to recreate in the mind's eye this great centre of Pictish power, now sadly overwhelmed by the village, built on the site in 1805–9, and its ugly, domineering maltings plant. It is best to begin by appreciating this magnificent promontory fort from the great, sweeping beach of Roseisle to the S (easily approached from the B9089). There one can readily imagine the impregnability of the fort and picture the Pictish fleet moored in the lee of the promontory.

Eighteenth-century engravings show the fort to have been medallion-shaped. Three great ramparts, 6m high, ran across the neck of the promontory for 240m in arrowhead formation, defending the landward side. These great walls were timber-laced and nailed at the joints. A further great rampart defended the seaward sides whilst the inner ridge was defended by a cross rampart. Part of this survives as the "Doorie Hill", now used for the village's mid-winter fire-festival, the Clavie, still held on 11 January.

So were 3 hectares enclosed, forming a considerable town. Of especial interest are the famous Burghead Bulls, Pictish animal carvings (two can be seen in the village library) and the subterranean Burghead Well, discovered and preserved in 1809 during the search for a suitable village water supply. It is known locally as "Bailey's Well", since it lay within the bailey (annexe) of the fort. The well, now in the care of HBM, is an impressive and essential site, pointing further to the grandeur and importance of Burghead: key from Mrs Anderson, 60 King Street, Burghead. Various uses have been ascribed to the well: a Roman well, an early Christian baptistry (note the bath in one corner and the pedestal in another), a Celtic then Pictish water shrine.

## Cullykhan

NJ 838 661. 16km W of Fraserburgh, 1km NW of Pennan. W of Pennan on B9031, turn N up first track to carpark. Walk along narrow path for 500m to fort. Unrestricted access.

Also known as Castle Point, Troup, this is another distinctive Pictish promontory fort of the school of Burghead, Dundarg (NJ 895 649) or Green Castle (NJ 488 687), although excavations have revealed occupation that may ante-date the Picts. The remarkable, natural defensive qualities of the site make it an obvious choice as a fortified refuge. Indeed, a medieval castle and then Fort Fiddes, an 18th-century shore fort, prolonged this memorable site's long history. Once again, the promontory must have afforded welcome shelter to the ships that carried the warriors of Buchan to war.

## Duffus

NJ 189 672. 6km NW of Elgin. Sign-posted to carpark, turning E off B9012 Elgin-Hopeman road. Unrestricted access: HBM.

This great feudal motte and its ruined 14th-century castle, a combination unique in Scotland,

rises unexpectedly and massively from the now-fertile flatness of the Laich of Moray. The motte and bailey was probably built by King David around 1130 before being given as a feu to Hugo Freskyn, a Fleming, around 1160. David himself stayed here in 1151, whilst visiting his new abbey at Kinloss. The English Commissioners sent north by Edward I of England to receive the Maid of Norway also stayed at Duffus.

The deep ditch that separated the motte from the bailey is still visible. After the castle's sack in 1452, a new curtain wall was built around the old bailey. Remains of the domestic buildings which sheltered behind it survive. The whole site, 3 hectares, is surrounded by an original defensive ditch.

## The Bass of Iverurie

NJ 780 205. 1.5km SE of Inverurie centre. Turn E onto B993 on southern outskirts of town. Motte unmistakable to N of road, in graveyard 100m after railway bridge. Access unrestricted.

This spectacular motte, sited to command the fords of the rivers Urie and Don, is, like Duffus, a product of the feudalisation of Grampian. Between 1179 and 1182, as Earl of Huntingdon, David was granted a fief in the still Pictish Garioch by his brother the King; David established his caput or seat at Inverurie and erected the castle whose motte and outer bailey survive as the Bass of Inverurie. Unusually, alongside the main motte is a subsidiary, oblong mound (known as the Little Bass) which may have housed the domestic buildings.

Thomas the Rhymer of Ercildoune prophesised of the Bass:

*The Dee and Don shall run in one,*
*The Tweed shall run in Tay,*
*And the bonnie water o' Urie*
*Shall bear the Bass away.*

Although, by means of a canal, the waters of the Don did mingle with the Dee in the mouth of Aberdeen harbour, the Bass stood fast!

## Peel of Lumphanan

NJ 576 036. 1km SW of Lumphanan on minor road to Dess as it passes under railway, off A980 Banchory-Alford. Unrestricted access: HBM.

Built by the Norman Durward family, this is a very large, flat-topped, medieval earthwork and a fine example of its type, 37m by 46m and rising for 9m above its encircling ditch, itself an unusual width of 15m. It is the stone curtain wall, girdling the very edge of the summit, that led to the Peel's identification as a shell keep; this may, however, be a late 18th-century dyke.

The great flood of 1829 revealed the sluice through which the water left the ditch and the position of the drawbridge, but both have now vanished. Until their removal for building material in 1782, the remains of a rectangular manor, Halton House, were visible on the top of the mound.

Apart from its associations with Macbeth, Lumphanan was also the scene of the submission, in 1296, of Sir John de Malvill (Melville) to a triumphant Edward I as he marched N, reinforcing his victory in the first of the Wars of Scottish Independence.

### Doune of Invernochty

NJ 351 129. 25km W of Alford on B973 at Strathdon, just after War Memorial by roadside. Unrestricted access.

Although two other Norman earthworks (Urr in Kircudbrightshire and Duffus) are of comparable size, the oval summit of this, the "capital messuage" of one of the five great feudal lordships of Mar, is unparalleled in size, 74m by 33m. Like Lumphanan, the summit is encircled by a curtain wall of stone, this time mortared and, therefore, almost certainly contemporary with the motte itself.

Within this wall lie the foundations of two rectangular stone buildings, one, near the S entrance, probably a tower and the other, oblong-shaped, a chapel. A carved basin or *piscina* and a romanesque fragment of stone were found near the chapel. These are two of the very few recorded examples of early Norman stone-work on a motte-castle.

Of more prosaic, but equal interest, is the feat of military engineering which enabled the motte's ditch to be flooded by a great earthwork dam nearby to the W (the eastern bank is still visible in the trees), the flow controlled by a complex series of sluices. Water remained in the moat until 1823, when the new road was built.

### Dunnottar

NO 881 838. 1.5km S of Stonehaven, sign-posted off A92 Stonehaven-Montrose road. Carpark, then 1km walk to castle. Privately owned. Open to public 9 a.m.– 6 p.m., Sundays 2–5 p.m.

For situation, history and architecture, Dunnottar Castle is all but unrivalled. No account of the history and development of the British castle would be complete without it.

The cliff-top eyrie of Dunnottar has been fortified since prehistoric times: it may be the *Duns Fother* of such early epics as the *Annals of*

*Castle Fraser, circa 1920*

*Ulster* and the old French *Romance of Fergus*. The castle's 3.5 hectares first enter recorded history with their capture from the English by Sir William Wallace in 1297 (see chapter 2). The English garrison sought sanctuary in the castle's church, built in 1276 on the site of an earlier chapel consecrated to St Ninian. Wallace burned them alive.

The earliest structure still standing is round to the right of the present brooding gatehouse: the L-plan keep, 15m high, was built by Sir William Keith early in the 14th century.

A declaration under the Privy Seal of 20 January 1531 recognised Dunnottar's importance, declaring it "ane of the principall strenthis of our realme and warrand of the cuntre quhar it lyis". Yet it was not until the 17th century that Dunnottar assumed importance on a national scale. By then the Keiths, Earls Marischal, had built themselves a formidable seat, adding in the late 16th and early 17th centuries many of the buildings that survive today – the great quadrangle or palace that forms a complete mansion house in the NE corner of the plateau of rock, the Great Hall in the N range and the Whig's Vault of 1645.

In 1639, his new buildings barely completed, the seventh Earl Marischal declared for the Covenant. Montrose was unable to change his old friend's mind. In 1645, he beseiged Dunnottar for his envoy had "stood at the yett, bot gat no answer, quhairat Montroiss was heichlie offendit". He found Dunnottar impregnable, but the earl had to "stand on his own battlements and see the fires of war devouring his broad acres". The Covenanting minister by his side, Andrew Cant, offered him this consolation: "Trouble not, for the reek will be a sweet-smelling savour in the nostrils of the Lord." The earl's response is unrecorded.

Defeated at Worcester in 1651, King Charles sent the Crown Jewels to Dunnottar for safe-keeping. By May of the next year, only Dunnottar still flew the royal flag in Scotland. It surrendered only after an eight-month siege. By then, the Regalia had been smuggled out of the castle and hidden under the floor of Kinneff Church. There they remained until the Restoration of 1660.

Two more episodes conclude Dunnottar's history: the notorious 1685 incarceration in the Whig's Vault of 122 men and 45 women of the

*Farmland from Barmekyn hillfort, Echt*

Covenant and the use of Dunnottar's cannon in the 1715 Jacobite rebellion. The tenth Earl Marischal, George, played a prominent part in that rising. His estates were forfeited as a result and Dunnottar came into the hands of the York Buildings Company who dismantled much of the castle, selling off the roofs and floors. The estate and castle were bought by the Cowdrays in 1919. In 1925 Viscountess Cowdray began to restore the ruins of this unequalled place.

### Drum Castle

NJ 796 005. 16km W of Aberdeen, sign-posted N off A93 Aberdeen-Banchory road. Open to public: April–October, Mon–Sat 9 a.m.–4.30 p.m., Sun 10 a.m.–4 p.m.

Of many tower houses and baronial residences in Grampian, Drum is definitive. Its original rect-

*Gravestones of the Lairds of Drum, Deeside*

angular tower, 16m by 12m, with its rounded towers, has no projections except that of a latrine on the wall-walk. A 1619 Renaissance mansion is attached to but does not overwhelm the tower, built around 1286 by Robert the Bruce to guard the Royal Forest of Drum.

The rounded battlements are very rare in tower-houses. To drain rain-water away, the stone flags of the parapet walk vary in height, thereby making for hazardous passage. In compensation, and this feature is unique, the inner face of the battlements is niched to provide a foothold.

The Jacobean wing of Drum rewards attention. A vaulted, stone-flagged passage extends along the length of the basement; in the drawing-room, once the great hall of the Renaissance castle, hang portraits of Irvine lairds (Bruce gave Drum to his armour-bearer, William de Irvine, in 1323) by Raeburn, Reynolds and Gilbert.

## Dunideer

NJ 612 281. 2km W of Insch, sign-posted from village: carpark by side of minor road from Insch-Clashindarroch. Unrestricted access. Stout shoes. 1 hour return walk.

There are many reasons for walking the brisk 267m to the top of the hill of Dunideer. The ram-part and ditch of a prehistoric Celtic fort and the remains of a second, possibly Pictish fort are of great interest, whilst the walk and the view alone are reward enough. Opposite, on the Hill of Christ's Kirk (NJ 601 274) are the remains of another prehistoric fort.

Under-rated, however, are the ruins of a very early tower castle of stone, almost certainly those of the "Castle of Dunidor" of 1260, referred to in the *Chartulary* of Lindores Abbey. This would make Dunideer the earliest authenticated tower-house in Scotland. The castle was a simple, rect-angular tower, unvaulted, with two narrow slit-windows in the basement.

## Kildrummy

NJ 454 163. 12km W of Alford on A97 Huntly-Ballater road. Unrestricted access: HBM

Gaunt and imposing ruins are all that is left of this, the earliest great castle of enclosure (enceinte) in Grampian. It was built around 1225 for Alexander II by the last Scottish saint, Gilbert de Moravia, Bishop of Caithness, to secure royal authority over the route to newly subjugated Moray. It is of seminal importance to Scottish history over six centuries. The stone was quarried from just N of the castle, the *lapicidarium de*

*Kyndromyn* of the Exchequer Rolls, and now a magnificent rock garden (see chapter 8).

Alexander had dictated for Kildrummy a plan based on the French Chateau de Coucy, once the home of his wife Marie. Hence the great keep or *donjon*, the Snow Tower. But, by the time Alexander and his successor had died, Kildrummy was unfinished and Scotland in the throes of her struggle for independence.

By an irony of history, the castle was completed in 1296 by the two gatehouse towers, identical to those of Harlech Castle in Wales, and other works of Edward I. Edward lived to regret the labour: for their safety, in 1306 Robert the Bruce sent his wife and children to Kildrummy under the care of his brother Nigel. A siege by Prince Edward was unsuccessful until the castle was betrayed by Osburn the Smith. He received his promised reward of gold in unexpected form: molten, it was poured down his throat.

Restored after the battle of Bannockburn in 1314, Kildrummy was again besieged in 1335 when held by Bruce's sister, Christian, wife of the then regent of Scotland, Sir Andrew de Moray. He relieved the castle and defeated the attackers at the battle of Culblean (see chapter 2), turning the tide in Scotland's favour in the second War of Independence.

Burnt in 1530, the castle was captured by Cromwell in 1654 and burnt again. In 1690, the forces of Viscount Dundee set light to Kildrummy rather than allow it to fall into the hands of William of Orange. Partly restored, it became the headquarters of the Earl of Mar's ill-fated Jacobite rebellion of 1715. Thereafter, it was dismantled and became the local quarry until Colonel James Ogston began repairs in 1898. In 1951, his niece gave the castle to what is now HBM.

## Delgatie

NJ 754 506. 3km E of Turriff. Turn E off A947 Turriff-Banff road along first minor road. Signposted to S after 1.5km. Privately owned: open to public Wednesdays and Sundays, 2.30–5 p.m., July–August.

Delgatie has been for 700 years the home of the Hays, a family which has given distinguished service to Scotland. The family is said to have gained its name from the battle of Luncarty in 971, when three of them alone held a pass against the Danes and were given the name Haye, from the Gaelic *garadh*, a palisade or wall.

Robert the Bruce rewarded the chief of the Hays for his part in the Wars of Independence with the title of Hereditary Lord High Constable of Scotland, still held today by the Countess of Errol. At Flodden, in 1513, the third Earl of Errol, Clan Chief, Sir Gilbert Hay of Delgatie, 88 other chieftains of the name and all their men were killed, fighting beside their King. Hay of Delgatie was executed alongside Montrose in 1650. The staunch devotion of the Hays to the Jacobite cause led to their persecution and diaspora all over the world.

Their original, four-storeyed tower-house of the 13th century was slowly added to until, in the 16th century, the castle was completely rebuilt on an L-plan. Besieged in 1594 after the battle of Glenlivet, the W wall was breached and restored in 1597. Chapel and kitchen were added to the main tower in the 17th century; 1720 saw further improvements, notably the Long Drawing Room on the N side. The castle's collection of armour is especially fine, as are three painted ceilings.

## Auchindoun

NJ 348 374. 4km SE of Dufftown, off A941 Dufftown-Rhynie road, up rough track to Upper Keithack/Parkhead. Private ground to castle, then HBM.

The remains of this L-plan tower castle, built late in the 15th century on an imposing hill, are as striking as any, alone and proud in the empty Cabrach. It is memorably viewed from Glen Fiddich, 2km to the S.

The castle is surrounded still by prehistoric earthworks. Nearby, King Malcolm II routed an army of Danes at the Battle of Carron in 1010. There is a fine lime-kiln on the W of the castle-hill, a relic of the agricultural improvements of the 18th century (see chapter 5).

The design of the castle is attributed to James Cochrane, Earl of Mar. It then became a home of the Gordons. Most infamous of these was Adam Gordon who, in 1571, intensified the long feud between the Gordons and the Forbes (see chapter 2) by besieging a Forbes seat, Corgarff Castle, defended by the wife of the absent Alexander Forbes. Since they would not surrender, Gordon set light to the castle, burning the lady, her children and household alive.

# GRAMPIAN
*A country in miniature*

## Druminnor

NJ 514 263. 1.5km SE of Rhynie. Turn E at junction in Rhynie of A97 with A941 onto minor road. Sign-post to castle. Privately owned. Open to public by appointment.

Although the first written record is a charter of 1271, the family Forbes had been established

*Braemar Castle, the Braes of Mar*

here since prehistoric times, their first castle probably 1.6km N of the present one where the Kearn Burn meets the River Bogie. (*Druminnor* is Gaelic for "ridge where two rivers meet".)

The castle we see today, and especially the E front, is substantially the 1440 palace house built for Sir Alexander Forbes (elevated to the peerage in 1445) by John of Kemlock and William of Inverkip, both from Renfrewshire. They received 151 of the 200 merks due to them for "ye makyn of ye house of Drumynour" before going on to build Huntly Castle (NJ 532 407) to much the same plan.

Druminnor was partly sacked after the battle of Tillyangus in 1571 (see chapter 2). The year 1660 saw very extensive alterations, such as the sub-division of the great, first-floor hall. The Old Tower was demolished in 1795. A Gothic wing, added in 1815 by the architect Archibald Simpson, was demolished in 1960 and the main block restored to its 17th-century glory. Of unusual note is the "happy room", so-called from a 15th-century inscription, possibly by King James II.

Driven deep into debt by the feud with the Gordons, the sixteenth Lord Forbes sold Druminnor in 1770 to Robert Grant, moving the seat of Clan Forbes to Putachie, now Castle Forbes (NJ 622 192). The Grants, in turn, were forced to sell Druminnor in 1954; of the 49 lots, the Hon Margaret Forbes-Sempill (of Craigievar Castle) bought the castle and began its restoration. It was bought in 1976 by Mr Andrew Forbes, through sixteen generations a direct descendant of the castle's builder.

## Glenbuchat

NJ 397 148. 18km W of Alford, sign-posted off A97 Huntly-Ballater road. Unrestricted access: HBM.

This is an outstanding and pure example of the Z-plan castle, built in 1590 by John Gordon and his second wife, Helen Carnegie. Though now illegible, their names and the date still stand above the ruin's gateway with the vainglorious motto: "Nothing on earth remanis bot faime". Fleeing to France with D1000 on his head after the 1745 Jacobite rebellion, the last laird of Glenbuchat, John Gordon, the famous "Old Glenbuchat", put the motto to the test. He died in poverty in 1750. The whole glen, sorely depopulated, bears sombre witness to the privations his people shared. (In fairness, the motto should be interpreted in relation to the then contemporary meanings of "faime" as "good repute" and "bot" as "without".)

One feature of the castle's architecture is especially interesting: arches, not corbels (projecting stones or timbers) support the staircase. This is more typically French than Scottish, explained, perhaps, by the fact that Helen Carnegie's father was Scottish ambassador to the Court of Henri II.

## Craigievar

NJ 566 094. 7km S of Alford. Sign-posted off A980 Alford-Banchory road. NTS. Opening hours: TBA.

Completed in 1626, this is certainly the finest and purest product of the Aberdeenshire School, an articulation of the welcome peace of the years between the Reformation and the Covenant. It is the ultimate achievement of Scots Baronial architecture, rightly and incomparably praised by Stewart Cruden: "As a testimony of taste

*Tolquhoun Castle, Tarves*

Craigievar ranks with any representative building in Britain. As a work of art it claims a Scottish place in the front rank of European architecture... There is a sort of sublimity...a serene assurance... No infelicity of mass or exaggeration of detail suggest room for improvement. Quite perfect, lightly poised upon the ground, it is the apotheosis of its type."

The castle's interior is no less remarkable. The Great Hall on the first floor is unsurpassed, its four-part, groined vault a masterpiece of the English plaster-workers whose work also adorns the castles of Glamis and Muchalls.

Craigievar's builder was "Danzig Willie" Forbes, the epitome of the new type of merchant lairds of the 17th century, rich from trade with the Baltic.

## Tolquhon

NJ 872 286. 8km E of Old Meldrum. Go N from Pitmedden on B999 Aberdeen-Tarves road. Castle sign-posted to W after 2km. HBM: Open April–September, 9.30 a.m.–7 p.m. on weekdays and 2–7 p.m. on Sundays.

Today's impressive ruins of pastel pink sandstone from Craigdam quarry are those of the Renaissance castle begun in 1584 by another William Forbes, seventh Forbes laird of Tolquhon,

whose tomb can still be seen in Tarves kirkyard. The site is an ancient one, seat of the Thange of Formature, the country between the rivers Don and Ythan, and came in 1420 to the Forbes family from the Prestons (of Craigmillar Castle, Edinburgh) by marriage.

Tolquhon's especial interest is in illustrating the great changes in comfort and civilisation that the 16th and 17th centuries brought to the castles of Scottish lairds. William Forbes was a civilised and godly man who founded and endowed a hospital in Tarves. His learning and culture were reflected in his home. Well-windowed and spacious with extensive service quarters on the ground floor of the S range, this quadrangular building (incorporating the 1420 Preston Tower) is more domestic than defensive; the triplets of pistol-holes are largely decorative, the twin towers that flank the main entrance are embellished with sculptures and the gatehouse, with its Forbes and royal arms, is designed more to impress the peaceful than to deter the warlike. Remnants of the castle's great garden or pleasance survive (see chapter 8).

Alexander, the tenth laird, was knighted in 1651 for saving the King's life at the battle of Worcester. His net income, however, was unequal to his gross habits and the estate had to be sold. His heir, another William Forbes, was forcibly ejected from Tolquhon in 1718 by redcoat soldiers. In 1929, the decaying remains of the castle were entrusted by the Marquess of Aberdeen to what is now HBM.

*Craigievar Castle, Alford*

# GRAMPIAN
*A country in miniature*

*Fife Arms Hotel, Braemar, circa 1910*

*The bridge over the Dee to Ballater, circa 1900*

# 5

# THE AGE OF IMPROVEMENT

When I look around me, I seem to live not only among a new race of men but in a new world.

> – Rev George Cruden,
> Minister of Logie Buchan, 1840

*Thy seasons moderate as thy Laws appear,*
*Thy constitution wholesome as the Year:...*
*Where Strength and Freedom in their Prime*
*    prevail,*
*And Wealth comes wafted on each freighted gale.*

> – The Isle of Wight,
> *A poem in three cantos, 1782*

One of Grampian's many paradoxes is that although it resonates the past, its landscape is relatively modern, with few features older than the late 18th century. That this should be so is the result of Grampian's age of improvement which began around 1760 and expressed the formative changes then sweeping through the whole of British society, affecting the structure of its economy and the nature of its government. Throughout Britain raged the fervour of, as the historian Macaulay put it, "physical...moral... and...intellectual improvement". Early in the 1800s, even the traditionalist Sir Walter Scott admitted an "improvement of national taste and delicacy"; the diarist GR Porter claimed that he had seen in his own life-time the "greatest advances in civilisation that can be found recorded in the annals of mankind". These were heady times; appealing to poets and industrialists alike, a new spirit was abroad.

Precisely because it had long been isolated and, in many ways, backward, improvements in Grampian were of a great pace, range and intensity. A frenzy of development saw new roads and spas and bridges and schools and canals and all manner of things. Caught up in a ferment of improvement, a burst of energy that left nothing untouched, Grampian was transformed. In the space of 150 years, the region moved from the medieval to the modern era.

The novelties were often incongruous: in an experiment typical of the spirit of the age, Sir Charles Forbes introduced a pair of kangaroos to Strathdon, determined to develop a kangaroo farm as opposed to a traditional sheep farm. The animals thrived but, alas, did not breed for they were, it transpired, of the same sex. Across the Garioch, Buchan made up in hats what it lacked in kangaroos. A local minister observed that in the 1750s, only two people in his congregation could afford hats: by the 1790s, every ploughman owned one.

Even the great empty uplands of Grampian were affected. In 1800, a consortium of the "new money" led by Sir John Maxwell took a 10-year lease of the Deeside estate of Abergeldie. Thirty years later, the number of advertised deer forests had trebled and much of Grampian's land above 300 metres was given over to sporting. The paintings of Landseer and the publication in 1834 of William Scrope's *Days of Deer Stalking* furthered demand, increasing the value of sporting ground.

Quaint evidence of the popularity of stalking is provided by two of Grampian's more curious monuments: on Duchery Beg, high above the Water of Tanar, stand two pillars, each with a stone ball resting on a pyramid. They are exactly 244 metres apart, commemorating Sir William Cunliffe Brooks' shooting of a stag at that formidable distance on 9 October 1877.

Wide moorlands such as those of Strathdon or Glen Gairn were changed by such men. Grouse shooting became as popular as deer stalking. With it came the heather burning that ensures the grouse its staple diet of young heather shoots and gives rise to the mosaic of different colours on many of Grampian's moors.

The winds of change reached every aspect of life in Grampian. This chapter chronicles some of the region's age of improvement by concentrating on six of its manifestations: transport, industry, great houses, agriculture, towns and architecture and social welfare.

### Transport

"Till good roads be established, agricultural and internal improvements can never proceed with energy." – James Anderson, *A General View of the Agriculture and Rural Economy of the County of Aberdeen*, 1794.

*Invercauld Bridge, Deeside*

In 1290 it took English envoys sent to meet the Maid of Norway 19 days to get from Newcastle to Wick. When Johnson and Boswell travelled through Grampian in 1763, matters were only just beginning to improve.

The clans broken, the battle of Culloden in 1746 marked the end of a way of life. Yet, paradoxically, the defeat eventually brought economic benefit to Scotland, for the campaign of military "pacification" that followed the '45 brought much-needed bridges and roads to large tracts of a land that had been, hitherto, impassable. The military engineers were of great benefit to Grampian. Their work, such as the fine bridges at Invercauld (NO 186 909), built in 1752 by Major Edward Caulfield, and Gairnshiel (NJ 284 008), began a process of improving the region's communications that had, 70 years later, transformed Grampian.

Meanwhile, Grampian's roads were still dependent on statute labour – legislation of 1699 required all labourers to work on the roads for six days a year, whilst the better-off were taxed to pay for the necessary materials. Neither party approved of the system: the labourers were "not sensible of the great advantage of good roads" and "go to the labour with reluctance and perform it in an awkward and slovenly manner". (*Old Statistical Account*, vol. VI.) As for the tax-payers, the grumble of one of them, James Beattie, writing in March 1790, speaks for the rest: "paid for myself and son something called road money, a premium perhaps to the Commissioners of Supply for keeping the roads in bad repair." (James Beattie's *Day Book*, 1773–98.)

It was 1845 before this archaic system was formally abandoned. Much earlier, however, landowners had begun taking matters into their own hands. When, in 1776, the road north-west from Aberdeen over Tyrebagger Hill was at last improved at a cost of £77 (including picks and barrows), it was local landowners who footed the bill. The fine Bridge of Alvah in the grounds of Duff House and the quaint Craigmin Bridge at Letterfourie (NJ 441 621) are but two examples of the initiative of landowners.

What really changed things, however, were the turnpike roads. The first to be built, in 1798, was the Deeside Road from Aberdeen to Drum. When Milltimber's Binghill estate was put up for sale, amongst its manifold attractions was the fact that "the turnpike road leading to this property renders it a very desirable purchase" (*Aberdeen Journal*, 31 March 1800.)

Several bridges, such as Potarch (1814) (NO 607 973) or Telford's 1817 bridge at Keig (NJ 617 186) were soon incorporated within turnpike roads. Help came from other quarters: established in 1803, the Parliamentary Commissioners of Highland Roads and Bridges paid half the cost of building bridges at Ballater (1809) and Alford (1811), even if people were still losing their lives attempting to ford the Deveron at Turriff as late as 1826.

By the mid-1800s, there were 795 kilometres of turnpike in Aberdeenshire alone; reviewing their efficacy in 1857, the Report by the Committee on Turnpikes was clear: "Without easy means of inter-communication no agricultural progress would have been made, improvement would not have been remunerative either to landlord or tenant, and in many cases would have been physically impossible." Yet they remained expensive to use (the Old Meldrum Road had to generate £400 a year in tolls merely to pay interest on the £8000 borrowed to build it) and unsuitable for transporting heavy goods. It took the railway to complete the transformation of Grampian.

*Steam engine rally, Alford*

By 1877, a railway network was well established throughout the region that finally brought even remote communities within reach of mainstream economic life. Between the Caledonian, Highland and Great North of Scotland railways, Grampian had a means of economic expansion that she was not slow to exploit. When the railway reached places that lacked any sizeable centres of population, they developed in its wake – the Alford valley line was completed in 1859. Alford was then but the merest hamlet, with an inn, a Friendly Society Hall and a few thatched houses. Thanks to the railway, it grew rapidly and had a population of 634 by 1901. Dyce, Torphins and New Maud are three more of Grampian's towns that owe their existence to the railways.

*Main Street, Banchory, circa 1900*

An unforeseen effect of the railways was tourism: when, in 1852, the line was extended to Banchory, the *Aberdeen Journal* rejoiced that the line would enable "citizens to escape at least occasionally from the stifling influences of a town into the fresh air of the country". How right it was. Ballater, reached by rail in 1866, became a popular tourist resort almost overnight. Cullen benefited in a similar way.

Alas, much of Grampian's railway fell to the axe of Beeching in the 1960s. Parts of the old Deeside line are laid out as footpaths (eg at NJ 897 030). The Buchan line is still obvious at NJ 894 180, whilst the Speyside Way, following the old railway from Spey Bay to Ballindalloch, is popular with walkers.

## Industry

It was with textiles that Grampian first entered the industrial age. Even in the 17th century, the immigration of Flemish weavers to Aberdeen had produced a successful industry, exporting plaiding and stockings to Germany and the Low Countries. Then better transport opened up the home market. In 1779, the first factory was built in Woodside, Aberdeen. In 1789, the first water-powered mill was built on the Don; by 1800 there were three more. The industry expanded outwards, with linen at Inverbervie and large wool mills in Keith and Elgin. Dunecht Estate had its own woollen mill; its engine survives at Garlogie (NJ 782 055).

The granite industry also developed. Rubislaw Quarry was being worked as early as 1741. The granite of Cairngall, 9 kilometres west of Peterhead, considered harder than Aberdeen granite, was first quarried in 1808. Railways led to a wide market for granite – the fountain at Charing Cross, London, the inside of the Victoria Tower in the Houses of Parliament and the great pillars in St George's Hall, Liverpool, are but some of the products of Craighall, whilst Rubislaw granite was exported as far as South Africa. The growth of the village of Kemnay was fuelled by its great granite quarries, still worked today. By 1900, the quarries of Grampian were producing over 500,000 tonnes of granite a year. It was used for London's Waterloo Bridge, the terrace of the Houses of Parliament and to line the walls of the British Museum's main staircase.

By the 19th century, the demand of Grampian's growing industries for paper allowed a paper industry to grow. There were mills at Mugiemoss and Culter late in the 18th century, joined shortly by two more on the river Don. Paper-making is still a major force in Grampian, the products of such modern mills as Taits near Inverurie or Wiggins Teape further down the Don in demand throughout the world.

At the same time, the whisky and fishing industries were industrialising, selling their wares to a growing home market and, as transport improved, exporting all over the world. Shipbuilding flourished and the economy of Grampian took on, in the age of improvement, an extraordinary diversity that, despite the dominance of oil, it has never lost. Food preserving was established in Aberdeen as early as 1822; by 1877 in Turriff "provision and fish-curing is successfully carried on." Long before Perrier, there were mineral water factories in Huntly, Strichen, Inverurie and Ellon; throughout the region, there were bone mill factories and shoe factories and breweries and flour mills and almost every form of industry known to man.

## Great Houses

As the improving age marched on, so did the profits it generated. Although the lot of the working man improved as a result, it was to the great landowners of Grampian that the greatest affluence came. Perhaps the most palpable remains of Grampian's age of improvement are the great houses built or re-designed in the period. Some 40 per cent of Grampian's land was owned by such great lairds as the Earl of Fife who, in 1879, had 103,063 hectares. Another 40 per cent was owned by smaller lairds who were also able to improve their properties with the profits of improved agriculture.

Looking back in 1910 upon this phenomonen, Revd Andrew Chalmers, a local minister and acute observer, was scathing:

> We nursed our admiration of the stately homes of the landed proprietors and...I had ample opportunities of seeing their interiors...The parks and ponds, and herds of deers, and delightful walled gardens were more fascinating than the laird's own private surroundings. The rooms were large and handsome, but there was usually a lingering odour of tobacco smoke and stale whisky punch...The lairds were...by no means superior beings, and food, drink and sport seemed to be the leading concerns of their lives. Looking back across the snows of many winters, I can recall the severity and discomfort that widely prevailed. The damp dusty churches, the squalid bothies and rudely constructed cottages have left a cheerless impression on my memory.

## Agriculture

"Takin't as it is, there's been grun made oot o' fat wasna grun ava; an ther it is, growing crops for the eese o man an beast." – Johny Gibb of Gushetneuk.

When James Anderson surveyed Aberdeenshire in 1794 for the Board of Agriculture, he painted a gloomy picture, reiterated by the minister at Alford: "all the old-fashioned prejudices of husbandry are still looked upon as sure and infallible rules of good management."

Yet, only 17 years later, George Skene Keith compiled a second *Agricultural Survey* that described a country utterly changed. Gone was the laborious cropping of high crooked rigs with primitive implements in the infield, gone were the stones and gorse and marsh of the outfield. This transformation says much not only for the determination of improving landlords but also for the staggering toil of ordinary folk.

The process actually began as early as 1716 when, disgraced in London, the young Sir Archibald Grant, son of the great improver and lawyer Lord Kaimes, retired to his estate at Monymusk. What he saw depressed him and he set about improvements with remarkable energy, draining, clearing stones and enclosing fields. On the home farm, he developed the practice of fallowing and of crop rotation; once perfected, he encouraged it on his let farms by low rents and long leases for suitably progressive tenants.

Such were the ideas of the Society of Improvers, diffusing those of Jethro Tull north of the border. They were taken up in Banffshire and Morayshire by such lairds as the Duke of Gordon and the Earl of Findlater. In Kincardine, Barclay of Ury and Silver of Netherley transformed the face of the land. In 1877, the tenant of Drumgeldie in Cairnie recalled that he and his father had reclaimed 450 acres of waste ground, built eleven miles of stone dykes and laid innumerable tile drains, perhaps aided by some of the £500,000 that Sir Robert Peel had made available to Scottish farmers in 1846 at an interest rate of 6.5 per cent as compensation for the repeal of the Corn Laws.

The Grampian farmer discovered the law of increasing returns: as the distinguished local historian JR Allan puts it, "the more stock, the bigger the midden; the bigger the midden the better the crops; the better the crops the more stock."

Once more, better transport was crucial. The agriculture of central Grampian at least received a vital boost from John Rennie's Aberdeenshire Canal. Canal-mania was a feature of the age of improvement throughout Great Britain. In 1790, it extended to Grampian with the passing of an Act of Parliament, sanctioning the construction of a canal from Inverurie to Aberdeen. The effect this canal had on the agriculture of the Garioch was incalculable; in 1811, Skene's agricultural survey maintained that the new waterway was the main reason for the active improvement of the Garioch countryside. It allowed the fertilisers lime and bone meal to be carried right to the heart of what soon became Grampian's granary. In 1836 alone, over 4,000 tonnes of lime were shipped up the canal; in 1840, 1,349 tonnes of bone meal passed up the waterway.

Whether farmers or not, the people of the Garioch benefited: in 1840, one of the canal's two boats carried 4,765 passengers as far as Kittybrewster to the bright lights of Aberdeen. The journey took four hours, but there were compensations, for the boat "being licensed for the sale of porter and ales was frequently tenanted by parties making a day's outing who spent the hours chiefly in playing whist". (J Davidson, *Recollections*.)

The canal was eventually made redundant by the coming of the railways. Bought in 1850 by the Aberdeen Huntly railway company, much of its bed was used for the railway line. A fragment of the canal survives north-west of Dyce at NJ 850 156. But, before its closure, the canal had played a seminal role in the transformation of agriculture in Grampian.

### Towns and Architecture

"Nothing was more likely to civilise the inhabitants of upland Aberdeenshire and Banffshire than the plantation of villages, all with linen works, post offices, markets and prisons." – The Inspectorate of Forfeited Estates.

One of Grampian's many fascinations is its series of well-preserved "planned towns", designed, usually, by improving landlords, and reflecting the full vigour of the age of improvement. Thus did New Keith (Lord Deskford, 1750), Archiestown, Laurencekirk (Lord Gardenstone, 1763), Cuminestown (Joseph Cumine of Auchry, 1763), Strichen, Fochabers (Duke of Gordon, 1776), Longside (James Ferguson, 1801), and Dufftown (Earl of Fife, 1817), amongst others, come into being in what had all the appearance of a competition amongst the lairds. Most were built with the dual purpose of pursuing agriculture and cottage industries. They created centres of population and employment that changed forever the face of Grampian.

Meanwhile, much was changed in the architecture of existing towns and villages as the improvements marched on. Many of Grampian's finer buildings date from this period, from Scotland's

*Sheep dog trials, Hazlehead, Aberdeen*

523 houses and Stuartfield's 530 souls had but 279 rooms between them.

Things were little better out on the farms. Writing in 1892, Dr Lawson of Midmar described typical accommodation for farm servants in his district: their rooms were in stable lofts, reached "behind the heels of half a dozen horses and then up by a rickety stair or ladder. Inside the room are two or more beds, according to the size of the farm, and if any space is left it is nearly all taken up with trunks...soiled clothes, bits of harness etc are lying about...there is no fireplace of any description. The place is lighted by a skylight... with broken panes...filled up with straw or a pair of trousers."

There was often an acute shortage of food for ordinary people. In 1782–3, for example, Insch Kirk Session bought meal for its parishioners to prevent their starving. Peterhead saw meal riots in 1812. As the new industries of Grampian's improvement went through their predictable troughs, unemployment soared and the traditional system of relief, the Church, was fully stretched. The Great Disruption made matters worse, for it diverted resources elsewhere. The Poor Law Enquiry of 1843 identified the problem, but advocated no solution: much illness stemmed from "no other cause than the filth and wretchedness of the people and particularly the want of a sufficient quantity of nourishing food". In his submission to the enquiry, Dr Thompson of Inverurie, a man with 30 years' experience of medicine in his burgh, stated that the poor were "very ill off for furniture, particularly for bedding and clothing" and suffering "a great deal from want of nourishment, more so...than from want of medicine". (*Poor Law Enquiry* (*Scotland*) 1848, Appendix II.)

Improving the lot of those not born to wealth was a slow business in Grampian. At last, in 1845, came legislation establishing Parochial Boards. The practice of raising money by compulsory assessment came to be accepted throughout the region while, gradually, public water supplies were installed and houses, hospitals and schools were built. A few buildings, such as the Buchan Combination Poorhouse, survive in Grampian to bear witness to the pain of the birth of the industrial age. Even as the 20th century advanced, life was still hard for the working class of Grampian,

premier example of Greek Revival, St Giles Church in Elgin (Archibald Simpson, 1825–8) to such fine vernacular architecture as Springbank on Bogie Street, Huntly, or the extraordinary Gothic orne of Dales Cottage, Peterhead.

### Social Welfare

If such were the benefits of an improving age, it brought its problems too, especially for "those whose lot it is to labour". When the polemicist Joseph Townsend stated categorically in 1783 that "no human efforts" could improve the state of the poor and that only hunger could induce "sobriety, diligence and fidelity", he was representing a substantial train of thought within the age of improvement. Townsend maintained that the larger part of the poor would continue to fulfil "the most servile, the most sordid, and the most ignoble offices in the community", perpetuating such ideas as that education of the working class threatened "the great law of subordination".

The lairds were well off in their great houses. But in 1868, towns like Old Meldrum still had open sewers, slaughter houses, dunghills and pig styes amid their houses. The hostility of a local landowner prevented the installation of a proper water supply to Old Meldrum until 1871. In the same year, Fraserburgh's 950 families lived in only as the novels of Jessie Kesson so memorably attest.

## TRANSPORT

### Craigellachie Bridge, River Spey, Moray

NJ 285 451. By A941 Craigellachie-Rothes Road, 0.3km W of village of Craigellachie.

Of all Thomas Telford's feats of engineering, this is amongst the most striking. Probably the earliest iron bridge in Scotland (built between 1812 and 1815), its single iron span seems to leap lightly over the Spey from the stone abutments that launch it. Its height and arch above the river are to accommodate the spates to which the Spey is notoriously prone. (The Spey is the most rapid river of its size in Britain: its average fall from its source, Loch Spey, to its mouth is 11ft per mile, compared, eg, to the Thames' 2ft). It takes its name from the Gaelic *speidh*, which means, appropriately, rapidity or strength. It was as a result of local advice as to the Spey's strength that Telford built his bridge 5 ft higher than he had originally intended – just as well, for it was only by inches that the bridge avoided being swept away in the great spate of 1829.

The story of the bridge's ironwork is remarkable in itself. It was cast at Plas Kynaston in Wales by William Hazeldine. The ribs of iron were floated over Telford's Pontcysyllte aqueduct on the Llangollen canal and then shipped round to the Moray Firth and up the Spey.

### Garchory Bridge, Strathdon, Gordon

NJ 304 098. 5km W of Strathdon on S side of B973. By-passed by modern road.

This is as beautiful a bridge as any and one unforgettably situated amongst old beech trees above a long slow wind of the Don. It spans the river in one arch of exquisite grace. The bridge is unusually large and well-constructed for one so early – it was built in 1715 by Alexander Forbes of nearby Inverernan House.

### Well of the Lecht, Kirkmichael, Moray

NJ 234 151. 2km N of Lecht summit on A939 Cockbridge to Tomintoul road.

The Lecht road is still notorious as the British road most regularly blocked by snow. It was from this inhospitable place, marked by a white stone plaque above a spring, that five companies of the 33rd regiment under the command of Lord Charles Hay built the road to the Spey in 1754. This was a crucial section of the network of military roads that ensured the pacification of the Highlands after the 1745 Jacobite rebellion. It was built at the rate of one yard per man per day, impressive enough even by today's standards. The road ran from Ruthven Barracks on the Spey near Aviemore, up and over the Lecht and then S past Corgarff Castle, over Gairnshiel and then S

*Telford's Iron Bridge, Craigellachie*

Invercauld Bridges to Braemar Castle and on to Perth. Sections, such as that which leaves the A939 at NJ 296 063, survive and make for a memorable walk.

### Speymouth Railway Viaduct, Urquhart, Moray

NJ 345 641. 5km N of Fochabers off B9104 Fochabers-Spey Bay road.

This great metal-trussed masterpiece of Victorian engineering, built in 1886, now forms part of the Speyside Way from Spey Bay to Ballindalloch. Its unusual length of 290m was a response to the constant changes of channel that were and remain a characteristic of the Spey's mouth. The viaduct's designer, Patrick Barnett, accordingly had built one great central bowed span of 107m, approached on each side by three shorter level spans of 30.5m each. All were supported by piers piled so deep that when the viaduct was tested before opening with a load of 400 tonnes of gravel, it deflected a mere 29mm.

### Cullen Railway Viaducts, Moray

NJ 51- 67-. 17km W of Banff on A98 Banff-Buckie road.

When, in the 1880s, the Great North of Scotland Railway was refused permission to run its line through what was then part of the grounds of Cullen House, the engineer PM Barnett was appointed to find a solution. Between 1882 and 1884, he built the great railway viaducts that still grace the 1820s New Town of Cullen.

One of these extraordinary constructions bisects the town in two great arches; the eight arches of the other cross the Burn of Cullen. This, the larger of the two, is 196m long and 24.8m high.

## INDUSTRY

### Lecht Iron Mine, Strathdon, Gordon

NJ 236 153. 6.5km SE of Tomintoul, off A939 Cockbridge-Tomintoul road. Park at Glenlivet Crown Estate carpark; walk 500m along track to mine.

The District Council has restored this square, two-storeyed building sympathetically. It was built in 1730 by the York Buildings Company, one of many English ventures to benefit from the forfeiture of Jacobite estates. The obvious shortage of timber, then as now, doomed the enterprise from the start: the iron ore had to be carried on horseback to near Nethybridge where there was enough wood to smelt it into Strathdoun Pigs. The mine closed in 1737. Having added a crushing mill and a mill lade, the Duke of Gordon reopened the mine for manganese in 1841, despite the troubles he had in having the vast mill wheels brought from Aberdeen up the steep Lecht road. The carthorses were unequal to the labour: the bull belonging to the minister of Corgarff was pressed into harness and the task accomplished.

At its peak, the mine's 26m-deep shaft employed 63 people. The manganese was exported by way of Portgordon, before cheap imports from Russia made the mine unviable. It closed in 1846.

### Old Mills, Elgin, Moray

NJ 206 630. In W end of Elgin: turn N at roundabout in front of Gray's Hospital and down Old Mills Road for 0.5km.

This is another fine example of District Council restoration: the mill is once more in full working order and represents an enviable opportunity to see something so integral to the age of improvement. For although mills survive throughout Grampian (eg the fine water-powered saw and mill on the Feugh at Finzean, NO 591 916), this is the only one restored to its former glory. Most of the mill dates from the 1790s. The walls of the main block are thick and of rubble in order to withstand the vibrations of the machinery. There are two fine "undershot" water-wheels, turned by a well-designed double lade.

An interesting comparison with this Old Mill is Elgin's Newmill, built in 1797 for the manufacture of "Scotch plaids, tweeds, kerseys and double cloth". By 1868 Newmill had become "the most important public work in the County, employing 1–2000 hands". It is still thriving today.

### Foudland Slate Quarries, Huntly, Gordon

NJ 602 336. 8km SE of Huntly off A96. Turn into Colpy off A96 and follow track NW past Jericho farm (where, NB, the ruins of the Bennachie whisky distillery). Park after 2km and strike W along path for 1km to quarries.

*These quarries afford employment to many industrious workmen and keep within the county a large*

*sum of money which used to be sent out of it, for this
very useful and now indispensable article.*

– James Blaikie,
*On the Slate quarries of Aberdeenshire*, 1847

Although now disused, from the 1830s these
quarries produced some 800–900,000 slates a
year, the roof, as it were, of Grampian's age of
improvement. Most famously, they were used to
roof Balmoral Castle. Less august buildings
throughout Grampian, from cattle courts to dovecots, attest their quality.

In the 1850s, the quarries employed some 65
men. Most of them worked at splitting and dressing the slates for 16 shillings a week. Many a local
farmer earned extra cash by carting the slates all
over the region. There were further slate quarries
on the Hill of Tillymorgan, 4km to the W.

### Rubislaw Quarry, Hill of Rubislaw, Aberdeen

NJ 991 056. 3km W of Aberdeen city centre.
Follow Queen's Road onto A944 and turn right at
first traffic lights, sign-posted "BP Exploration".
Quarry screened by trees immediately to your right.
Easiest access is up the bank by the bus stop round
the corner on Queen's Road.

Semi-circled by some of the buildings of
Aberdeen's more recent industry, oil, Rubislaw
Quarry is the largest man-made hole in Europe,
some 150m deep and 90m across. Closed in 1971,
controversy continues about its potential as a
tourist attraction. At present it is formidably
fenced off. Robert II granted the lands of
Rubislaw "to the Burghy of Aberdeen to be held
in fee and heritage and free Burgage" in 1379.
Quarrying began here in 1741. The *Aberdeen
Journal* of 16 May 1791 advertised "the whole
stone quarries on the estate of Rubislaw will be
set in tack [leased] by public roup [auction] for
the space of seven years." Yet still in 1889, the
deposit of granite was described as being "practi-
cally inexhaustible: within 8 acres of the centre of
the property, 3,910,347 tons of superior rock have
been removed by the present proprietors, and the
best rock has not been touched."

Quarry workers used to say "the half o'
Aiberdeen has come oot o' that hole." Its unmistakable silvery granite is certainly much in evidence throughout Aberdeen. Rubislaw granite
was also used for the Bell Rock lighthouse and for
the docks at Portsmouth, Sheerness and
Southampton.

## GREAT HOUSES

### Cairness House, Fraserburgh, Banff and Buchan

NK 039 609. 7km SE of Fraserburgh. Take B9033
N off A952 Peterhead-Fraserburgh road. After 3km,
turn left (NW) up drive to house. privately owned:
telephone for appointment.

Built between 1791 and 1797 by James
Playfair for Charles Gordon, who had made his
fortune in Jamaica, Cairness is "arguably the finest
neo-classical mansion in Scotland" (Charles
McKean). It would have to be, for Gordon was a
demanding and capricious client: Robert Burn
had just designed him a new house. Dissatisfied
with Burn's work, Gordon engaged Playfair to
design a granite house of remarkable austerity and
grace, almost arrogantly unadorned. Playfair died
during the commission.

### Fasque House, Fettercairn, Kincardine and Deeside

NO 648 775. Sign-posted from B974, 1.8km N of
Fettercairn. Open daily, May–September.

Built in 1809 and standing proud in its surrounding parkland, Fasque embodies all the assurance of the age of improvement. It was bought in
1829 by John Gladstone, who added the Doric
portico to the base of the house's main block. His
younger son was WE Gladstone, four times Prime
Minister, and the house contains many memorabilia of the man.

Although the architecture of Fasque, with its
soaring double staircase, is fascinating in itself, it
is above all as a living relic that Fasque is unique
in Grampian. Gladstones still live there; they
appear never to have thrown anything out and
here as nowhere else can one reconstruct the life of
a great Victorian house.

The kitchen, with its rows of gleaming copper
pans, is unforgettable. The whole ground floor is
given over to domesticity, sculleries and pantries,
still rooms and larders, a great machine for servic-
ing the every comfort of such Gladstones as Sir
John's grandson who lived for shooting and sporting. In 1905, he and seven friends shot more than
3,000 pheasants in one day. At today's prices of
some £20 per bird shot, such a day, if it could be
had, would cost £60,000 or £8,571 per gun. After
a day like that, Sir John's great canopied bath
would have been welcome indeed.

## Duff House and Policies, Banff

NJ 690 633. 0.5km S of Banff, sign-posted off A97. HBM. Open April–September 9.30–7 p.m., Sundays 2–7 p.m. Closed October–March.

For all its flamboyant magnificence, this is yet a sad and sombre house which betrays its sorry past. Now marooned between a golf course and rugby pitches, the house was never finished. Its architect, William Adam, and owner, the *nouveau riche* William Duff MP, who later became the first Earl of Fife, fell out over costs, design and fees. In 1741 the case went to law and work stopped, the planned colonnades and wings unbuilt.

The simple quadrangular block is massively, brashly adorned with a pediment, Corinthian capitals, metopes, balustrades and urns. Inside, the customary rooms – hall, dining room, drawing room, a massive 9m cubed saloon – are splendid, if intimidating and, somehow, cold. That many fine features, doors, fireplaces and plasterwork survive is surprising, since the house was much abused as a sanatorium and war-camp before Lord Fife gave it to Banff and MacDuff in 1906. Its contents were sold in 1907. Plans are now afoot to turn Duff House into a major art gallery.

An hour's return walk S leads through what were the house's policies, past its ice house and fine mausoleum, beautifully situated above the slow winds of the Deveron, on to the Bridge of Alvah (1772) and back to the Fishing Temple on an island in the river. Such were the works of a man so proud of his Scottishness that he had loads of Scottish soil spread on the site of his London house. Even if soured by Duff House, William Duff was always able to claim that he lived on Scottish soil.

## AGRICULTURAL

"This countrey is well peopled, for all things necessary to life are easily had here." – *A Report on Grampian* in the reign of Charles II.

### Dovecots

The many dovecots in Grampian are of varying date, for of course man enjoyed the flesh of doves before and after the age of improvement. Yet many of the finer examples date from this period. Those at Lessendrum, Huntly (NJ 581 414), Findlater (NJ 539 667), Urquhart Manse (NJ 283 626) and Gallery, Marykirk (NO 675 653) form a representative sample.

## Lime Kilns

The practice of liming to counteract soil acidity and balance pH was crucial to improved agriculture. Many limekilns survive in Grampian: a homespun and simple one survives at Auchindoun Castle (NJ 348 374) and contrasts with the elaboration of Pitmedden's (NJ 885 280). A series of kilns run up Glenbuchat (NJ 367 175).

## Consumption Dykes, Kingswells

8km west of Aberdeen. Turn north off A944 at Kingswells roundabout, sign-posted Dyce. After 0.8km, park at head of farm track. Dyke runs due west after 50m.

One can only marvel at the labour that must have been involved in creating this remarkable relic, "one of the most impressive monuments of the agricultural improvements in the north-east" (IAG Shepherd). It was begun around 1854 in order to "use up" the many stones on the unimproved estate of Kingswells. It is 477m long, 10.5m wide and 2m high with a paved central path, steps and water-bays. A drive through any of Grampian's farmland will still reveal stone-clearing in operation, even if the stones are not put to so novel a use.

## Aden Country Park, Old Deer, Banff and Buchan

NJ 981 479. 0.3km NE of Old Deer. Sign-posted off A950 Mintlaw/Old Deer road. Open all year.

With its ice house and mansion house, cartsheds and stables and excellent interpretative material, Aden allows the visitor a comprehensive understanding of life on an improved 19th-century estate. The two dark rooms of the farm's last horseman, furnished as they were in the 1930s, form a telling contrast with the opulence of the now-gutted mansion house, re-designed by John Smith in 1832. Writing in 1910, the Revd Andrew Chalmers was, once more, blunt: "Most of the Buchan lairds of the 1850s kept up establishments of a needlessly ostentatious and expensive style...their imposing mansions with their extensive policies were in painful contrast to the squalid homes of those who contributed to their maintenance."

The stables, now the heart of the park, are magnificent, matched in Grampian only by those at the home farm of Altyre, Forres (NJ 028 553).

*Farming up Glen
Derry, Deeside*

They form half of a rounded square, dominated by a four-storeyed central tower surmounted by an elaborate doric-columned cupola.

## Towns and Architecture

### Strichen Village, Banff and Buchan

NJ 94- 55-. 11km SW of Fraserburgh.

When Lord Strichen designed his planned village in 1764, his desire was "to promote the arts and manufactures of this country and for the accommodation of tradesmen of all denominations, manufactures and other industrious people". He picked an ideal location, deep in the sheltered valley of the North Ugie, and the village maintains the vivacity its founder intended, hosting the Buchan Heritage Festival and the Doric Drama Festival each May. The town's Z-plan, with the main road passing through a central square, is typical of Grampian's many planned settlements. The "planned" houses that survive have a standard frontage of 13.7m, in accordance with Lord Strichen's feu. The restored Mill of Strichen (1791) by the old bridge is especially pleasing. On closer inspection, the High Street loses its planned austerity, for many of its houses are intricately adorned with cornices, eaves, cantilevered dormer windows and even "cherry-cocking" (setting small stones systematically between larger blocks).

### New Leeds, Banff and Buchan

NJ 99- 54-. 12km S of Fraserburgh on A92.

If Strichen was a success, its neighbour New Leeds was a disaster. Almost incredibly, its founder Captain Fraser of Strichen intended it to rival the city of Leeds in Yorkshire. Little remains of his dream. In a letter to him in 1852, Christian Watt pulled no punches: "You had dreams of huge spinning factories rising in Buchan not, as you say, to give work to the poor, but to further your own wealth and interest." Perhaps this was why, according to an account of 1879, New Leeds had become no hive of industry but a "nursery of idleness and vice". This, in turn, may have had something to do with the fairs that the captain ran in order to generate much-needed enthusiasm for his project: to commemorate the first fair in 1799, the captain offered a prize of an eight-day clock not to the best-dressed or best-behaved, but to the drunkest man.

He soon tired of his new town, turning instead to laying out the white horse on Mormond Hill (NJ 962 566) to commemorate a white charger shot from under him in battle. Meanwhile, back in New Leeds, the local joiner had taken up residence in a ruined byre where he slept in a coffin. When Dr Pratt wrote about the village in 1886, he described a "straggling and miserable" place. Not long after, the villages houses were torn down and their stone used to construct farm buildings on Strichen estate.

### Temple of Theseus, Pitfour, Mintlaw, Banff and Buchan

NK 975 486. 3km W of Mintlaw. Park at Saplinbrae Hotel, off A950. Walk up track for 500m to temple by lake.

Few buildings in Grampian are more expressive of the expansive extravagance of the age of improvement than this wonderful folly, a bath house for its builder, Admiral Ferguson of Pitfour. He kept alligators in it. Built in 1835, the tem-

ple's 34 granite columns of the Tuscan Doric order support a wooden entablature and roof. Across the lake the House of Pitfour, with its great glazed verandah, was demolished in 1927. Mercifully, the temple remains to attest the former glories of the "Blenheim of Buchan" (McKean).

### Marischal College, Broad Street, Aberdeen

Although it is now confronted by the modern hideousness of St Nicholas House, the audacity and verve of Marischal College transcend its surroundings. The building is granite's zenith, an astonishing feat, its pinnacled façade (finished in 1906) the epitome of the self-confidence of Aberdeen's spirit of improvement. Marischal College was founded in 1593 by George Keith, Earl Marischal (of Dunnottar Castle) in response to the Reformation of 1560: it was to be a purely Protestant rival to the traditionalist King's College. The college used the buildings of the old Greyfriars monastery until the older buildings of the present quadrangle were completed in 1844. It is here that "battle" still rages every four years between the supporters of the candidates for the Rectorship of the university. In 1860 Marischal joined with King's College to form Aberdeen

*Mid Street, Keith, circa 1910*

University. The union was almost undone recently when, faced with a £2,500,000 cutback in government funding, the university considered selling Marischal.

## SOCIAL WELFARE

**Robert Gordon's College**, Schoolhill, Aberdeen.
Robert Gordon (1665–1731) made his fortune, like William Forbes of Craigievar, from trading with the Baltic port of Danzig (now Gdansk, Poland). He was a grandson of his namesake Sir Robert Gordon of Straloch, the cartographer. He never married and was famed, in his lifetime, for his meanness. Yet he left his entire and considerable fortune for the foundation of a college (a "hospital") for the education of poor boys from Aberdeen.

No less an architect than William Adam was commissioned; he designed a pedimented block of three storeys, flanked by pavilions and surmounted by a cupola. Work was completed by 1739; one panelled room of this period survives on the first floor. In the 19th century the foundation benefited from a series of generous endowments. John Smith was commissioned to add the two advancing wings and colonnade in 1833.

In the 1880s, Gordon's Hospital became Robert Gordon's College, a private school operating along English public school lines, and greatly expanded its numbers. Its founder's intentions are maintained, however, by generous scholarships for the deserving.

**Grays Hospital**, Grant Street, Elgin

NJ 209 625. W of town centre. Follow A96. Hospital overlooks fourth roundabout.

The soaring tower, topped by a dome and cupola, dominates western Elgin. This was altruism on a grand scale. The hospital was founded by the 1809 benefaction of Dr Alexander Gray, a native of Elgin, who had made his fortune in the Honourable East India Company. His endowment included £2,000 for "the comfort of virgins whose hope had decayed". The building was designed by

*Union Bridge and Terrace, Aberdeen, circa 1920*

James Gillespie Graham and built between 1815 and 1819. Pleasingly, it has just been refurbished and continues life as a hospital, even if smallpox patients are no longer to be found on the second floor.

**Anderson's Institution**, Elgin

NK 228 626. On S side of A96 as it enters Elgin from the E.

As Gray's Hospital enriches the W, Elgin's E is also distinguished by beneficence, the "Elgin Institution for the Support of Old Age and Education of Youth". The building's two-storeyed H-plan was the work of Archibald Simpson between 1830 and 1833. Its vast Ionic entrance colonnade epitomises Simpson's Greek Revivalism, already gracing Elgin in the form of Simpson's triumph of the genre, St Giles Church on the High Street. Here, however, the lines are upset by the curious and somehow unsettling domed bell-tower that caps the building.

The institution, like Gray's, is eponymous: General Andrew Anderson's own mother had never been educated and had been left destitute.

# — 6 —
# FISHING – MORTAL MAN, IMMORTAL SEA

Even by the late 19th century, Grampian dominated the fisheries of Scotland. Now, late in the 20th century, its fishing industry is the largest and most important in western Europe. Grampian catches and lands; it cans and it smokes, it processes and freezes some £150 million worth of fish a year, two-thirds of the Scottish total and almost half the British.

The diversity of this vast industry is astonishing; in its wake come boat-building, ice-making, marine engineering and electronics enterprises pioneered in Grampian for the rest of the world. Here too are the world's most distinguished institutes for fishing research: marine bio-chemistry, stock conservation, fish processing, including the world's only fish head processing plant, and all manner of enquiry to ensure the vitality and primacy of fishing in Grampian.

Small flint flakes, used to make fish-spears of bone, garnered from the the sand at Forvie and the haughs of the Dee and the Ythan, are our first evidence of fishing in Grampian. The cycle of the salmon, caught in the rivers and estuaries, was as important to those early hunter-gatherers as that of the plants and animals in the forest.

The salmon remained important; by medieval times, the salmon fisheries in Grampian's rivers had become the largest in Scotland, considered a major national resource. The Priory of Urquhart held the fishings of the Spey by grant of Royal Charter, whilst the burgh of Aberdeen held those of the Dee and Don. The fish were caught by net and coble in the estuaries and, beyond the tidal limits, by cruives or weirs. By the 19th century, the practice had begun of catching the salmon in "fixed engine" nets as they swam along the coast. Much the same method predominates today and is well illustrated in the stake nets on the Drums Links, 3kilometres south of Newburgh at NJ 999 225.

Yet the North Atlantic salmon, part of fishing tradition in Grampian for 8,000 years, is under threat from over-fishing, inadequate conservation, poaching and pollution. A great fish, probably a salmon, is carved on the Pictish Craw Stane (near Rhynie at NJ 497 263). As the carving fades, the fish that inspired it and that remains so important to Grampian cannot be allowed to disappear.

The history of sea fisheries in Grampian is a more recent one, beginning around 1600, when the region began to challenge the previous dominance of the Clyde and Forth. Sea fishing in Grampian began with tiny coastal villages, often clinging to the cliffs, whose inhabitants were both crofters and fisherfolk. Initially, fishing was by baited hook and line. "Great lines" were cast from six-man boats (the curve-stemmed "skaffie" on the Moray coast, the straight-stemmed "fifie" elsewhere in the region) for the catch of cod in the spring and "sma' lines" from four-man boats for the catch of haddock and whiting.

The women and children played their part, collecting mussels and other bait which they used for baiting miles of line. If the men's task in catching the fish was onerous and dangerous, to the women fell the thankless job of gutting and cleaning, salting and curing and then walking many miles with heavy creels of fish for sale.

These first fishing communities worked from coves or shingle beaches and sold their produce locally; gradually, with support from Church and

*Sunset from Aberdeen beach*

*Opposite Mussel fishermen on River Spey*

# GRAMPIAN

*A country in miniature*

state, the industry developed and harbours were built. By the middle of the 18th century, over 55 full-time fishing communities were established along the coast of Grampian, catching mainly haddock and cod for the growing market of central Scotland.

Then came the age of the herring. The Dutch had been fishing for the "silver darlings" with drift nets for some time. Grampian, however, lacked the infrastructure to cope with the short-lived summer glut of herring until, in the 1790s, merchants and curers established enough pickling and curing sheds to deal with the bounty of the sea. By 1820, over 1,000 boats crowded the east coast for the two-month season and by 1913 there were 10,000 boats involved in the Scottish herring industry, most of them fishing from ports in Grampian. At the peak of the herring boom in 1907, 2.5 million barrels of herring were exported, most of it to Germany and Russia. The industry by then was no longer seasonal: Grampian's boats followed the herring shoals clockwise round the coast of Britain, from the Minch in the spring to Shetland and the east coast in the summer, to East Anglia in the autumn. Grampian's fishing industry boomed without check until the Russian Revolution in 1917 brought about a collapse in the market for herring.

As the industry grew, so did its technology. In 1879, a boat-builder from Lossiemouth married a fisher-lass from Fife. Amongst other things, their marriage produced something that revolutionised fishing in Grampian: the Zulu, named after the

*The Craw stone Rhynie: Salmon has been important to the Grampian economy since the earliest times.*

war that ended that year, was a boat that combined the best of both fifie and scaffie and is known as the most noble sailing craft ever designed in Britain. "The sense of grandeur and power that they conveyed...has never been surpassed by any other craft under canvass." (Anson.) The Zulu enabled Grampian's fishers to fish further and faster than ever before, whilst her innovative decking made her safer into the bargain.

Nets, too, advanced. From the Dutch, Grampian borrowed the drift net for catching herring. Then, after 1822, came the trawl net, a bag dragged along the sea bottom to catch the deep-swimming white fish, principally cod and haddock. A variant on this is the "pair trawl", a lighter net towed by two boats to catch the shallower-swimming mackerel and herring. From Denmark, around 1922, came the seine net, a drag net like the trawl. Then, most recently, the lightweight purse-seine net, often as big as six football pitches. Operating like a draw-string purse, it is designed to catch whole shoals of pelagic fish, herring and mackerel.

A momentous year for fishing in Grampian was 1882. A consortium of Aberdeen fish merchants bought the region's first steam tug, the Toiler, converting her "for the purpose of prosecuting trawl fishing." Within a few years, the Zulu was superceded and the traditional fishing villages of Grampian became dormitories, much as they are today. Although lobster and crab and small boat line-fishing continue in some of the fishing villages, the sea-going boats tend to congregate in some 20 ports. The vast majority of fish are landed at Peterhead, Fraserburgh or Aberdeen. The fishermen may still live in the village of their ancestors, but they drive from there to the port where their boat is based.

Today Grampian's boats are safer and incomparably advanced with their winches and echo-sounders, refrigeration plants and navigators. But if the work is less arduous and the dangers less threatening, to the perennial problems of fisherfolk have been added those of bureaucrats, with an EEC Common Fisheries Policy, total allowable catches (TACs), quotas and exclusion zones, quite apart from the staggering costs involved in building and operating a modern fishing boat. Yet, as even cursory inspection will show, Grampian's fishing industry is innovative, resourceful, adaptable and vibrant, still thriving in all its many guises.

*Fishing boat, MacDuff*

selves are no longer made of flax. Five boats still work in this ancient way and the fish from Gourdon is greatly prized. You can buy it at the harbour most weekday afternoons, depending on the tide. The harbour was built in 1820; it has a sheltered inner basin and, on the hillside above it, a beacon to guide the boats home in the dark.

### Catterline

The coastline, from Gourdon northwards, is so inhospitable that the fishing villages cling to the cliff-tops (known in Grampian as the *heugh-heid*), with their tiny harbours or jetties down below. Catterline, recorded as "Katerlin" as long ago as the 12th century, is amongst the best-preserved of the *heugh-heid* villages. Its pier was built by the local laird, Viscount Arbuthnot, around 1810 and

*The beach, Stonehaven, circa 1900*

There is no better way of appreciating the range and history of fishing in Grampian than to follow the coast from St Cyrus north round the knuckle of Buchan into Morayshire. There is interest too for the geologist and ornithologist. Above all, the coast of Grampian instills respect for the indomitability of man as he sought and seeks still to wrest a living from the sea.

Starting from the south, this route covers a selection of the villages and ports, dead and living, that adorn the craggy coast of Grampian. The coastline does not lend itself to habitation, let alone fishing. It is open, exposed to the prevailing east wind, devoid of the shelter afforded by offshore islands. There are few coves or gentle bays. For the most part, great fissured sandstone cliffs confront a cold grey sea; in other places, rock gives way to long and windswept strands. That fishing should have been and continues to be so successful here is a marvel.

### Gourdon

This village is an essential visit, for the old long-line method of fishing for haddock and cod lives on here. The baiting of the lines with mussels is still known as "redding", even if the lines them-

is still used for landing salmon, whilst one lobster boat still works from it. In 1881, 30 men and eight boats worked from here. More recently, Catterline has been associated with the distinguished painter Joan Eardley who lived, worked and died here.

### Stonehaven

The best natural port between Arbroath and Aberdeen, Stanehyve must have been one of the earliest centres of fishing. It takes little imagination to visualise a huddle of fishermen's huts on the raised beach below the Bervie Braes. The town takes its name from a great rock, Craig-na-Caer, which rose from the sea at the mouth of the har-

*The fishing fleet, Stonehaven, circa 1905*

At the height of the herring boom, however, over 100 boats worked out of Stonehaven. There are now five trawlers, one seine-netter and seven crab boats, although several other Stonehaven boats work out of Aberdeen. The harbour is a fascinating, bustling place, alive with sailing boats and sea-anglers. The Tolbooth Museum, near the harbour, is well worth visiting. (Closed on Tuesdays.)

### Cowie

Although now connected to Stonehaven by a promenade, from about 1367 Cowie was a royal burgh in its own right, with its own castle built by King Malcolm Canmore in the 11th century. Even then a *laigh* (low) *toun*, the medieval village stood further from the sea than the 19th-century fishing village which once boasted more boats than Stonehaven. But disaster struck it on Sunday, 11 September 1864. A Swedish cargo boat, bound for Montrose, was wrecked near the village. Its crew, and the cholera they carried, were taken in by the villagers. Within weeks, most of the inhabitants of Cowie were dead; the village never recovered and there is still a sense of desolation about the semi-ruined harbour.

bour until, because of the danger it posed to shipping, it was blown up in 1816 by the engineer Robert Stevenson, grandfather of Robert Louis Stevenson. Fishing was the engine behind the town's development, even if the *Old Statistical Account* (1791–9) records rather gloomily that there were only three boats and yawl working from the harbour, for the fishermen's – "morals were being ruined through the excessive drinking of spirits".

*Herring fleet, Aberdeen, circa 1860*

## Aberdeen

The medieval harbour was the fulcrum of Aberdeen's growth. Improved by the engineers Smeaton (late in the 18th century) and Telford (early in the 19th), the harbour remained a centre of trade, rather than of fishing. Visiting Aberdeen in 1784, John Knox bemoaned this surprising fact: if 50 or 60 vessels should be "employed in the herring and white fisheries, the port of Aberdeen would, in a few years, become the most celebrated mart of fish now existing". The syndicate of Aberdeen businessmen who bought the tugboat, Toiler, in 1882 proved Knox right: by 1900, there were 205 trawlers fishing from Aberdeen and by 1930, Aberdeen had 40 great steam liners, able to reach the vast fishing grounds of Iceland and the Arctic. The port became one of the most important in the world. Many factors contributed to Aberdeen's decline, now the home of only some 50 boats. The extension of territorial waters made her long-range fleet redundant, whilst the inflexibility of the Dock Labour Scheme saw her landings diminish. Yet the bustling Aberdeen Fish Market on Albert Quay (open all year, weekdays from 4 a.m., sales approx. 7–9 a.m.) still makes an essential visit. The Aberdeen Maritime Museum in Provost Ross'

*The Cruel Sea*

*Crab boat, Aberdeen*

House, Shiprow (open all year, Mon–Sat, 10–5 p.m.) is also very interesting.

### Footdee

Their windowless backs to the sea, the houses of "Fittie", as it is known, form a perfectly preserved 19th-century fishing village at the head of Aberdeen's North Pier. At the turn of the century, 584 people lived in Fittie, an average of nine people to each two-roomed cottage!

### Collieston

In 1696, there were 36 adult fishermen resident in "Collestowne", making it the largest fishing

*Queen Street, Peterhead
circa 1900*

settlement in Aberdeenshire and one of the largest north of the Tay. Its prosperity was secured by its deep natural bay, St Catherine's Dub (so called after a Flemish galleon of that name was wrecked there in 1594). By the 1880s, over 100 fishermen worked from Collieston and the village's lightly dried haddocks and whitings (known as s*peldin*s or *blaavin fishies*) were famed throughout the land. Yet despite the construction of an impressive harbour in 1894, at a cost of over £6,000, the village mysteriously declined. Around 1900, many of the remaining fishermen moved *en masse* to Torry, the result perhaps of Collieston's strange "incurable malady", known as "the stone". Although the village thrives today, it is no longer a place of the fisherfolk; the Lang Reel o' Collieston, danced by the whole community at Forvie Sands after each Collieston fishers' wedding, is seen no more.

### Old Castle of Slains

NK 054 301; turn left, sign-posted "Whinnyfold", just before Collieston, past church. After 1km, turn right up track to "Mains of Slains" to end.

Just N of Collieston, defying reason and nature on a cliff-top promontory, stand the remains of "the most curiously situated village on the east coast of Scotland" (Anson). Three of the old cottages remain, even if two have been restored almost beyond recognition. Two more modern houses continue centuries of habitation at this strange and eerie place. The fishing village was built from the early 18th century onwards with stones taken from the Old Castle of Slains. A narrow track winds down to the shingle beach from which, in 1850, some 30 fishermen wrested their living — when, that is, they weren't smuggling. This stretch of the Buchan coast was a haven for smugglers until the coastguards, the "preventative force", were able to quash the trade early in the 19th century. But in the heyday of smuggling, around the 1850s, so much smuggled liquor came ashore here that, it was claimed, "the meanest kind scorned whiskey on the Buchan coast"!

### Whinnyfold

Pronounced "Finnyfa", this is still a classic *heugh-heid* community, its four parallel rows of what are now mainly holiday cottages facing the sea from the cliff-top. There are no new buildings to spoil the village's authenticity. Landward, however, the Whinnyfold pumping station, sending the oil it receives from BP's Forties field to Grangemouth, could not be credited with being a sensitive example of industrial architecture. "Old" Whinnyfold was actually situated 1km inland: it must have been a "farmtown", before its inhabitants forsook farming for fishing — or smuggling! — and moved seaward. New Whinnyfold was laid out in the 1860s and overlooks the Cruden Skares, a notorious reef. Far below, its shingle beach is tiny and suitable only for small boats which had to be winched up beyond the reach of the tide. You can still see the remains of the winches and slipway. On the beach to the N are the remains of an old tackle shed.

### The Bullers of Buchan

These coves and creeks and inlets, and especially the great "Pot" or cauldron, wrested by the sea from the ragged cliffs, are a dramatic sight and rightly a popular attraction. Yet in 1886 some 36 fishermen lived in the *heugh-heid* village of Bullers and nearby North Haven, using the tenuous strand below, then as now all but deafened by the multitude of kittiwakes, gulls, fulmars and shags which soar and sweep about this prodigious place. The name "Bullers" is often thought to come from the French *bouillir*, to boil; others claim that "bullers" is an old Scots word meaning a "rushing of water". What is beyond dispute, is the view of Dr Johnson who, in 1773, visited the Bullers, "which no man can see with indifference, who has either sense of danger or delight in rarity".

## Peterhead

Peterhead's first harbour was begun as a bulwark at Port Henry in 1593, but it was as a trading port that the town first flourished. In the mid-1600s, astonishingly, Peterhead was a fashionable spa and fishing was distasteful to its genteel clientèle. Yet, by 1680, "in this town is one of the best fishings that is on the north coast…the fishermen have a singular skill… so that their fishes are a proverb in the nation." For all that, the great sailing ships drew away the fishermen to act as crew or pilots and it took the emergence of whaling to confirm Peterhead as a major fishing port. Between 1788 and 1823 Peterhead became Britain's premier whaling port, with as many as 31 whalers out of a total British fleet of fewer than 60. The Arbuthnot Museum on St Peter Street (open all year, Mon–Sat 10–12 a.m. and 2–5 p.m.) preserves some fascinating whaling memorabilia. By the late 1830s, the herring industry was Peterhead's cornucopia; at its peak, 480 boats and 27 curing stations secured the town's place as the most important herring port of Scotland. Today, Peterhead is Europe's principal fishing port. Some 400 boats, mainly of middle-range, work out of it; to see them leave for the fishing grounds late on a Sunday night is an unforgettable experience. But it is the town's fish market that secures its future, handling up to 15,000 boxes of mainly white fish each day (open all year, Mon–Sat from 8 a.m.).

## Rattray

NK 106 582, up minor road off A952 just after St Fergus gas terminal.

It is hard to believe that this windswept and desolate place, all but devoid of human habitation, was once a royal burgh. Yet in medieval times, before the great sand-dunes grew and when the beach was of shingle and before the Loch of Strathbeg was formed, the estuary of the Burn of Rattray connected with the sea near the modern farm of Old Rattray, affording ships a welcome anchorage on an otherwise barren coast. Such was the importance of Rattray in the 13th century that two castles were built to guard the harbour. The remains of one survive at NK 088 580, whilst the ruins of the village chapel, St Mary's, built around 1200, are found at 085 575. In 1721, Alexander Hepburn visited the place and tells us of "the village of Rattray, famous for codfish which the inhabitants take in great plenty and have the best way of drying and curing them." Yet, sand gradually closed the estuary and the village died.

## Inverallochy and Cairnbulg

Like their sister villages, St Combs and Charlestown, 2km to the south, these siamese twins are separated only by a small burn known as "the Strype" and now, ignominiously, contained within a pipe.

The houses of the seatown of Inverallochy (still known locally as "Cotton") stand close to the shore, windowless gables backed to the sea. After

*Pennan*

years of drinking to great excess, the folk of the villages foreswore alcohol late in the 19th century and made the highlight of their year a Temperance Walk, Inverallochy's on Christmas Day and Cairnbulg's on New Year's Day. Temperance was all they had in common; although the villages always needed a harbour, they could not agree on where to site it. The Cairnbulg fishers suggested Westhaven, but Inverallochians could not bear to think of spending their money on a harbour at Cairnbulg, wanting it at Whitelinks. Not surprisingly, no harbour was ever built, although Cairnbulg folk built their own pier in the 1920s. The true rivalry between the villages rested, however, in golf; Inverallochy fishers would work the summer herring but spend the rest of the year playing golf. Cairnbulgers eschewed such frivolity, preferring to make money all year round instead.

### Fraserburgh

Known locally as "the Broch", the town was founded in 1546 by Sir Alexander Fraser who even built a university here. Like Peterhead, Fraserburgh was not a fishing port of note until the late 18th century; before then, its older neighbour to the west, Broadsea, held that prerogative. By 1881, though, over 1000 boats thronged the Broch for the summer herring. Today the town is still important for its fish processing.

### Sandhaven and Pittulie

The large harbour here, both inner and outer, point to what once was a thriving fishing port. Pittulie remains the epitome of an unspoilt Buchan fishing village and lobster fishing still goes on. Forbes and Co. still manufacture wooden fishing boats by the quayside, continuing centuries of craft and tradition.

### Pennan

Anson, as always, puts it perfectly: "Of all the fishing villages on the east coast of Scotland Pennan must...come first for picturesque situation." The beauty of Pennan catches the breath as you follow the steep track down the cliff-side to discover the village clinging, so unexpectedly, to a ledge so hard by the sea. Since David Putnam filmed *Local Hero* here, the village has been much visited and admired, yet has lost none of its charm. One small boat, *Guide Me*, still works for lobsters and crabs and line-fishes for cod from its tidal harbour. When they weren't fishing, the 19th-century inhabitants of Pennan had a major, if improbable, sideline – manufacturing millstones hewn from their red sandstone cliffs.

### Crovie

Pronounced "Crivie", this tiny village of 40 cottages is the jewel in Grampian's fishing crown, a perfectly preserved relic that clings so tightly to its cliff-foot as to leave no room for gardens, let alone cars. Some of the cottages seem to snuggle into the sheer cliffside "like a brood of young seafowl nestling with their heads under their dams", as the *New Statistical Account* of 1845 so memorably puts it. The village's death-knell was the great storm of 30–31 January 1953. Many of its cottages were ruined and many of its villagers moved away. Now restored by "incomers", Crovie is alive once more and rightly recognised as one of Europe's architectural gems.

### Gardenstown

Known in Grampian as "Gamrie", the village was founded in 1720 by Alexander Garden of Troup. It is quite unique, not least because it is still thriving, and is reputed to be the richest village in Britain. The newest homes crown the terraces

*Opposite page:*
*Crovie, Buchan*

*Fisher's house, Gardenstown, Buchan*

of cottages that rise up the hillside from the sea. Gamrie's vitality and success are all but inexplicable; it has not followed the decline of the other small ports, but still has its own fleet of some 12 boats and a boat-building yard, while the harbour was dredged as recently as 1984. The primacy here of the Plymouth Brethren is a factor; many of

*MacDuff, Buchan*

the village's brethren are "closed", refusing even to eat with non-brethren. Whatever the reasons, Gamrie preserves an admirable and austere independence, remarkable in this age.

### Macduff

Much of the present town was built in the 1780s by James Duff, second Earl of Fife, for whom the original town of Doune was re-named. The harbour, one of the best on the Moray Firth, with four separate basins, was at the heart of the town's construction. The town shook off the herring slump, eagerly taking up the seine net and motorised boat when others were clinging to the old ways. Watt, the shipbuilder, is still making boats of wood or steel, after four generations. Centred around its bustling harbour, Macduff retains a dignified prosperity.

### Banff

This is an ancient and elegant town, granted a charter in 1163 and made a royal burgh by Bruce in 1324. From the middle ages until the early 19th century, it conducted a busy and lucrative trade with the Low Countries, then the Mediterranean and Baltic. Thus Banff was never too dependent on fishing, even though it played its part in the herring boom. Around 1850, the river Deveron changed its course; the harbour silted up and the remaining fishing boats moved to nearby Macduff, leaving the town, as it was well-accustomed, to its own ample resources.

### Whitehills

This too has long been a resourceful place. Although the present harbour was not built until 1900, the village had long maintained a fair fleet of boats and still does. Its success comes from retailing: rather than moving their boats to larger ports as so many did in the 1920s, the people of Whitehills bought vans, selling their own fish themselves inland and, as they still do, at the Whitehills harbour. If this is unusual, so too is the harbour, one of few in Grampian to be owned not by the local authority but by the villagers themselves. It is run by commissioners elected from the village by the village.

### Portsoy

At the turn of the century, Portsoy's 17th-century harbour was semi-ruined and its many fishing warehouses were derelict. It is now greatly restored and reinvigorated, even if no longer serving as a fishing port. Its harbour, considered one of the safest on the coast, was once the home of tall ships whose trading with the Baltic brought the town the prosperity that is still reflected in its many fine buildings.

### Sandend

This small village is rightly famed for its fine beach. The tiny fishing cottages stand at right angles to the sea on a "berch" or strip of land between the ocean and the hill; about them are curing-sheds and smoke-houses, whilst fish merchants still trade around one of the prettiest and smallest harbours in Scotland.

## Portessie

Founded by a local laird in 1727, the village has now been absorbed by Buckie. Yet it retains its own character, its fishing cottages standing at right angles to the sea. Built beside a natural bay, the village never had a harbour.

## Buckie

Like Peterhead, though without the recent panoply of oil, Buckie is once more a thriving fishing port, boasting 116 registered boats. Here, the chandlers, fish merchants, boat-builders and ice-makers still carry on their timeless trades. Before the First World War, Buckie, whose name comes from the Gaelic *bocaith* for "bucking" or "leaping", was the fastest-growing town in Scotland. The town was formed from a group of three hamlets, Ianstown, Yardie and Buckpool. Its Maritime Museum and Peter Anson Gallery in the Town Hall West, Cluny Place (open all year, Mon-Fri 10 a.m.–8 p.m., Sat 10–12 a.m.) is well worth visiting.

## Spey Bay

This long spit of land, right at the mouth of the Spey, has supported salmon fishing for centuries. A great ice house, built in 1830, has been converted into an excellent museum of salmon fishing; its exhibits also reveal much of the turbulent history of the Spey. (Open daily June–Sept, 10 a.m.–4 p.m.).

## Burghead

A great place of Pictish strength, this is as old a coastal village as any in Grampian. It was once a busy fishing port, with 43 boats based here in the 1840s when the old pier was replaced by a harbour. The yellow sands of Roseisle run far from the lee of the Burghead promontory.

## Findhorn

Although there is still a salmon fishing station here and some subterranean ice houses to the N of the village, this beautiful place has never supported a serious fishing community; nature is too fickle. The first village was engulfed by the sea and the second by the great shifting sands of the estuary. Even today, only small craft can cross the sand-bar at the mouth of the bay. Findhorn's fleet is now one of pleasure craft, especially those of the Royal Yachting Club.

*The coast at Pennan*

*Fishing boats, Buckie*

# WHISKY: WATERS OF LIFE

*Wi' tipenny {ale}, we fear nae evil.*
*Wi' usquabae, we'll face the devil.*

                – Burns, *Tam o'Shanter*

*Beying moderatelie taken, it sloweth age; it strengthenth youthe; it abandoneth melancholie; it relisheth the harte...trulie it is a soverainge liquor.*

        – Holinshed, *Chronicles*, 1578

Grampian is to whisky what whisky is to Scotland. Of Scotland's 90-odd malt whisky distilleries, 67 are in Grampian, most of them in or near the Spey Valley. Grampian dominates not only the distilling of whisky but also the manufacturing of the copper stills that are used for distilling throughout Scotland.

Water, barley, peat. That these three essential elements of whisky should be found in such abundance and purity in Grampian explains in part why whisky production so flourishes in the region. The addition to these natural resources of centuries of skill and experience ensures the quality and popularity of such Grampian malts as Glenfiddich, Macallan or Glenlivet.

In keeping with the mystery of the spirit itself, no-one quite knows when whisky was first distilled in Scotland or in Grampian. The earliest recorded reference to whisky is in the *Scottish Exchequer Rolls* of 1494 which describe the provision of "eight bolls of malt to Friar Cor wherewith to make aquavitae". Whisky was certainly well known – some would say too well known – to the court of King James IV of Scotland by 1500.

What is certain is that, long before the 15th century, the small crofter's still was common in Scotland, producing what was known in Gaelic as *Uisge Beatha*, the "water of life". The Gaels' *uisge* is anglicised to "whisky".

The first tax on whisky was imposed by the Scots Parliament in 1644 to raise money for the Duke of Montrose's army. The tax cannot have been very lucrative, for most distilling was on a very small scale and usually, for that matter, undeclared. Grampian's remote hills and glens were an ideal location for illicit distillers.

After the Act of Union between England and Scotland in 1707, the London government decided to bring whisky distilling under legal control, establishing the Board of Excise and passing successive Acts of Parliament which imposed harsh penalties on those caught illegally distilling "the Cratur". The Scots were not well pleased, for the Articles of Union maintained that malt should not be taxed in Scotland. Resentment culminated in the Malt Tax Riots – the army had to be brought in to subdue riots all over Scotland. The most notorious were the Porteous Riots in Edinburgh, during which a Captain Porteous of the Edinburgh City Guard was lynched in 1736.

Although the roads built by General Wade throughout the Highlands in the wake of the failed 1745 Jacobite rebellion made life easier for the excise men, there was little else to help them. The geography, the hostility of the inhabitants and the portability of the stills made their task a hard one.

Distilling was seen by most Scots as a God-given right. Just how common it was is well attested by the *Old Statistical Account*. In 1794, for example, it reported of the inhabitants of Tomintoul: "All of them sell Whisky and all of them drink it." There were no fewer than 300 illicit stills within an eleven-kilometre radius of the village. The same held true of many other villages in Grampian, for there was a strong imperative – money. As a crofter in Grampian claimed in 1796, "Distilling is almost the only method of converting our victual into cash for the paying of rents."

As a result, the great formal distilleries of Grampian and the rest of Scotland might never have come into being. That they did so is thanks largely to the fifth Duke of Gordon, a great Banffshire laird. He argued in the House of Lords that, since it was not possible to stop the Highlander distilling, favourable opportunities for distilling whisky legally should be provided. He promised that, if this were done, he and his fellow landowners would do everything in their power to suppress illicit distilling and encourage their tenants to license their stills.

*Opposite*
*Tormore Distillery,*
*Speyside*

So, in 1823, an Act was passed which sanctioned the distilling of whisky on payment of duty of 2/3d per gallon and a licence fee of £10 on all stills with a capacity of 40 gallons or over. The Act worked, it seems – 14,000 illegal stills were detected in 1823, but only six in 1874.

It was with the passing of the 1823 Act that Grampian first came to dominate the distilling of Scotch whisky, a position it has never lost. For when, in 1824, George Smith of Glenlivet took out a licence to establish a legal distillery, it was the first in Scotland. His action, however, was one which must have given him pause for thought.

Faced with intense local opposition, Smith carried a pair of pistols in his belt to deter the local stillsmen who opposed what they thought to be his currying of favour. Smith persisted with his distillery even though, of the two distilleries opened in the next two years, one closed because of local hostility and the other was actually burnt down.

His determination paid off. King George IV drank "nothing else but Glenlivet whisky". So many distilleries sprang up in what became known, cynically, as the "longest glen in Scotland" that, in 1880, the Smiths sought and won a legal decree confirming their whisky as the only one entitled to call itself "The Glenlivet". Nonetheless, many Speyside distilleries still bear the name "Glenlivet" as a proud suffix, like "Abelour-Glenlivet".

By the late 1800s, assisted by the phylloxera disease which destroyed France's vines and cognac, Scotch whisky was established and with it, Grampian's place at its heart. There have been peaks and troughs, of course – the American Prohibition, the shortage of barley for malting in the Second World War – but, if some distilleries have closed, others have displayed great stamina and Grampian remains proud of its central role in the success of Scotch whisky.

There are two kinds of Scotch whisky: malt whisky, made from malted barley in a pot still, and grain whisky, made from barley, maize and other cereals in a patent still. We owe grain whisky to the invention of the patent still in 1833 by one Aeneas Coffey, ironically a retired Customs Inspector. His still, an advance on the 1826 Stein still, was capable of producing far greater quantities of admittedly poorer spirit than the pot still.

Apart from "Choice Old Cameron Brig", the only pure grain whisky on the market, all grain whisky is used for blending; the grain whisky is mixed with the pure malts which give the blend its flavour. Blending had begun as a random process, effected by publicans and merchants to produce a cheaper drink. But by the 1860s, with their consistency of taste and bouquet, blended whiskies achieved a recognition they have never lost.

Yet to many, pure malt and blended whiskies are heaven and hell. The hostility of the purists towards blended whiskies is of long standing. In 1905, a London magistrate ruled that a blended whisky, 90 per cent the product of a patent still and 10 per cent of a pot still, was not legally "Scotch", which delighted the pot distillers. Such was the controversy that, in 1908 a Royal Commission was appointed to settle the matter. Its decision – that both patent and pot still whiskies were "Scotch" – determined the future of whisky production, even if many continue to regard grain whisky, predominant in blends, as a poor cousin of true pot-distilled, single malt whisky. As Aeneas MacDonald lamented at the time: "The tasteless distillate of grain, made at one process in a patent still, is now equally entitled to call itself whisky as the exquisite pot-still malt whisky, dried above a peat fire."

All of Grampian's distilleries are malt distilleries. With the exception of Invergordon, all grain distilleries are in southern Scotland, near ports and railways. Most of the production of Grampian's distilleries was used for blending, but the last decade has seen increased demand for pure, single malts. Yet whether blended or not, Grampian's malts remain fundamental to the variety and subtlety of Scotch whiskies, a range to satisfy every palate.

The best way of coming to understand how malt whisky is made is to visit Grampian's distilleries and see for yourself. At its simplest, the process involves (1) Malting the barley by soaking it in water and causing it to germinate, thereby releasing its sugars. (2) Arresting the process of germination with the heat of a peat kiln. (3) Gristing (milling) the malted barley. (4) Soaking the grist in hot water. (5) Draining off the liquid, known as "worts", cooling it and mixing in yeast to cause fermentation. (6) Distilling this liquid, known as "wash", by heating it in a still and causing the alcohol to vaporise.

There are always two distillations – the first, in a "wash still", results in "low wines" with an alcohol content of about 25 per cent. Much of the low wines is discarded (of 11,000 litres of wash, usually only 2,500 litres are kept). The second, in a "low wines" or "spirit still", turns the low wines into "fore-shorts", the first flow from the still, the "middle cut" and "feints." Only the "middle cut" has the quality and strength for malt whisky. It will contain about 70 per cent alcohol. The "fore-shorts" and "feints" are returned to the "wash still" for re-distillation in the next batch of wash. Choosing the "middle cut" or "heart of the run" is crucial and highly skilled. You will often be able to see the still-man making this momentous decision, assisted by his hydrometers, turning taps in the spirit safe to begin or end the middle cut.

The whisky is then stored (for at least three years before it can even be legally known as whisky) in oak casks. Some distilleries swear by casks which previously held sherry; others prefer those that once stored bourbon.

Some malts are drinkable after eight years in the pure, damp Highland air which imparts so much to the maturing spirit. Usually, 12 years of maturation is regarded as the optimum. Finally, at the bottling stage, spring water is added to reduce the strength of the whisky, usually to 40 per cent volume.

Exactly why each malt whisky should vary so much remains a great imponderable. Chemists can isolate some 300 constituents in whisky, but they acknowledge that there are likely to be at least 100 more which defy scientific analysis.

"Water running off granite and through peat" is said to be the best for making whisky. Grampian is amply endowed with both granite and peat. The peat has a second use when added to the kilns which dry the malting barley. Its smoke has a characteristic aroma which transmits a flavour to the barley as it dries. Grampian's barley is well known to be high in fat and protein, contributing further to the fruitiness of Grampian's whiskies.

These essential, local ingredients are used in a variety of ways, which you may witness at individual distilleries, but the skills and traditions of each distillery's maltsters are a closely guarded secret. At Balvenie, you can still see "floor malt-ing", although "Saladin boxes", so named after the Frenchman who invented them, are much more commonly used for malting. In different distilleries you will see oil, coal or gas used to heat and distill the spirit.

There are as many explanations of the mystery of whisky as there are people to give them. One is best, perhaps, to agree with Walter Bagehot: "Do not let in daylight upon magic."

Grampian's Tourist Boards have prepared a "Malt Whisky Trail", covering seven distilleries located on a suggested route of 112km. Leaflets describing the trail are readily available at tourist offices.

The trail's distilleries have the advantage of being well-prepared for visitors. Distilleries outwith the trail are not and you should telephone in advance of your visit. You will find that most distilleries close for between 2 and 4 weeks each summer for maintenance: the custom comes from the days when they did so as they awaited the new season's barley. Nonetheless, you will still be welcomed and shown round, even if the distillery isn't actually distilling. Many distilleries are a joy to visit for their locations alone.

### Old Fettercairn

Telephone: Fettercairn (05614) 244. Opening hours: 1 May–30 September, 10 a.m.–4 p.m. Visitors Centre.

The entrance to the village of Fettercairn is through a magnificent arch built to commemorate the visit of Queen Victoria and Prince Albert to the village in 1861. The original distillery was built on the slopes of the Cairn o' Mount by the brothers Guthrie in 1820 and moved in 1824 to its present site near the river Esk. One of Old Fettercairn's many distinctions is that it was the first to use oil-heating for its stills.

The Old Fettercairn company was formed in 1887 under the chairmanship of the owner of the nearby Fasque Estate, Sir John Gladstone, brother of the great Liberal Prime Minister, William Gladstone. Until the First World War, when the practice was made illegal, the distillery's employees used to be given the perquisite of old casks. Into these they would pour a few gallons of boiling water before rolling the casks along the street to work the whisky out of the wood! This was known as "grogging the cask".

# GRAMPIAN

*A country in miniature*

The distillery was bought by the well-known blenders, Whyte and MacKay, in 1971. It produces a full, dry malt. Bottled at five years old, it is known as "Old Fettercairn 575" to denote its age and strength, just as 875 denotes an eight-year-old whisky.

## Lochnagar

Telephone: Crathie (03384) 273. Opening hours: all year, 10 a.m.–5 p.m. weekdays and 11 a.m.–4 p.m. weekends.

Lochnagar distillery lies a little SE of Balmoral Castle on Royal Deeside. It opened a formal Visitors' Centre early in 1988. The name comes from the mountain above the distillery, immortalised by Lord Byron:

> *England, thy beauties are tame and domestic*
> *To one who has roved o'er the mountains afar.*
> *Oh for the crags that are wild and majestic*
> *The steep frowning glories of dark Lochnagar.*

and, more recently, by Prince Charles' story, *The Old Man of Lochnagar.*

The only other distillery on Deeside was burnt down in 1825 by "those who sympathised with the illicit trade". The first distillery at Lochnagar was also destroyed by fire in 1841. Its successor, visited by Queen Victoria (who liked to lace her claret with Lochnagar) and Prince Albert in 1848, was granted permission to use the prefix "Royal".

*The river Spey from Macallan distillery*

Bought in 1916 from its founding family of Begg by one of the great blending houses, John Dewar and Co, the distillery in turn became part of what is now Distillers plc in 1925. Its whisky, with a subtle flavour of sherry from the casks in which it matures, is famed for its richness and is reputed to be the second-best selling malt in West Germany. The distillery is a small one, with only two stills. Its product is used in the famous blended whisky, John Begg.

Like the other distilleries owned by Distillers plc, Lochnagar buys in barley that has already been malted in a central "maltings". For all that, the product of each distillery owned by Distillers plc is, as you will taste, remarkably different.

## Glen Garioch (pronounced "Glen Geerie")

Telephone: Old Meldrum (06512) 2706. Opening Hours: 2.30–4.00 p.m., all year except July (closed for maintenance).

The distillery stands where it was built, in 1797, on Distillery Road in the village of Old Meldrum, the capital of the valley of the Garioch, famed since Roman times as Grampian's granary.

In 1937, Distillers plc bought the distillery but, sadly, had to close it in 1968. In 1970, it was bought by Stanley Morrison Ltd, who added a third still in 1973, and has since developed a formidable reputation for its 10-year-old, rich and fruity malt. It also produces a 21-year-old malt, 43 per cent alcohol, taking its water, as it has always done, from the Percock Hill. As the distillery's charming booklet puts it: "Glen Garioch is suited to any man's mood and has a taste equal to any occasion."

The distillery heats its stills with gas. In a remarkable venture with master-gardener Jim McColl (of the BBC's *Beechgrove Garden*), the surplus warm water is used to heat greenhouses which grow tomatoes and other plants. A Visitors Centre was built in 1975.

## SPEYSIDE MALTS

### Aberlour-Glenlivet

Telephone: Aberlour (03405) 204. Opening hours: by arrangement, 9–11 a.m. and 1–4 p.m., Monday to Friday. Closed for maintenance, 1 July–15 August.

Re-built after a fire in 1879, there has been a distillery here on the banks of the Lour, just before it joins the mighty Spey, since 1826. The grounds, however, have much older associations. The Christian missionary, St Drostan, baptised his converts here as early as 929, before leaving to take up office as Archbishop of Canterbury. The Well still bears his name. Who knows what effect this well has on the distillery's smooth and round produce, now bottled at 12 years old and 40 per cent alcohol? The distillery was bought by Pernod in 1974.

Hidden by landscape and trees, it is easy to pass the distillery without noticing it. While you are there, you might succumb to the temptation of taking a bottle with you and climbing the 843m of Ben Rinnes, from whose summit 10 counties are visible (on a clear day!)

*Whisky barrels, Cardhu distillery*

## Balvenie

Telephone: Dufftown (0340) 20374. Opening hours: mornings preferred, by arrangement with Glenfiddich Visitors Centre.

The distillery takes its name from the ancient castle hard by. The castle's ruins are well worth visiting. Edward I stayed here in the course of his campaign against Robert the Bruce. Mary, Queen of Scots also based herself here in 1522.

When William Grant had made a success of nearby Glenfiddich, in 1892 he converted some of the castle's ruined outbuildings into what is now Balvenie Distillery. Legend has it that he did so because a Catholic priest told him of the remarkable properties of the Robbie Dubh spring, from which the distillery still draws its water.

There is no better example of the mysterious differences between Grampian's malts than that between Balvenie and its very near neighbour, Glenfiddich. The same water and barley are used for both, yet the product is very different.

Balvenie still uses a traditional malting floor – the malting barley is dried on the floor, turned by hand with wooden shovels. Perhaps this, in part, explains the difference. Perhaps, too, the difference lies in the stills. Balvenie's eight stills are much bigger than Glenfiddich's and are heated by steam, rather than coal.

Several malts come from Balvenie. "Founder's Reserve" is the produce of "vatting" or mixing from 60 or more casks, each eight or nine years old. "The Classic" is bottled in a flagon, said to represent the doors of the old peat kiln. It is transferred from oak to oloroso sherry casks at least a year before bottling. This explains its darker colour and richness.

## Caperdonich

Telephone: Rothes (03403) 494. Opening hours: by arrangement, Monday–Friday, April–October.

Built in 1897 by the son of the founder of Glen Grant, Caperdonich (from the Gaelic for "secret well") closed in 1901 when recession blighted the whisky industry. It was not to re-open until 1965 and was bought, in 1978, by Seagram, who continue to leave production under the control of Chivas Brothers Ltd.

Caperdonich was originally so deeply suspected of illicit distilling by the excise men that they insisted its product be piped to and mixed with Glen Grant. This "whisky pipe" ran under the main street of Rothes.

The distillery, which used to be known as "Glen Grant 2", is now as modern and its product as rare as any. It is only available from independent bottlers – Gordon and MacPhail, of Elgin, bottle the 1979 distillation at 40 per cent and William Cadenhead an 18-year-old at 46 per cent. If you can find a bottle, keep it. It is usually left undrunk by serious collectors. Sampled alongside a glass of Glen Grant, it is an excellent example of the subtle differences between two adjacent whiskies.

### Cardhu (pronounced "Kaardoo")

Telephone: Carron (03406) 204. Opening hours: all year, weekdays, 9.30 a.m.–4.30 p.m. May to September, weekends by arrangement.

Although not on the official "Whisky Trail", Cardhu should be. Unlike some, this is a distillery, not a factory. It makes for an outstanding visit, memorable not only for the beauty, peace and order of the distillery, but for the friendliness of the staff. Its twin pagodas (kiln towers) and its six, shining stills are as striking as they are photogenic, whilst the distillery's layout makes it easy to understand the whisky-making process. Its reception area is most attractive, an example of how such conversions can and should be done. The old malting kiln has been converted to a dining-room which can be hired for private functions.

Owned since 1893 by John Walker and Sons (and now the "heart whisky" for blended Black and Red Label), the distillery was founded around 1811 by the man who farmed there, John Cumming. An innovative and enterprising man, Cumming took out a distilling licence in 1824 and began to ship his produce to Leith, Edinburgh's port, where he found an appreciative and large market for what is still a mellow, sweetish malt, rightly suggested to go exceedingly well with haggis. Cumming's great-grandson, Sir

Ronald Cumming, was Chairman of Distillers plc from 1963 to 1967.

The distillery's water is still piped from springs on the Mannoch Hill. The whisky, 12 years old and 40 per cent, comes in an unusual, decanter-shaped bottle that is corked and not screw-capped. The name is from the Gaelic for "black rock".

### Dufftown-Glenlivet

Telephone: Dufftown (0340) 20224. Opening hours: by arrangement, Monday–Friday.

With seven distilleries in or near it, it is hardly surprising that Dufftown gave rise to the popular rhyme:

*Rome was built on seven hills,*
*But Dufftown stands on seven stills.*

The Dufftown-Glenlivet distillery, now owned by Arthur Bell and Son Ltd, stands just outside the town in what must be one of Scotland's bonniest glens, Glendullan. A walk along the Dullan Water's peaty banks, past the distillery and the Lady's Apron Waterfall up to the Giant's Seat, is unrivalled for peace and beauty.

The distillery's water actually comes from Jock's Well nearby, famed for its purity. Although the Dufftown-Glenlivet is much in demand for blending, a single malt is bottled at eight and 14 years. Slightly sweet, it is considered a perfect after-dinner malt.

### Glenfarclas

Telephone: Ballindalloch (08072) 257. Opening hours: 9 a.m.–4.30 p.m., Monday to Friday, all year.

With a popular and well-designed Visitors' Centre, furnished with panelling from the liner *Australia*, Glenfarclas remains one of the last independently owned distilleries. John Grant bought the tenancy from the distillery's founder, Robert Hay, in 1865. The current managing director of a product so popular with blenders that it is almost all sold before it is made, is still a Grant and, indeed, named John.

The distillery's name comes from the Gaelic, "Glen of the Green Grassland", and its water from the Green Burn which rises in Ben Rinnes, the hill behind the distillery. Particularly worth noticing are Glenfarclas' unusually large, gas-heated stills and its old, confiscated illicit still –

on loan from Customs and Excise and, by regulation, with small holes bored through its base!

Glenfarclas is not "topped up" whilst it matures in the cask and therefore evaporates. This, in part, may justify the advert's boast: "Of all the Whiskies, malt is King. Of all the Kings, Glenfarclas reigns supreme." It is bottled at varying strengths at 8,10,12,15,21 and 25 years.

Single malts bring out the poetry in people. After a visit to the distillery in 1912, "Whisky Tom" Dewar proclaimed that "in its superiority" Glenfarclas "is something to drive the skeleton from the feast and paint landscapes in the brain of man".

## Glenfiddich

Telephone: Dufftown (0340) 20373. Opening hours: 5 January–20 December, 9.30 a.m.–4.30 p.m., Monday–Friday. Also, 14 May–16 October, Saturday, 9.30–4.30 a.m. and Sunday 12 a.m.–4.30 p.m.

The founder of Glenfiddich, William Grant, epitomises the canny industrious Scot. The son of a soldier who served under Wellington in the Peninsular War, he was originally apprenticed to a shoemaker but left to spend 20 years working at Mortlach distillery. There he not only learnt about distilling but saved some money.

In 1887 he bought the equipment from the old Cardow distillery for £120 and built his own distillery on the river Fiddich. Rebuilt and expanded in 1955, it now produces Scotland's biggest-selling malt and houses one of its busiest Visitors Centres in the original distillery buildings.

Sheer weight of numbers makes for a regimented but nonetheless interesting visit. Fifty thousand free drams a year are as much evidence of traditional Highland hospitality as of canny public relations.

Glenfiddich is one of only two malts to be bottled on site. It draws its water, like its neighbour Balvenie, from the Robbie Dubh spring on the lower slopes of the Conval hills. The age of the whisky is not on the triangular bottle, but it is mostly eight years old, with a small quantity of 12-year-old added to each "vatting" or mixing.

## Glen Grant

Telephone: Rothes (03403) 494. Opening hours: 15 April–7 October, 10 a.m.–4 p.m., Monday– Friday.

The Grants of Strathspey have been making malts, legally or otherwise, since distilling began. They built this distillery, one of the most picturesque, in 1840, moving from the nearby farm of Dandaleith where they first licensed a still in 1834. The distillery still draws its water from the Caperdonich well.

Some Glen Grant is matured in sherry casks and some in plain casks, giving it an unusually clear colour. Single malt Glen Grants are available up to 33 years old in varying strengths and are always best when well matured. It is a light, dry malt – a good all-rounder.

When Seagrams acquired the distillery in 1977, they added four more stills. Unusually, Glen Grant uses both coal and gas to heat its stills. The rummagers in the wash stills are still driven by a water wheel, the last one in use.

## The Glenlivet

Telephone: Glenlivet (08073) 427. Opening hours: 1 April–1 November, 10 a.m.–4p.m., Monday– Friday.

The largest-selling malt in the United States, this famous distillery draws its name from the Livet Water nearby and its water from local wells where, interestingly, you will see little granite or peat in evidence, This whisky is justly famed for its mellow, full flavour and delicate aroma. The distillery's peat is still cut at the nearby Faemussach Moss, whilst its barley comes from the Laich of Moray.

The founding family of Smiths owned The Glenlivet right up to 1978, when Seagram bought both it and Glen Grant, The malt's reputation remains enviable, as recognised by a local rhyme:

*Glenlivet has its castles three,*
*Drumin, Blairfindy and Deskie*
*And also one distillery*
*More famous than the castles three.*

It was widely known that George VI drank "nothing else but Glenlivet whisky", whilst James Hogg, the Ettrick Shepherd (1770–1835), had very pronounced views on the subject: "The human never tires o' Glenlivet... If a body could just find oot the exact proper proportion and quantity that ought to be drunk every day, I verily trow that he might leeve for ever."

Mellow and with a hint of the peat over which its spring water (drawn from the Letter Burn) passes, Inchgower is bottled at 12 years old and 70 degrees proof. It has sucessfully fortified the fishermen of nearby Buckie for many generations. A visitor in 1896 described the space in front of the stills of Inchgower as "sufficient to seat a small congregation to witness the progress of the work and spiritual mission carried on within its boundaries".

## Knockando

Telephone: Carron (03406) 205. Opening hours: by appointment, 10 a.m.–4 p.m., Monday–Friday. Closed for maintenance, July.

Pronounced "Cnoc-an-Doo" from the Gaelic for "the little black hillock", or possibly from *cnoc ceannachd* for "market hill", whisky has been distilled here since 1898, the water coming from the Cardnach Spring. Again, only recently has it been marketed as a single malt, winning great local approval.

Knockando's austere label states not only the bottling date but also the distillation season. This is of great importance to true connoisseurs of malt whisky, for they believe that malt whiskies have vintage seasons, just like wine. The distillery's owners since 1962, Justerini and Brooks, would agree and bottle when they think a particular distillation ready, rather than at a pre-determined age. They also market an "extra old", distilled at least 21 years before bottling.

## Linkwood

Telephone: Elgin (0343) 7004. Opening hours: by appointment. Closed, 4 July–22 September.

Linkwood stands in the wooded outskirts of Elgin, where the Linkwood Burn runs into the small loch which used to power the distillery's mill. For some reason, this malt is not well known. Once discovered, though, its light fruitiness is long remembered. Built in 1821, the distillery has been owned by Scottish Malt Distillers since 1933 and still draws its water from springs near Millbuies Loch.

The name comes from a mansion house that once stood on the site. The distillery's founder, George Brown, was six times Provost of Elgin and surveyed most of the many roads built in Grampian by Thomas Telford.

*Whisky Country* **Inchgower**

Telephone: Buckie (0542) 31161. Opening hours: by arrangement. Closed for maintenance, 1 July–7 August.

As mentioned earlier in this chapter, most malt whisky used to be used for blending. Inchgower is an excellent example – it has only been available as a single malt since 1972.

Built in 1871, Inchgower was bought by Buckie Town Council in 1933 when its owners went into receivership. The council, in turn, sold it for the snip of £3,000 to Arthur Bell, in 1936. Bell increased his bargain by buying a nearby mansion for £1,000. The Provost of Buckie later admitted "it was the first time I was done twice in one day."

The quality and consistency of the whisky is largely thanks to one Roderick MacKenzie, a Gaelic-speaking native of Wester Ross, who supervised the distilling for many years with "unremitting vigilance". He allowed no equipment to be replaced unless absolutely necessary and nothing, it was said, not even a spider's web, to be removed, lest it detract from the quality of his product! When the distillery was completely rebuilt in 1962, Mackenzie insisted that the new stills should be exact replicas of the old.

## Macallan

Telephone: Aberlour (03405) 471. Opening hours: by appointment at either 11.30 a.m. or 2.30 p.m., Monday–Friday. Closed, 1 July–15 August.

Many consider this the finest malt whisky. In a *Sunday Times* tasting of the 20 most popular malts, The Macallan emerged with an "excellence quotient" (whatever that is) of 93.78 per cent, well above the runner-up. It certainly has a smooth richness of flavour that is quite unique. Its sweetness comes from the oloroso sherry casks in which it matures and for which the distillery goes to a great deal of trouble, sending someone to Spain each year to buy casks and arrange to have them seasoned for three years. Macallan is the last distillery still maturing its spirit only in sherry casks.

Which type of cask is best for maturing malt whisky? Some believe that over-exposure to sherry casks is detrimental to the delicacy of the maturing spirit. Yet in 1864, the vintner William Sanderson could claim that "whisky stored in sherry casks soon acquires a mellow softness it does not get in new casks." Some connoisseurs prefer a malt that has been matured in a cask that once held amontillado sherry; others prefer fino.

Nowadays, as containerisation makes sherry casks harder to come by, most whisky is matured in oak barrels that once held American bourbon: Macallan's strict adherence to its sherry casks is the more admirable. In their hands, these casks certainly enhance the delicacy of their fine malt. Its quality may be futher explained by the fact that Macallan's stills are unusually (and expensively) externally heated instead of being heated in the normal way by internal steam coils.

Built in 1824, the distillery stands above an ancient ford of the river Spey. Since 1892 it has been in the hands of the Kemp family. The first

Kemp at Macallan had previously owned and managed the Talisker Distillery on the Isle of Skye before bringing his skill and experience to Speyside. To cater for rising demand, the Kemps built a second distillery on the site between 1964 and 1966 and have always been and remain excellent marketers of their product. To celebrate the royal marriage in 1981, for example, they produced a special Wedding Malt, vatting together malts from 1948 (the year of Prince Charles' birth) and 1961 (that of Lady Diana).

The distillery goes to considerable trouble to make a visit there as individual and special as its whisky. Of particular note is the warehouse, still with a traditional earthen floor to maintain humidity. The audio-visual presentation may not be to everyone's taste, but is as extraordinary as it is memorable.

## Miltonduff

Telephone: Elgin (0343) 7433. Opening hours: by appointment, weekdays 10.30 a.m. or 1 p.m.. Closed for maintenance, July.

This distillery stands in the fertile vale of Pluscarden, not far from Pluscarden Abbey, founded in 1230. The Benedictine monks there were famed for the quality of the ale they brewed. It "made the hearts of all rejoice and filled the abbey with unutterable bliss".

The water for the brewing came from the Black Burn which runs off the Black Hills behind the distillery and through Pluscarden plain. Legend has it that an abbot knelt on a stone by the burn and blessed the waters. From that time on, the drink distilled from them was aptly known as "aqua vitae", the water of life.

The local belief is that the stone on which the abbot knelt was later built into the malt mill, whilst the distillery's old mash house, rebuilt in 1824, was once the monks' brewhouse. The distillery's old mill wheel is still kept in exemplary working order; the huge compounds of barrels round the distillery are memorable alone.

The Pluscarden plain is known as the "Garden of Scotland". The quality of the barley it grows may, in part, account for the quality of the fine Milton Duff malt, now licensed to George Ballantine and Sons and bottled at 12 years old and 40 per cent. Another single malt, Mosstowie, used to be produced here and is still available from Gordon and MacPhail.

### Mortlach

Telephone: Dufftown (0340) 20275. Opening hours: by appointment. Closed, June–August.

It was here, in 1010, that Malcolm, second King of Scotland, defeated the Danes. He had dammed the river Dullan upstream and broke the dam in the night, flooding the unsuspecting Danes who were camping in the valley below – Mortlach means "bowl-shaped valley". In his gratitude, Malcolm gave a generous endowment to Mortlach Church (founded in 556 AD).

The distillery is one of the earliest, built in 1823, and still draws its water from springs in the Conval Hills above it and from the famous Priest's Well which is associated with St Drostan.

The Distillers plc no longer issue Mortlach, a fruity luscious whisky, as a single malt in the UK. Bottles can still be had though, either through Gordon and McPhail in Elgin or William Cadenhead in Aberdeen.

### Strathisla (pronounced Strath-eye-la)

Telephone: Keith (05422) 7471. Opening hours: 9 a.m.–4.30 p.m., weekdays, all year.

This beautiful distillery nestles in the outskirts of Keith. Its owners, Chivas Brothers (part of Seagram), have restored the old water wheel that dominates the distillery's frontage and keep the whole site in pristine condition. The stillhouse, with its old roof and wooden beams, is especially charming. Two of the stills are steam heated; the other two are directly coal-fired.

Established in 1786, the distillery regards itself as the oldest Highland distillery. It produces a splendid, full, fruity malt with a taste of honey. Strathisla's production as a single malt is in relatively small quantities, though the Spar grocery in Keith stocks it. It is bottled at 12 years old, 40 per cent, and, under-rated, deserves to be better known. It is a whisky of which the Gaelic poet might have been thinking when he wrote:

> *Is coisiche na h-oidhche thu*
> *Gu leapannan na maighdeannan:*
> *Righ! gur h-iomadh loinn a th'ort*
> *Gu coibhneas thoirt a grugach.*
> (You are the prowler of the night
> To the beds of virgins;
> Oh God! what powers you have
> To gain kindness from girls.)

### Tamdhu (pronounced "Tam-doo")

Telephone: Carron (03406) 221. Opening hours: 10 a.m.–4 p.m., Monday–Friday, 1 April–1 October.

Although built in 1897, the depression forced Tamdhu's closure in 1927 and it wasn't reopened until 1948. Its owners, Highland Distillers, rebuilt the distillery in 1970 and converted the old railway station of Knockando into an attractive Visitors Centre and shop. The distillery is particularly worth visiting because of the large gallery around the main working area which makes it easy to understand how whisky is made.

Note, too, the spaces between the slates on the warehouse roof – these allow better air circulation, thereby contributing who knows what to the mysterious process of maturation. Don't miss the wonderful collection of old malts in the cases at the end of the viewing gallery.

Tamdhu still does its own malting, although it gave up floor-malting in 1952 in favour of Saladin boxes. Its peat is cut on a local hillside and its water comes from springs high above the distillery.

The malt is a typical light Glenlivet, well-flavoured and not too peaty. It is bottled at 10 years, 40 per cent and 15 years, 43 per cent.

### Tamnavulin (pronounced "Tam-navoolin")

Telephone: Glenlivet (08073) 285. Opening hours: 10 a.m.–4 p.m., Monday–Saturday, 1 March–7 October.

Although this concrete buiding looks strangely out of place, Tamnavulin (from the Gaelic for "mill on the hill") is particularly well worth visiting and tasting in order to test the theory that good malt whisky can only come from old distilleries.

Tamnavulin was built as recently as 1966 by

Invergordon Distillers and has a formal Visitors Centre in a converted mill-house of great charm, together with a beautiful picnic area. The distillery's designers went to great trouble to ensure that the stills they built were suited to the local waters.

Every distillery's stills are different, both at the point of boiling the liquor and in the "stretching" and control of the rising vapour so that unwanted elements fall away. You must taste this malt's rich and fruity bouquet and judge for yourself whether the designers of Tamnavulin have succeeded in applying modern technology to an ancient art.

### Tomatin

Telephone: Tomatin (08082) 234. Opening hours: all year, by appointment, 10 a.m.–1 p.m. and 2 p.m.–4 p.m., Monday–Friday.

This is the largest of the malt whisky distilleries, with an annual capacity of 5 million gallons. Strictly speaking, it lies just outside Grampian Region in Highland. Built in 1897, it was owned by an independent company but went into voluntary liquidation in 1984 before being bought in 1986 by two Japanese companies.

Its situation is surprising, 313m up on the northern slopes of the Grampian Mountains. There has been a distillery here, however, since the 15th century, when it served the needs of cattle drovers on their long trek south to the great cattle markets or "trysts" at Crieff and Falkirk.

Despite being owned by Japanese, this is a whisky of great individuality, made from local peat and local water that passes through peat and over red granite. It is light-bodied and, though peatier, not unlike Glenlivet.

### Tormore

Telephone: Advie (08075) 244. Opening hours: strictly by appointment with the manager, Mr Reid. Closed in July.

This was the first new Highland distillery to be built this century, in 1958. The architect, Sir Albert Richardson, past President of the Royal Academy, managed to design a building that blends well with its environment.

When the distillery was finished, its builders buried a time capsule in the shape of a pot still. Within are memorabilia of distilling, together with a magnum of Long John – perhaps to give sustenance to the extra-terrestial archaeologists who, one day, will find the time capsule!

The distillery's water comes from the Advockie Burn, whose source is high near Loch an Oir, the Loch of Gold. Coming from the "Golden Rectangle" in the heart of Speyside, one would expect a fine whisky. Bottled at the distillery at 10 years, 40 degrees, that is what one gets – a whisky that is not noticeably peaty, but very rich. It is owned by Long John International.

# PARKS, GARDENS AND FLORA

*Cela est bien dit, répondit Candide, mais il faut cultiver notre jardin.* (That is well said, replied Candide, but we must cultivate our garden)

— Voltaire (1694–1778), *Candide*

The earliest antecedent of the formal garden in Scotland is the medieval deer park, an import of Norman feudalism. Grampian preserves Scotland's finest example in the Deer Dyke that runs westwards for 4 km from the Clatterin' Brig at NO 664 783 and is part of the wall that enclosed Kincardine Park to the north of Kincardine Castle. William I first laid out this royal park. Alexander II extended it in 1266.

Such enclosures ranged from 20 to 20,000 hectares. They enclosed both red and roe deer, providing not only a ready source of meat in the winter but also captive animals to be released in season for the hunt.

By the 16th century, such parks were an increasing concern of central government. By royal edict, landowners in Scotland were encouraged to "have parkis with dere and plant at the leist ane aker of wood". The second injunction not only reflects an increasing concern with the lack of adequate resources of timber but also led naturally to the concept of the controlled landscape and the planned garden.

It was doubtless difficult for the government to enforce such regulations in remote Grampian. Yet Johan Blaeu's *Atlas Novus* of 1654, in part based on the work of Robert Gordon of Straloch in Aberdeenshire, shows that a great deal of planting and emparking had occurred in Grampian by the mid-17th century. As for smaller gardens and orchards in the region, although none are documented it is improbable that none should have existed – there is much historical and archaeological evidence for late medieval terrace gardens in the policies of even small castles elsewhere in Scotland, whilst we do have reference to the Knights Templars' "Gardenne of Physik", a medicinal herb garden, at Maryculter near Aberdeen in the 14th century.

By 1620, certainly, Sir Robert Gordon was urging the young Earl of Sutherland to "build a house in Dunrobin... Ther yow may easilie mak a fyne delicat park." In Blaeu's *Atlas* the map of Morayshire gives particular prominence to the parks at Gordon Castle where, in the 1630s, the Marquis of Huntly is said to "give himself whollie to policie, planting and building". A century later, the gardens of Gordon Castle were finer still, with grass terraces, statues, a canal, fountains, bowling greens, orchards and a park which contained a dovecot and enclosures for horses and swans. We know this not from any written account but from the original plans of the garden which survive in the Scottish Records Office.

But the best description of a Grampian garden in the 17th century has a sad provenance. In 1640, the Civil War came to the royalist Sir George Ogilvie's Banff Castle. The town itself was occupied by the Roundhead General Munro who "no sooner came thither but he sett downe his qwarter in the laird of Banfe his beautiful garden, which was a great ornament to the towne of Banfe, and, being gallantly planted and walled...enclosed the east syde of that towne. The souldiours wer no sooner sett downe there but they fell to macke havocke of all the standing trees, younge nor old, and cutting upp all the hedges to the rootes." Another contemporary describes the garden as "inclosed with excellent stone walls, and planted with the best fruit-trees then could be had".

If such was the garden of Banff Castle, it would not be unreasonable to assume that other great houses of Grampian were similarly furnished. But it is with the 18th century, the wealth that trade brought to Grampian and, above all, exposure to France in the wake of the restored and French-educated Charles II that Grampian's gardens, in common with the rest of Scotland, came of age.

The pioneer of French influence on Scottish gardens was the distinguished Scottish architect Sir William Bruce of Balcaskie (1630–1710) who completed a great French garden at his home near

*Opposite*
*Crathes Castle garden, Deeside*

Kinross in 1690. A staunch royalist, he had used business on the continent as an excuse for carrying many messages to the court of the exiled Charles II. In the course of these, he had seen and admired the gardens designed by Le Nôtre at the chateau of Vaux-le-Vicomte. He passed his experiences on to such of his friends as Sir Alexander Seton who gave it voice at Pitmedden.

In 1683, John Reid published *The Scots Gard'ner* in Edinburgh, giving Scotland not only her first gardening book but also a thorough statement of the principles of French garden design. It fell on fertile ground as Scottish and Grampian lairds became more cosmopolitan, travelling not only to Charles II's restored palace of Holyrood and its new French garden designed by Sir William Bruce but to the court in London and further afield.

They were able to see for themselves the effect of John Reid's advice that "all the buildings and plantings should ly so about the house as that the house may be at the centre...whatever you have on the one hand, make as much of the same form and in the same place on the other." The *patte d'oi* or goose-foot, triple lines of trees, was all the rage. William Adam designed a particularly fine example around 1720 for the Earl of Breadalbane at Taymouth Castle in Perthshire. In Aberdeenshire, the garden and parkland at Tyrie that were planned in 1690 gloried in "large orchards and arming of barren planting (ie a goose-foot) and at foot of the parks, below the house eastward, is a pretty cannal or water draught of 12 foot broad, near a mile in length."

Nearby at Boyndlie, according to the same account, there were "3 handsome terraces" on each side of the river with "a pair of stairs ascending by 12 steps to the hous from a handsome avenue and square from the utter gate". The house was "invironed with fyne gardens well-planted and walled with rounds on every corner...with a summer hous and ducat".

Early in the 18th century, conifers new to Scotland began to be imported from the expanding American colonies. They were taken up with enthusiasm by landowners in largely tree-less Grampian. At Urie Castle near Stonehaven, the Barclays planted "a great many trees of several sorts, particularly fir trees, which thrive very well, he is supposed to have near an hundred thousand". At Monymusk, the great agricultural improver Sir Archibald Grant (see chapter 5) took up tree-planting with particular gusto. In 1760 he was described by Bishop Pococke as "a very great improver in the farm and garden... He has made a fine plantation; first you come into an orchard, then to an avenue of firrs with parterres on each side: there is also a pleasant walk by the river; and the hills to the south are covered with trees."

A walk through the Woods of Paradise near Monymusk from NJ 678 180 still allows a glimpse of Sir Archibald's vision and is a welcome alternative to its modern equivalent: the forest walks through the Forestry Commission's rows of sitka spruce on the other side of the river. It is heartening, too, that the Monymusk Walled Garden (NJ 685 153) is being restored and now thrives as a commercial proposition.

The next stimulus to the development of the garden in Grampian came from increasing English influence in the region after the 1745 Jacobite rebellion. Many estates were forfeited and given to or bought by Englishmen or Anglophiles. Families such as the Gordons lay low and turned from politics to improving their estates. The English ideal of landscaped policies, given its finest expression by "Capability" Brown, came to the north by way of such men as Robert Robinson, who had served his apprenticeship under Brown and was introduced to Grampian by Sir Archibald Grant. Robinson planned the new gardens at Castle Grant in 1764 and also worked at Banff, Glamis and Cullen House.

Grampian's most spectacular example of the new style was not, however, the work of Robinson but of Thomas White who, from 1786, completely transformed the landscape of Gordon Castle and Fochabers at the behest of the fourth Duke of Gordon. The castle's old formal gardens were eradicated; the canal was filled in and the parterres were levelled. By 1792, White had completed a ha-ha or sunk fence more than 2 kilometers long to divide the lawns of the policies from the pastures of the parks beyond. But such re-ordering of the landscape did not stop with the castle and its policies.

With what now seems an incredible arrogance, the duke wished to destroy the flourishing and ancient little market town of Fochabers and replace it with one that would be an edifying extension of his landscape. Furthermore, the old

*Buttresses of yew at Pitmedden*

village was too close to the castle for the Gordons' liking. As early as 1773, the architect of the new Gordon Castle, John Baxter, had presented to the duke a "sketch of a new town agreeable to your Grace's idea of having it square and compact". By 1802, the last of Fochaber's inhabitants had been driven out and the old town was demolished. The new Fochabers, according to Lord Cockburn, was but "a kennel for the retired lacqueys and ladies' maids of the castle and for the natural children and pensioned mistresses of the noble family, with a due proportion of factors, gamekeepers and all the other adherents of such establishments".

Fortunately, most of Grampian's landowners were more conservative. The 19th century saw a renewal of interest in the older style of 17th-century garden such as that at Brotherton in Kincardineshire, described in 1813 by G Robertson: "On the coast side is another garden in the ancient style. This is bounded and subdivided not by hedges but by stone walls; and is raised terrace above terrace with a strength of masonry which might serve fortification."

When Prince Albert re-built Balmoral in the 1850s and had a formal garden laid out round the castle, he was expressing an attitude to gardens in Grampian that had described a full circle. Off the hill, the whole landscape of Grampian had changed; in a sense, it was all a park, enclosed and dyked and hedged, very much the landscape of today.

The story of Grampian's flora is a simpler one, but no less interesting. Largely because of its topographical range, from sea level to 1309 metres at the top of Britain's second highest mountain, Ben Macdui, the region contains a variety of flora that is without parallel elsewhere in the British Isles. Although more than 900 species of vascular plant have already been identified in Grampian, there are more to be found. Botanists have been much drawn to the region since Victorian times but there is still no comprehensive catalogue of Grampian's flora.

Three thousand years ago, perhaps as much as 80 per cent of the region was afforested — oak (*quercus petraea* and *q. robur*) on the fertile soils of

conifers. As the 17th century advanced, the timber that had survived became a valuable cash crop. In 1776, Charles Cordiner passed Luibeg and noticed "many thousand stumps of trees, the remains of woods which have been floated down Lui Water to the Dee". In 1797, the "rents of Rothiemurchus were small…but the timber was beginning to be marketable; three or four thousand a year could easily have been cut out of that forest and hardly have been missed." At Glen Tanar, many thousands of trees were felled, demand fuelled first by the Napoleonic Wars and then by the railways.

Fortunately, most of these woods either regenerated naturally or were re-planted. Some of Scotland's finest remnants of the "Old Wood of Caledon" are in Grampian, at Ballochbuie on the Balmoral estate and Glen Tanar in the south, at Nethybridge and Dorback Moor in the north. As Steven and Carlisle say in their *The Native Pinewoods of Scotland*, "To stand in them is to feel the past." Where the pines are not dense, the individual trees can attain great girth. There are particularly fine boles in Glen Quoich and Glen Lui. Fragments of the region's natural or semi-natural oak forests survive at Craigendarroch near Ballater, further down the valley at Dinnet, at Drum Castle and at Darnaway in Moray, although the sorry state of the Craigendarroch trees is a matter of grave concern. The primary birchwood at Morrone near Braemar is "extraordinary…probably unique in Britain" (Dr Gordon Miller, *The Grampian Book*). It is a birch wood in which anyone from Scandinavia would feel perfectly at home.

Many interesting flora thrive in these woods. Dinnet safeguards the unusual wild strawberry (*fragaria vesca*), stone bramble (*rubus saxatilis*) and common wintergreen (*pyrola minor*). The Morrone wood's dense ground cover of juniper (*juniperus communis*) shelters some rare plants such as northern bedstraw (*galium boreale*), alpine ladies' mantle (*alchemilla alpina*) and alpine cinquefoil (*potentilla crantzii*). In the pine woods, the sight of the soft pink of twinflower (*linnaea borealis*) is especially pleasing. Two small orchids, lesser twayblade (*listera cordata*) and creeping ladies' tresses (*goodyera repens*), are especially fond of the pine woods' acid and humus-rich soils.

Apart from trees, the variety of plant life in Grampian is remarkable. Despite its smooth coastline the region contains, at St Cyrus near

*Kildrummy Castle garden* the Mearns and Deeside, oak and Scots pine (*pinus sylvestris*) in inland Aberdeenshire, Moray and Buchan and pine on the higher hills. A patch of natural pine wood still survives today as high as 640 metres on Creag Fhiaclach. Birch (*betula pendula* and *b. pubescens*) grew throughout these forests, probably as scrub at the upper altitudinal limit. Alder (*alnus glutinosa*) and willow (*salix spp*) grew in marshy ground.

Most of these forests were gone by the early 17th century. Blaeu's *Atlas* of 1654 shows very much the same woodlands as we have today, saving of course the very modern regiments of

*Opposite, top: Oyster plant (mertensia maritima)*

Montrose and Findhorn in Moray, two fine salt marshes with stands of eelgrass (*zostera spp*) and glasswort (*salicornia spp*). Some of Buchan's many sea cliffs sustain colonies of the arctic species purple saxifrage (*saxifraga oppositofolia*) and roseroot (*sedum rosea*). The very rare Dickie's Fern (*cystopteris dickieana*) can still be found in sea caves near Aberdeen, whilst the equally rare oyster plant (*mertensia maritima*) survives on the shingle beaches of the Moray Firth.

On the region's high peat moors, the month of June rewards the walker with the brilliantly white flowers of the yellow-fruited cloudberry (*rubus chamaemorus*). The moor of Muir of Dinnet is distinguished by its abundance of intermediate wintergreen (*pyrola media*). But it is for its wealth of rare mountain flora that Grampian merits special attention.

High in the Cairngorms, hiding in clefts and crannies of the rock, feeding off small deposits of chalk, calcite or epidote in the otherwise acid granite, is as fine a range of exquisite arctic and alpine flora as can be found anywhere. Particularly

rare are alpine milk-vetch (*astragalus alpinus*), alpine fleabane (*erigeron borealis*), tufted saxifrage (*saxifraga cespitosa*) and mountain sandwort. These and many others display a variety of form and colour to delight even the most jaded.

The Cairngorms have been attracting naturalists and botanists for more than two centuries. The great pioneers from the 1770s, men like George Don, William MacGillvray and Thomas Edward, were often great collectors. It is heartening that today those with the will and the patience to seek out the flora of Grampian prefer to photograph their trophies, rather than pick them. If the vital questions of conservation and land use in Grampian can be resolved, the region's flora will attract the lover of beauty for many centuries more.

### Crathes Castle Gardens, Banchory, Kincardine and Deeside

NJ 733 969. 31km W of Aberdeen. Well signposted off A93 Aberdeen-Braemar road. NTS. Castle open 11 a.m.–6 p.m., May–October; garden 9.30–sunset, all year.

"A happy Region…covered with a wonderful Profusion of Flowers that, without being disposed into regular Borders and Parterres, grew promiscuously, and had a greater beauty in their natural Luxuriancy…than they could have received from the Checks and Restraints of Art."

– Joseph Addison, *The Tatler*, 1710

The gardens of Crathes Castle are an astonishment, a horticultural and aesthetic triumph to rival even the great gardens of England like Sissinghurst or Hidcote. They are admirably kept by four NTS gardeners. Although the present gardens are largely 20th century in conception and execution, there has been a formal garden here for a very long time. Part of the old garden survives in the great Irish yew hedge that frames the croquet lawn in the upper garden. It was planted in 1702 by the third Burnett baronet whose wife bore him 21 children in 22 years. The very old Portugese laurel tree (*prunus lusitanica*) in the white borders is another relic; the hub of five paths, it was an important part of the 19th-century garden plan.

The present garden owes its form to the 19th century and two distinguished Victorian gardeners, William Robinson and Gertrude Jekyll. Miss Jekyll was particularly influential: in a number of books, especially *Colour Scheme in the Flower Garden* (1908), she established what became canons of taste for late Victorian and Edwardian gardens. She visited Crathes in 1895; the gardens still conform to many of her *dicta* – that earth should never be visible in a flower-bed (at least not in summer), that flowers which bloom at the same time should be placed near each other.

Crathes gardens epitomise the controlled vibrancy that Addison advocated. Although there are eight main formal beds, combining with borders to form an enclosed rectangle, within these restraints are a profusion of plants and a riot of colours. Most of the modern garden owes its quality to Sir James and Lady Sybil Burnett of Leys, the last Burnetts to live in Crathes Castle and who began to re-form the garden in 1926. They laid out the remarkable Colour Garden in 1932 yet retained the best of the Victorian garden, preserving, for example, the Blue Garden with its centrally placed fountain and statue. The work of Sir James and Lady Sybil was continued by their Burnett heirs: the June Borders with a fine dovecot as their focal point were begun in 1945.

The Golden Garden, begun in 1973, was the dream of another Burnett, its inspiration from Gertrude Jekyll. To the right of the June Borders is a garden begun in 1977 and devoted to plants with red flowers or foliage.

Amongst the gardens' 14,000 different species of plant are many fine and rare species. The nursery boasts an especially tall and strong strain of Himalayan lily (*cardiocrinum giganteum*). The June Borders contain several old varieties of oriental poppy. By the path between the Double Shrub Borders is a splendid tree from China, *staphylea holocarpa rosea*, best seen in late spring when its deep pink flowers grace the world. A notable North American "Indian bean tree" (*catalpa bignonionides*) stands in the Blue Garden. Such rare plants first came to Scotland in the mid-19th century when the invention of the sealed glass "Wardian case" enabled the tenderest plants to survive long sea voyages. Their survival at Crathes, in the age of the garden centre, is a great tribute to the Burnetts of Leys, the NTS and its devoted gardeners.

### Pitmedden Garden, Ellon, Gordon

NJ 885 280. 30km N of Aberdeen. Take A947 towards Old Meldrum. Garden sign-posted. NTS.

Open 10 a.m.–6 p.m., 1 May–30 September. Museum of Farming Life and other facilities open 11 a.m.–6 p.m., May–September.

Pitmedden makes for an interesting contrast with Crathes in many ways, not least because whilst at Crathes the NTS took over a garden which had been lovingly kept up, at Pitmedden they were faced with resurrecting a garden whose remains were vestigial. The three central acres of the great garden that Sir Alexander Seton began here on 2 May 1675 had become a vegetable garden; a disastrous fire in 1818 gutted Pitmedden House and destroyed the plans of the original garden. When the NTS accepted Pitmedden in 1951 and undertook to restore the garden, they had only an architectural skeleton, the walls, stairs and pavilions of the original garden to work from.

The garden today, an authentic and comprehensive restoration, is the fruit of remarkable co-operation between scholars, gardeners and masons from 1955 to 1974. Restoration continues. Most recently, a herb garden has been laid out in the upper garden to the design of the man, the late Dr James Richardson, who re-created Sir Alexander Seton's plans.

The garden is laid out as four great parterres, each delineated by box hedges (there are nearly 5km of them!) and divided by grass paths, the whole enclosed by a wall with viewing terraces to N and S in the manner of such other 17th-century Scottish enclosed gardens as Holyrood, Pinkie, Seton and Winton. As was intended, the garden is best seen in its entirety from the lawn above.

The colours in the parterre's designs are provided by a staggering 40,000 annuals, grown in the estate's own greenhouses and frames and planted out each May. Three of the parterres' designs are taken from Gordon of Rothiemay's drawings of the gardens at Holyrood. The fourth pattern is an original tribute to Sir Alexander Seton, a heraldic design based on his coat-of-arms: the mottos *"sustento sanguine signa"* (with blood I bear the standard) and *"merces haec certa laborum"* (this sure reward of our labours) refer to the death of Sir Alexander's father, a staunch Royalist, in the service of Charles I at the skirmish of Brig o' Dee in 1639.

Of particular interest is the re-built fountain at the heart of the upper garden. Seven of its carved stones once formed part of the fountain at Linlithgow Cross, designed to commemorate the restoration of Charles II. It was built by Robert Mylne who also constructed the pavilion at Kinross House for Sir William Bruce. Pitmedden's two pavilions echo his work and provide another link between Seton and Bruce. The restoration of the split-pebble pavement round the fountain required long-lost skills.

### Kildrummy Castle Gardens, Alford, Gordon

NJ 456 166. 12 km W of Alford. Sign-posted off A97 Huntly-Ballater road. Open 10 a.m.–5 p.m., April–October.

At the heart of this fine water garden is a replica of Aberdeen's famous Brig o' Balgownie which bridges the gorge around which the garden is laid out. Underneath the bridge, in a series of dammed pools, is a Japanese water garden. Charming paths lead through the garden's acres, brooded over by the ruins of Kildrummy Castle.

The garden was created by Colonel James Ogston, an Aberdeen soap manufacturer, who bought Kildrummy estate in 1898. Having built himself a house (now Kildrummy House Hotel) and a bridge, he and his wife planted silver firs, hemlocks and larch to act as shelter for the gorge that had been formed when the stone for Kildrummy Castle was quarried here. At the foot of the den they made an alpine garden. In 1936 their heirs began a rock garden, using carefully sought glacial boulders and other unusual stones. In 1968 a charitable trust was established to look after the gardens; since then, grants from the Scottish Tourist Board have enabled further improvements.

### Edzell Castle Gardens, Edzell, Angus

NO 593 687. 2km W of Edzell. Sign-posted off B966 10km N of Brechin. NTS. Garden open all year round, 11 a.m.–sunset.

This is Scotland's definitive 17th-century pleasance and an outstanding example of Renaissance art. Its sculptures and flower baskets, recessed into the garden's wall, are unique in Scotland. The garden was laid out in 1604 by Sir David Lindsay whose coat-of-arms is carved above the doorway in the NE corner of the enclosing wall. Within the pleasance, the walls are decorated with bas-relief sculptures of the Liberal Arts on the S, the Planetary deities on the E and the Cardinal Virtues on the W. The beautiful box hedge in the garden's centre was replanted in 1932 and spells

# GRAMPIAN
*A country in miniature*

*Winter Gardens,
Duthie Park*

*Pitmedden*

*Granite and roses,
Aberdeen*

out the Lindsay family motto *"Dum spiro spero"* (while I live I hope).

A most unusual luxury by 17th-century standards, a bath house stood in the garden's southern corner. Long since knocked down, its foundations were exposed in 1855 and show that the bath house had three apartments: a sitting room with a fireplace, a dressing and a bath room. The Summer House survives in the eastern corner. Its water-closet boasts twin privies.

### Public Parks and Gardens, Aberdeen

With Hazlehead, Victoria, Walker, Seaton, Duthie and Westburn Parks and Johnston, Rubislaw Terrace, Union Terrace and the university's Cruikshank Gardens, Aberdeen is especially well endowed, justifying her claim to be the "Flower of Scotland". The many flowers in these places and along such roads as Anderson Drive have won for the Granite City first place in the "Britain in Bloom" competition so often that Aberdeen gracefully forebears to enter.

Duthie Park's celebrated Winter Gardens are the third most visited attraction in Britain (after Kew Gardens and the Tower of London); its "Rose Mountain", over 100,000 roses growing on a terraced mound, is remarkable by any standards. The pink granite obelisk that towers above the Dee was removed to the park from the quadrangle of Marischal College in 1906. Originally the mini-estate of Arthurseat, the land was given to Aberdeen by Miss Charlotte Duthie on condition that a park was formed; it was opened formally by Princess Beartrice in 1883.

In Victoria Park is a garden for blind people, its plants specially selected for their strong scent and the labels beside them written in Braille. Hazlehead, aquired by the city in 1920, is Aberdeen's largest park and contains Scotland's only maze, with over a mile of paths. In Union Terrace Gardens is a working floral clock; Seaton Park is memorable for its sinuous paths beside the river Don and its fine views of St Machar's Cathedral.

*James Leslie Mitchell*
*— the author*
*Lewis Grassic Gibbon*

# A CULTURED LAND

Even if it lacks world-famous festivals or opera houses, museums or libraries, Grampian has a culture of a vibrancy and diversity lost to much of the western world. What is more, Grampian's culture is largely indigenous, distinctive in a homogenised world. Its roots are strong and many seek to ensure its survival in an age of uniformity.

## Language

When he alighted from the Edinburgh coach at the canny twa and twae toun of Aberdeenawa, he had some doubts if the inhabitants spoke any Christian language.

– John Galt, *The Entail*

At the heart of Grampian's culture is its tongue, the Doric. The name comes from the ancient Greek dialect of that name: the Dorians invaded Greece from the north around 1100 BC and their dialect, "Doric", has long been used to describe northern tongues or accents. The adjective "Doric" entered English as a description of any rustic dialect in the 16th and 17th centuries in, for example, the poems of Spenser and Milton. In the 19th century, Ramsay was the first to use it singularly to denote the Scottish tongue. By the 20th century, the word had come to be applied only to the tongue of Grampian, with "Scots", "Lallans" or "braid Scots" accepted descriptions of the language elsewhere in Scotland. For in Grampian, as ever relatively isolated from the forces of industrialisation and immigration, the Doric lived on, its bastions the fishing and farming communities.

Today, even the most passing of visitors to the region will hear the "gweed aal spik o the fowk", for its strength is still great and its usage all but universal. Its vitality distinguishes it sharply from the dying dialects of much of the rest of the United Kingdom. Heard not only in the factories and farms, the ceilidhs and the markets, Doric is naturally the everyday speech of doctors and lawyers, scientists and teachers in a region that is all but bilingual. The social stigma that attaches to dialect speech elsewhere has yet, mercifully, to afflict the Doric.

Those who would deride the speech of Grampian in its many forms as some corruption of "true" English demonstrate only their own ignorance. Doric has as long a lineage as any other Anglo-Saxon tongue, coming to Grampian with the Normans in the 12th century and gradually displacing Gaelic as the process of feudalisation continued. It is, as Derrick McLure puts it, "nobody's bad attempt at anything": the language in which John Barbour wrote his poem *The Brus* in 1375 (see chapter 2) maintains its vigour today. Doric poetry competitions in many of Grampian's schools, for example, augur well for the survival of the tongue amidst the babel of pop culture. In a country where the establishment still favours "English" and promulgates such decrees as: "If you allow the use of Doric by your pupils…you could be a contributor to what can only be described as a sorry state of affairs" (Scottish Education Dept. circular to teachers, March 1985), attitudes are blessedly different in Grampian. One of its recent Directors of Education, James Michie, far from discouraging the Doric, gave great encouragement to *Ten North East Poets*, a book edited by Leslie Wheeler of Aberdeen's Northfield Academy and now widely used in Grampian's schools. Headteachers like the redoubtable Gillespie Munro of Monymusk are devoted servants of the Doric, whilst the region's tongue is blessed to have such tireless advocates as Duncan Muirden of Clatt.

Although sharing many of the characteristics of Lowlands Scots and notwithstanding its many variants throughout Grampian, Doric is much more than a mere accent, maintaining still a rich vocabulary of its own. If someone from Edinburgh asked in Aberdeen for gym shoes, using the Edinburgh word *gutties*, he would be given golf balls: he should have asked for *jimmies*. Gardeners still improve their soil with *sharn* (manure) and water their plants with *roozers* (watering cans). Much as they always have, some people still *scutter* (work in a disorganised way) and *ficher* their time away, thinking, perhaps, of *rowies* (flat crispy rolls) or *baps* (floured rolls). Even if much of Doric's rural vocabulary has perished — a Grampian schoolchild is unlikely to know *yaavins* (bristles of barley) or *boodies* (scarecrows) — youngsters still enjoy a *cappie* (an ice-cream cone), play with *dazzies* (marbles) and occasionally *wheenge* or even *peenge* when denied their desires. As for those who talk posh, they're aye jist *gnappin* or even *gneppin* awa.

Doric is further distinguished by several fetching idiosyncrasies. Ubiquitously, *wh-* is replaced by *f-*: where, for example, is *far*, what is *fit*, who is *faa* and when is *fan*.

Throughout Grampian, one hears the greeting *fit like?*, a welcome alternative to "how are you"? "Why" becomes *"fit wye"*: whistle and weasel are

*'Catterline in winter',*
*by Joan Eardley*

*fussel* and *futrat*. This "f" substitution is an old and distinguished one: in his *Chronicle of Aberdeen*, Walter Cullen describes seeing King James VI in 1580: "...I paist to Dunnottar, fair I beheld his graice."

Equally distinctive of Doric is the use of *vr-* for the English *wr-*: wrong is *vrang*, write is *vreit*, wretch is *vratch*. For the English *-th-*, Doric reads a *-d-*: father, mother and brother are *fader*, *midder* and *breeder*. Heather is *hedder* and so on. A girl is a *quine* and a boy a *loun*; when other forms of Scots have ee- or ae- vowels, Doric uses an *ey-* diphthong: chain and wait become *chyne* and *wyte*. As it is in German but not in English, Doric sounds an initial "k" as in "**k**nock; in parts of Buchan still an initial "g" is likewise sounded, as in "**g**naw".

From the Esks to the Moray Firth, albeit with significant variations from district to district, Doric lives defiantly on. It bears with it the folk memory, the culture of an entire people from which there is much to be learned.

### Literature

The primary corpus of written Doric is poetry. Its earliest known progenitor is Barbour's *Brus*, by any standards poetry of the highest order:

> *A, fredome is a noble thing,*
> *Fredome mays man to haiff liking,*
> *Fredome all solace to man giffis;*
> *He levys at es that frely levys.*

But Barbour was not alone: in his study *The Bards of BonAccord* (1887), William Walker lists more than 70 other poets writing in Doric between 1375 and 1860 . Alexander Ross, born in 1699, is still well known for his poem *Helenore*, the tale of two lovers separated when one is carried away by Highland raiders. John Skinner, minister at Longside and friend of Robert Burns, is remembered for such of his fine poems as *The Monymusk Christmas Ba'ing*.

By the late 19th century, the agrarian life of Grampian was changing fast; in the wake of the 1872 Education Act, literacy spread and with it, of course, came "standard" English. In reaction to this, poets like Charles Murray (1864–1941) formed the vanguard of a vernacular movement, writing and publishing in Doric even from as far away, in Murray's case, as South Africa. His collection *Hamewith* is still in print. Murray's poetry has been criticised as facile, juvenile and nostalgic: Hugh McDiarmid, for example was scathing: "I say Charles Murray has not only never written a line of poetry in his life, but that he is constitutionally incapable of doing so." Yet many of its poems make such sweeping criticism questionable. There is a fine and sparse tautness about the eight lines of *Winter*, for example:

> Noo that cauldrife Winter's here
>   There's a pig in ilka bed,
> Kindlin's scarce an' coals is dear;
> Noo that cauldrife Winter's here
> Doddy mittens we maun wear,
>   Butter skites an' winna spread;
> Noo that cauldrife Winter's here
>   There's a pig in ilka bed.

Murray often makes much of the Doric, working the words to great effect, as for example in his poem after Horace's *Odes I, 9*:

Drift oxter-deep haps Bennachie,
Aneth its birn graens ilka tree,
The frost-boun' burn nae mair is free
    To bicker by.

Presenting a bust and a portrait of Murray in 1926, John Buchan said: "there is one quality about his work I would like to emphasise, and that is its catholicity. Like Robert Burns he produces all the great lines of Scottish tradition...Charles Murray gives us the broad Scots."

Others did likewise. Amongst them, JM Caie, David Rorie, Mary Symon, Flora Garry and JC Milne are still remembered. Now a hale 90, Garry has described Doric as a "spiritual birthright". Her poem *Bennygoak* is particularly fine:

It was jist a skelp of the muckle furth,
A skylter o roch grun,
Fin grandfadder's fadder bruke it in

Fae the hedder an the funn {whin}
Granfadder sklatit barn an byre,
Brocht water to the closs {farmyard}
Pat fail-dykes ben the bare brae face
An a cairt road tull the moss.

Of contemporary Doric poets, Sheena Blackhall is rightly respected.

But the largest corpus of Doric poetry is to be found in the oral tradition, in the works of people who could neither read nor write. Grampian's many ballads, composed from the 14th to the 18th centuries, were first collected by Gavin Greig and JB Duncan. Work is continuing on an eight-volume edition of the *Greig-Duncan Folk Song Collection*, edited by Patrick Shuldham Shaw, Emily Lyle and Peter Hall. Volume III has been recently published. The collection of some 3,500 texts and 3,300 tunes includes such magnificences as *Edom of Gordon*, *The Fire of Frendraught* and *The Baron of Brackley*.

The new life of the 19th century produced a new form, the bothy ballad, and in these too Grampian is especially rich. It is heartening to hear these old tales passed on at such events as the

Buchan Heritage Festival, held each May in Strichen.

In prose, George MacDonald was the first of Grampian's writers to win international acclaim. Now largely and sadly ignored, he was lionised by the Victorians, a close friend of Tennyson, Arnold, Ruskin and Lewis Carroll. Several of his 25 novels draw deeply on his origins in Grampian – he was born in Huntly in 1824. *Alex Forbes of Howglen,* for example, uses much Doric dialogue.

Still a recognised classic, the novel *Johny Gibb of Gushetneuk* by William Alexander (1826–81) is not only a triumph of prose Doric but also, set in the time of the Great Disruption (see chapter 4), a penetrating commentary on profound social changes. The novel is a remarkable achievement for a man who began life as a humble farm servant and ended it as editor of the *Aberdeen Free Press*. His book remains a magnificent embodiment of the language of Grampian, beginning, unforgettably, with the "orra loon" Tam Meerison helping Johny to yoke his cairt:

> Heely, heely, Tam, ye glaiket stirk - ye hinna on the hin shelvin' o' the cairt. Fat hae ye been haiverin at, min? That cauf saick'll be tint owre the back door afore we win a mile fae hame...

In the 20th century, Grampian has produced many novelists: Ian MacPherson, John R Allan, Nan Shepherd and Hunter Diack all have their following. But a great writer by any standards was Lewis Grassic Gibbon, born James Leslie Mitchell, under which name he had published four novels before a pseudonym and *Sunset Song* (1931) brought him huge acclaim. Two more novels (*Cloud Howe*, 1933, and *Grey Granite*, 1934) made up *A Scots Quair* and continued the story of Gibbon's principal character, Chris Guthrie. Gibbon's work is fine by any standards. Its mastery and exploitation of the Doric is compelling, an achievement that Gibbon recognised:

> Often the Scots writer is quite unaware of this essential foreignness in his work; more often, seeking an adequate or phrase, he hears an echo in an alien tongue that would adorn his meaning with a richness, a clarity and a conciseness impossible in orthodox English. That echo is from Braid Scots, from that variation of the Anglo-Saxon speech which was the tongue of the great Scots civilisation.

It is fitting that, at last, Gibbon is being given the formal recognition in his native place that he has long deserved. A memorial is to open shortly in Arbuthnott.

Almost as famous a novelist is Grampian's Jessie Kesson whose novels are based largely on her own childhood in the region. *The White Bird Passes* (1958), *Glitter of Mica* (1963) and *Another Time Another Place* (1983) are rightly acclaimed. Once more, one of their strengths is the application of the particularities of Grampian, its tongue, its customs, to the universalities of life. David Toulmin, still writing, is more in Gibbon's mould: his novel *Blown Seed* also has a central female character and compliments his many essays on farming life in his native Buchan. Alanna Knight's career began in Aberdeen with the publication in 1969 of her first novel, *Legend of the Loch*, based on Deeside, and followed since by 25 more books.

### Artists

For an isolated and sparsely populated region, Grampian can boast a formidable number of renowned artists. The earliest is George Jamesone (1589–1644), who dominated Scottish portraiture in his day. Horace Walpole called him "the Van Dyck of Scotland". Several of his portraits hang in Aberdeen's Trinity Hall on Holburn Street, testament to his early commissions by the guilds and burgesses of Aberdeen.

Sir George Chalmers, who died in 1791, was a direct descendant of Jamesone. He lived in Cults near Aberdeen and, like his progenitor, painted portraits. John Phillip (1817–67) transcended his humble origins as the son of an Old Meldrum shoemaker and became one of Queen Victoria's most favoured Scottish artists: she commissioned from him a portrait of Prince Albert. JB MacDonald (1829–1901), born in Morayshire, is rightly famed for his retrospective paintings of incidents during the Jacobite rebellions. Few Scottish paintings can be better known than those, much re-produced, of sheep in snow by Joseph Farquharson (1846–1935), Laird of Finzean on Deeside.

James Coutts Michie (1861–1919), a pupil of

Farquharson's, specialised in landscapes and was a founder member of Aberdeen Arts Society. David West (1868–1936) was born in Lossiemouth, the son of a ship's captain. Apart from participating in the Alaskan Gold Rush and making one visit to South America, he lived and painted in his native town.

James Cowie (1886–1956) moved from being art master at Fraserburgh Academy to becoming arguably one of the 20th century's most influential Scottish painters, even if his reputation has never scaled the heights of James McBey's (1883–1959), Newburgh's most famous son. Joining a bank at 15, McBey attended evening classes at Aberdeen's Gray's School of Art but was otherwise self-taught. North Africa was the inspiration for his best work, of which Aberdeen Art Gallery has an unparalleled collection.

Equally famous is Joan Eardley, despite her tragically early death in 1963. She studied under and was much influenced by James Cowie. From her house on the coast at Catterline, she painted haunting sea and landscapes.

Of contemporary Grampian artists, Ian Fleming is a former Principal of Gray's School of Art, as is Alastair Flattely, who now divides his time between Aberdeen and Spain. Ian MacKenzie Smith combines painting with his post as Arts Officer for Aberdeen City Council, having been Director of Aberdeen Art Gallery. On her farm near Newtonhill, Catherine Imhof-Cardinal paints in a semi-abstract manner and deserves her growing reputation.

## Music

Harp and fedyl both he fande
The getern and the sawtry
Lut and rybid ther gon gan,
Thair was al maner of mynstralsy.

        – Thomas the Rhymer

Nae man's a rale fiddle player till he can mak folk greet.

        – Niel Gow (1727–1807)

Notwithstanding her enduring contributions to the language, literature and art of Scotland, it is without question in the field of traditional music that Grampian has long been unsurpassed. Her fiddle music was and remains seminal, now at the heart of the vibrancy of the Scottish folk music revival.

For how long stringed instruments have been played in Grampian or, for that matter, anywhere, no-one knows. Whether plucked or bowed, stringed instruments are as old as recorded history. The *rebec* and the *croud* were early progenitors of the *fedyl* or fiddle. Melrose Abbey, begun in 1136, contains a carving of a female figure bowing a rebec. The Museum of Antiquities in Edinburgh houses a woodcarving of around 1600 which depicts a *fitheler* or fiddler.

One of the earliest fiddle tunes to become known and played throughout Scotland was composed in Grampian: *MacPherson's Rant*, if the improbable but fine tale is to be believed, was composed by the fiddler and freebooter James MacPherson on the eve of his execution at Banff's mercat cross in 1700. Standing on the gallows, he played his tune and offered his fiddle to the crowd. None would take it. With a curse, he broke it across his knee and went proudly to his death. Robert Burns wrote words for the tune in 1788:

Sae rantingly, sae wantonly,
Sae dauntingly gaed he,
He played a spring, and danc'd it round,
Below the gallows tree.

One of the earliest published collections of Scottish fiddle music (*A Collection of Countrey Dances*) was the work of another, though rather more respectable, Grampian loon, David Young, who was born in Aberdeen and educated from 1722 to 1726 at Marischal College. But the first of many distinguished north-east fiddlers of whom much is known was William Marshall of Fochabers (1748–1833).

Marshall was an extraordinary man. Of humble origins, he rose to be first butler then steward to the last Duke of Gordon at Gordon Castle. He was not only a most accomplished fiddler and composer, but also a self-taught mathematician, architect, astronomer and clockmaker. Robert Burns called him "the first composer of strathspeys of his age": the strathspey was and is a tune to which Scottish reels were danced. It arose in the 1760s around the river Spey in Grampian and is especially associated with two 18th-century fiddling families, the Browns of Strathspey and the Cummings of Freuchie. The strathspey is characterised by certain dotted rhythms, particularly the "Scots snap".

*Portrait of*
*James Scott Skinner*
*by David Waterson*

James learnt his craft, however, from his older brother Sandy and another great Grampian fiddler, Peter Milne (1824–1908), the "Tarland Minstrel".

Like Marshall and others before him, Skinner was not only a fiddler but an accomplished classical violinist as well. The many concerts that he gave, not only in Britain but America, were often a combination of classical and fiddle music. As the Inverness newspaper *The Highlander* recorded on 4 April 1879, "Mr Skinner really does the instrument justice. His performance of Mozart's *Figaro*, Paganini's *Rondo Pizzicato* and De Beriot's concerto were simply magnificent. And when he turned to the Strathspeys and the Reels, oh, what spirit and what finish."

Skinner has left over 600 compositions. He was indefatigable, giving at least 36 concerts in his 81st year and, once and for all, taking the fiddle beyond the bounds of an accompaniment to dance to find a voice of its own. His own words are his best valediction:

> The music that reaches and lives in the hearts of the people is the music that they whistle or sing at their daily toil or in their hours of recreation, that the mother croons o'er the cradle and that accompanies her children, a joyous companion, through life. Music thus entering into the hearts of the people proves by this test its real worth.
> – *People's Journal*, 21 April 1923.

Despite the other demands on his time, Marshall composed 257 recorded tunes, published in two volumes of 1781 and 1822. One of the most famous is his strathspey *Craigellachie Brig*, inspired by Telford's new iron bridge over the Spey (see chapter 5).

Less renowned than Marshall was his contemporary, Isaac Cooper (1754–1820), who lived in Banff and earned a living as a teacher of "the Harpsichord, the Violin, the Violincella, the Psaltery, the Clarionet, the Pipe and Taberer, the German Flute, the Scots Flute, the Fife in the regimental Stile, the Hautboy, the Irish Organ Pipe…And the Guitar, after a new method of fingering…"!

But Grampian's greatest fiddler and composer, still a man of international renown, was James Scott Skinner (1843–1927), the "Strathspey King", most famous of a distinguished fiddling family. His father had been a gardener at Banchory-Ternan until an accident with a gun cost him three fingers of his left hand. Undeterred, he learnt to play with his right hand.

The First World War and, then, the advent of radio and records saw a decline in fiddle music. Its survival in Grampian and in other parts of Scotland was due to the enduring efforts of fiddlers like John Murdoch Henderson (1902–72), Hector MacAndrew (1903–80) and William J Hardie (1916–) whilst the formation of the Scottish Country Dance Society in 1923 (it became "Royal" in 1951) and such other groups as the Highland Strathspey and Reel Society also contributed greatly to the fiddle's revival.

Henderson was born on the farm of Nether Oldwhat, near New Deer in Buchan, and educated at Peterhead Academy and Aberdeen University. A teacher, he was not only a prolific composer but also an avid collector of traditional music. His collection is preserved in the National Library, Edinburgh. His favourite tunes, *Flowers of*

*Scottish Melody*, including 40 of his own compositions, were reprinted in 1986 by the Buchan Heritage Society.

MacAndrew was born in Fyvie, Aberdeenshire to a famous fiddling family. His father was a fiddler and a piper, his grandfather a pupil of the renowned Niel Gow's last pupil, James MacIntosh of Dunkeld. In his day, MacAndrew was regarded as the finest living exponent of the fiddle. Although he composed some 80 tunes, none have yet been published.

Bill Hardie, apart from playing, teaching and broadcasting, passed on to his son Alastair the knowledge of the fiddle accumulated by generations of Hardie fiddlers. Alastair's publications on the fiddle and its music have preserved much of the knowledge and techniques of fiddle playing in Grampian.

MacPherson did not play his rant in vain. Almost 300 years later, the place of traditional music in the culture of Grampian and the rest of Scotland seems assured. Throughout the region, there are active Fiddle and Accordion Clubs, for example Keith's (Seafield Arms Hotel, 7.30 p.m., first Tuesday of each month), MacDuff's (Knowe's Hotel, 7.30 p.m., fourth Wednesday of each month) and Boddam's (Buchanness Hotel, 8 p.m., second Wednesday each month). Perhaps even more important to the vitality of fiddle music are Grampian's many Strathspey and Reel Societies (in Aberdeen, Elgin, Banchory, Huntly, Inverurie and Fochabers). These meet weekly and do much, with their competitions, to encourage young fiddlers.

A swelling of the art manifests itself each May with the Buchan Heritage Festival in Strichen, a prime mover thereof being a man only in his 30s, John Sorrie of Tarves, a fiddler himself and a wonderful repository of the tongue and ways of Grampian. Aberdeen's Robbie Shepherd is well known as a broadcaster and a devoted, tireless servant of traditional Scottish music. With such as these and the many young promising fiddlers of Grampian, William Marshall and James Scott Skinner may lie easily in their graves.

*Buchan Heritage Festival*

# REST AND RECREATION

If Grampian is all but unrivalled for the sheer variety of her leisure pursuits, she boasts too of the ease with which they may be pursued. Whether fishing on the Spey, walking up Clachnaben or listening to opera at Haddo, there is an absence of haste, a welcome ease. Indeed so relaxed is the matter of leisure in Grampian that preparation for rest and recreation in the region is a pleasure in itself.

This chapter seeks to make it easier still, describing in alphabetical order some of the range of leisures that Grampian affords.

### Accommodation
From the grandest castle to the humblest cottage, four-star hotel to youth hostel, there is accommodation available in Grampian to suit every taste and pocket. Full lists can be had at local Tourist Information Centres, which make no charge for booking accommodation. Grampian's main Tourist Information Centre is in St Nicholas House, Broad Street, Aberdeen. Like those in Banchory, Banff and Elgin, it is open all year round.

### Art
Aberdeen Art Gallery, Schoolhill, Aberdeen (open all year: Mon–Sat 10 a.m.–5 p.m., Thurs 10 a.m.–8 p.m., Sun 2 p.m.–5 p.m.) is an outstanding provincial gallery and the most important part of Grampian's art heritage, for all the many fine paintings which can be seen in those of the region's castles and stately homes that are open to the public. The eclectic permanent collection contains the paintings given to the city in 1872 by the eccentric philanthropist and granite merchant, Alexander MacDonald of Kepplestone. Amongst these is a unique collection of 92 uniform portraits of British artists. Otherwise, the gallery is especially strong on the works of Scottish painters and houses the largest collection of the works of James McBey (1883–1959) and fine examples of indigenous silver and glass.

There are, furthermore, a number of interesting private galleries in the region. The McEwan Gallery, Glen Gairn (open daily 10 a.m.–6 p.m.) concentrates on 18th–20th century oils, watercolours and prints. In Strathdon, the Candacraig Gardens Gallery (open 9 a.m.–7 p.m., 1 May–31 Oct) always displays interesting local work. The Tolquhon Gallery, near Tarves, Ellon (open Mon–Sat 11 a.m.–6 p.m., Sun 1 p.m.–6 p.m., closed Thurs) deals not only in paintings but in prints, sculpture and crafts. In Stonehaven, the Riverside Gallery on David Street (open Mon–Sat 9.30 a.m.–5.30 p.m.) is always exciting. On Aberdeen's Castle Street, Peacock Printmakers and Artspace Galleries (open Mon–Sat 9.30 a.m.–5.30 p.m.) has a wide selection of prints by Scottish artists. In Lumsden, the Scottish Sculpture Workshop (open daily 10 a.m.–4 p.m.) contains a small gallery for displaying sculpture made on the premises.

### Beaches
A great joy of Grampian is her many uncrowded and (relatively) clean, unspoilt and sandy beaches, for all that one hopes the councils will take their assets less for granted and pay more attention to pollution control and cleaning. From the lava cliffs of Milton Ness, the golden sands of **St Cyrus** (NO 75- 65-) sweep S for 3km to the mouth of the Esk. That the cliffs, dunes and beach fall within the St Cyrus Nature Reserve means that the beach remains unspoilt and undeveloped.

The easiest access to the beach is from the A92 at St Cyrus: a carpark is sign-posted and a path leads along the clifftop to the beach. Access to the southern end is off a side-road from the A92 to parking at Nether Warburton where boards are laid across the salt marsh to the dunes.

The beach at **Cruden Bay** (NK 09- 36-) is as fine and as long, even if debris from fishing and oil-related boats can prove unsightly at times. Further up the coast, the 6km of beach from Cairnbulg Point to **Rattray Head** (NK 06- 63-) are almost always awesomely deserted and wind-swept. Another 11km of beach stretch from Rattray Head S to Peterhead. Swimming is dangerous off both stretches, for the currents are infamous. **Sandend** beach (NJ 55- 66-) is Grampian's most sheltered, popular and picturesque, signposted off the A98. The beaches at **Burghead** (NJ 11- 69-) Findhorn and Roseisle (Forestry Commission) are fine, though once more local currents can be capricious.

### Birdwatching

With so much wild open country and so little industrialisation, Grampian is an ornithologist's paradise. Any walk on any of the region's hills (see **Hillwalking**) will afford sightings of many birds. But for coastal birds, three sites are especially rewarding: St Cyrus National Nature Reserve, near Montrose (open Tues–Sun 9 a.m.–5.30 p.m.), Sands of Forvie Nature Reserve, near Newburgh (open at all times) and Fowlsheugh RSPB Seabird Colony, Crawton, Stonehaven (open at all times but especially worth visiting April–July). For woodland birds, the Braeloine Visitor Centre, Glen Tanar, Aboyne (open April–Sept 10 a.m.–5 p.m.), the Loch Muick and Lochnagar Wildlife Reserve near Ballater and the Morrone Birchwood National Nature Reserve near Braemar are especially worth visiting. In more esoteric vein, Grampian allows the rare sight of trained falcons: the North East Falconry Centre, Bruntbrae Farm, near Banff has flying displays at 11 a.m. and 2 p.m. daily.

### Clay Pigeon Shooting

There are excellent shooting schools at Kingscliff near Methlick and Glenrinnes, Dufftown. Both have comprehensive layouts and regular competitions. Glenrinnes has a Starshot. Several country house hotels now have clay pigeon ranges or, at least, traps. Most hotels in the region can arrange clay pigeon shooting for guests.

### Eating out

Sadly and notwithstanding the coming of oil, Grampian is still something of a culinary desert. Fried fish and chips, served with tinned peas, predominates, whilst the microwave is everywhere too much abused. There are, however, a few oases. Most are expensive. In Aberdeen, the Silver Darling fully deserves its excellent reputation, especially for seafood. Furth of Aberdeen are some distinguished country house hotels and restaurants: Invery House, near Banchory, Pittodrie House, Pitcaple (especially fine wine list), Meldrum House, Old Meldrum, Raemoir House, Banchory, Kildrummy Castle Hotel near Alford and the Bishops Mill House Hotel, Elgin are all very fine. None are cheap. Yet all have an ambience that make them the perfect venue for a special occasion.

Lower down the range, the Atholl Hotel on Aberdeen's Kingsgate does fairly priced bar lunches and suppers of welcome and traditional quality. Bar meals at Ardoe House Hotel, just outside Aberdeen on the South Deeside road are good value. The meals at the Lairhillock near Maryculter, Aberdeen are worth the journey. The fish at the Marine Hotel, Stonehaven is always fresh. Bar meals at the Grant Arms Hotel, Monymusk are the only ones worth eating for miles around. In Newburgh, the Udny Arms Hotel deserves the highest praise. Near Turriff, the Towie Tavern tries hard and in Udny Station the Muffin and Crumpet Bistro is well worth visiting. The Redgarth in Old Meldrum does sound and affordable bar lunches and suppers. In Huntly, Luigi Zani does not advertise the fact that, by prior arrangement and at very moderate expense, he will serve you the finest Italian supper this side of Milan in his Springbank Guest House. Art lovers will enjoy his extensive and eclectic collection of paintings.

### Fishing

Grampian is blessed with fresh and sea-water fishing to suit every pocket, taste and mood. Sea-fishing can be easily done from any of the many coastal piers or from a hired boat. The latter, though, can be dangerous: current and wind on the north-east coast are notoriously fickle. One is best to sea-fish by boat in such a sheltered place as Findhorn Bay where boats can be hired from Moray Water Sports.

For salmon and seatrout, the season on most rivers is 11 Feb–31 October. Of recent years, the spring run of salmon has been poor: the autumn run is a safer bet. The brown trout season runs from 15 March–6 October. It is illegal to fish for salmon on a Sunday. Although some proprietors allow brown trout fishing on the Sabbath, it is not encouraged. Some beats are restricted to fly-fishing. Others prohibit certain types of bait: seek local advice.

Grampian contains a great many fishable waters, the Bervie and the Bogie, the Feugh and the Lossie, the Ugie and the Ythan. Local hotels and tackle shops supply permits and advice. But famous the world over, especially for their salmon, are the rivers Dee, Don and Spey. Sporting agencies like Macsport in Aboyne or Meadowhead in New Machar can arrange extremely exclusive and expensive fishing on the best beats of these rivers. One rod for a couple on certain beats of the Spey in prime season can cost as much as £1,500 for a week. Equally, it is possible to fish on these three great rivers much more cheaply.

Most fishing on the Dee is privately owned, although the Aberdeen and District Angling Association has a good beat. Cheaper beats are available by the day or week from £12 or £60 respectively from the Scotia Sporting Agency. For the prime months of August and September, rates rise to a typical £40 and £200 respectively, for example on the Glen Tanarbeats .

The Don, however, is much more varied in price: a season ticket (available from the Kintore Arms Hotel) for the 4km of the right bank and 5.6km of the left bank at Kintore is outstanding value at £60 for visitors and £20 for residents. A weekly permit is £23 and a day's fishing £8. The Monymusk beat costs £21 per day or £90 per week (permits from the Grant Arms Hotel, Monymusk). The services of a ghillie are available on the Monymusk beat for £20 per day.

The Spey, like the Dee, is more exclusive. The best buy, at £10 per day or £50 per week, is for the Aberlour beats. Permits are only available, however, to guests staying overnight at either the Aberlour, Lour or Dowans Hotels.

In addition to river fishing, Grampian boasts a number of lochs and reservoirs. The Glen Tanar Loch is picturesque and well stocked with rainbow trout. A day permit is £14 to include a boat. The 5-acre loch at Mill of Strachan is stocked with rainbow trout and costs £10 per day. Near Lhanbryde, Loch Na Bo offers fine brown trout fishing (fly only) for £3 per rod per session plus £2.50 for boat hire. Grampian's best pike fishing is on Aboyne Loch for £3 per day. Loch Kinord offers both pike and perch.

The reservoirs at Fedderate, near Cuminestown and Glenlatterach near Elgin offer brown and rainbow trout fishing at very reasonable prices.

## Flying

For paragliding in Grampian, contact Scottish Paragliders at 4 Candacraig Square, Strathdon AB36 8XT. The Deeside Gliding Club organises conventional gliding from its airfield near Dinnet. There are two microlight flying clubs in the region: tel: 0224 642520 or 0224 722517. For conventional flying, contact the Dyce Flying Club. The Scottish Hang Gliding Championships are held each July at Cairnwell, Glenshee. The Cairnwell Hang Gliding School provides both equipment and tuition.

## Golf

There are at present a staggering 46 established golf courses in Grampian, not including the one currently under construction nor the private nine-hole course at Balmoral. There are courses to satisfy both the occasional hack and the professional. The region's courses are unrivalled in their diversity, ranging from the traditional links course (Royal Aberdeen tel: 0224 702221 where, in 1538, golf is first recorded as being played in Grampian; Cruden Bay tel: 0542 40685 or Peterhead tel: 0779 72129) to parkland courses like Hazlehead (tel: 0224 317336), Deeside (tel: 0224 867697) or Keith (tel: 05422 2469) and natural terrain courses like Braemar, at 366mthe highest 18-hole course in Britain (tel: 03397 41618), Torphins ( 03398 82493, eves & w/ends) or Ballater (03397 55567).

The municipal courses are open to the public at all times. The private clubs may be played by prior booking or by reserving a tee-off time on arrival. Advance booking for weekends is advisable. Green fees vary, from £5 for a round on municipal courses to £15 on the private championship courses.

Whilst it is invidious to single out courses, most golfers would agree that every golfer should experience the magnificence of Duff House Royal near Banff on the Moray Firth (tel: 02612 2062). A complete but charming contrast are the nine holes and 1,988m of Auchenblae (no telephone). Royal Invercauld, near Braemar (opening 1 April 1992) is dominated, just beyond the 18th green, by a huge granite obelisk to one of Prince Albert's corgis. Stonehaven (tel: 0569 62124) is splendidly set along the sea cliffs.

The earliest thorough description of the game of golf in Scotland, referring to bunkers, iron clubs, holes and sand for teeing up, is in a 1632 Latin grammar for Aberdeen schools. It is, then, all the more fitting that golf should now so thrive in Grampian.

## Highland Games

Although not strictly in the Highlands, nonetheless Grampian now hosts a number of fine Highland Games where the traditional contests – tossing the caber, piping, wrestling – go on. All are open to the public for a small admission fee. The most famous is the Braemar Royal Highland Gathering, held on the first Saturday of each September and still attended by the royal family from their nearby Balmoral Castle in perpetuation of a royal presence at the Games that began in 1848. Locals claim, however, that their Royal Gathering has antecedents as old as 973 when King Kenneth II held a race on the nearby hill of his name, Craig Choinich.

Aberdeen holds its Highland Games in June; in July, there are Games at Dufftown, Elgin, Forres, Stonehaven and Tomintoul and in August at Aboyne, Aberlour and Ballater. In Strathdon, each August's Lonach Gathering has a character all of its own: its March of the Clansmen, from Inverernan

3km to the W, is unique and unforgettable. The Lonach Games began in 1836, four years after the founding of the Lonach Highland and Friendly Society for the "preservation of the Highland garb and language". One of the Lonach's contests is "putting the stone", an adaptation of the ancient Highland Lifting Stones: before formal Games began, Highland lads tried their strength by lifting well-known stones like the *clach thogolach* on Deeside, near the confluence of the Luibeg and the Derry.

## Museums

With some 35 museums, large and small, Grampian is amply endowed. A wealth of material enhances our understanding of the region's past and, therefore, its present.

The Marischal Museum within Marischal College, Broad Street, Aberdeen (open Mon–Fri, 10 a.m.–5 p.m.; Sun 2 p.m.–5p.m.) houses a fine collection of anthropological artefacts from all over the world. The Aberdeen Maritime Museum in Provost Ross's House, Shiprow, Aberdeen (open Mon–Sat, 10 a.m.–5 p.m) tells the story of local shipbuilding, fishing and the more recent one of North Sea oil.

For those interested in transport, the Grampian Transport Museum in Alford (open 10.30 a.m.–5 p.m. every day, 1 April–30 Sept.) houses a fine collection of vintage cars, motorcycles, buses and tractors. Adjacent is the Railway Museum, from which runs Britain's only 2ft narrow gauge railway. The Moray Motor Museum, Bridge Street, Elgin (1 April–31 Oct, daily 10 a.m.–5 p.m) houses fine vintage cars, mororcycles and memorabilia. In Buckie, the Maritime Museum and Peter Anson Gallery (Mon–Fri 10 a.m.–8 p.m, Sat 10 a.m.–noon) tells the story of fishing in Buckie from 1800. The gallery displays a selection of the museum's collection of the artist Anson's work. Still on the sea, the Arbuthnot Museum, St Peter St, Peterhead (Mon–Sat, 10 a.m.–noon and 2 p.m.–5 p.m.) has a fascinating collection of whaling memorabilia and Eskimo artefacts of international importance.

The Elgin Museum (1 April–30 Sept, Mon–Fri 10 a.m.–4 p.m) has had since 1836 to amass notable collections of archaeological material; its fossil collection, which includes the Elgin Reptiles, is of international standing. The Falconer Museum, Tolbooth Street, Forres (1 May–30 Sept, Mon–Sat 9.30 a.m.–5.30 p.m.; July and August, Sun 2 p.m.–6 p.m.; Oct–April Mon–Fri 10 a.m.–4.30 p.m.) has an outstanding collection of local and natural history.

More recondite but well worth visiting are the Gordon Highlanders Museum, Viewfield Road, Aberdeen (all year Wed and Sun, 2 p.m.–5 p.m.), the Blairs College Museum near Aberdeen (last Sat of every month 2 p.m.–5 p.m, other times by appointment: tel: 0224 867626 or 861177) and "Remains to be Seen", an astonishing collection of Victorian, Edwardian and 20th century clothing, lace and jewellery housed in Quilquox Croft, Ythanbank, Ellon (daily all year 10.30 a.m.–4.30 p.m.: tel 03587 229). Two small but fine agricultural museums are Ladycroft Farm Museum, Archiestown, Moray (daily all year, 10 a.m.–5 p.m) and Northfield Farm Museum near New Pitsligo (June–Sept, daily 1.30 p.m.–5.30 p.m.).

## Music

There are regular concerts in Aberdeen's Music Hall (tel: 0224 641122 for programme and bookings). The Royal Scottish National Orchestra, for example, brings the Scottish Proms there each year. Haddo House Hall near Tarves (tel: Tarves 770, 10.30 a.m.–2. p.m.30, weekdays) has developed an international reputation for the quality and diversity of its productions, especially of "scaled-down" opera. Programmes and tickets are available at the Aberdeen Box Office on Union Street, Aberdeen (0224 641122).

Each May, Banchory holds a Festival of Scottish Music and Strichen a Buchan Heritage Festival. Keith holds a Traditional Music and Song Festival in June and Aberdeen an Alternative Music Festival each October. Details of all these may be had from Tourist Information Centres.

## Pony Trekking and Riding

Taking advantage of the peace and space of Grampian, there are many riding and trekking centres which offer the sport in splendid countryside. A full list is available from Tourist Information Centres, but five of the region's 20 centres, selected for the beauty of the rides they afford are: Glentanar Riding Centre, Aboyne, Balmoral Estates, Crathie, Garmouth Riding Centre, Spey Farm, North Gellan Stables, Tarland and Kirkton Riding Centre, Turriff. Brideswell Riding Stables, Cushnie offers instruction in carriage driving. All rates on application.

## Religion

The majority of churches in Grampian are Church of Scotland (Protestant). Most hold Sunday services at 11 a.m., although in rural areas where one minister might serve two or even three churches, services are typically at 10 a.m. or 11.30 a.m. Grampian's Church of Scotland Cathedral is St Machar's, Aberdeen. Of particular interest to many visitors is Crathie Church, 14.5km E of Braemar on the A93, and attended by the Royal Family when they are in residence at Balmoral. Sunday service is at 11.30 a.m.

Grampian's Catholic Cathedral is St Mary's, Huntly Street, Aberdeen. It holds mass on Sundays at 8 a.m. and 11.15 a.m. and 6 p.m. Amongst others, there are Catholic churches in Aboyne, Ballater, Banchory, Braemar, Dufftown, Ellon, Huntly, Inverurie, Keith (St Thomas: partly copied from Rome's Santa Maria degli Angeli) and Stonehaven. Despite the closure of the school, Mass is still sung in Blair's College chapel at 9.30 a.m. each Sunday.

The Church of England (Anglican) in Scotland is the Episcopalian Church. Amongst others, there are Anglican churches in Alford, Ballater, Banchory, Braemar, Dufftown, Insch and Keith. Check church notice boards for the times of sevices. A "high" Anglican church is St Margaret's on Aberdeen's Gallowgate.

For Muslims, Aberdeen has a Mosque on the Spital. There is a Tabernacle on Hope Street, Peterhead. At Findhorn, the Findhorn Foundation (open 10 a.m.–5 p.m weekdays, 2 p.m.–5 p.m. weekends) welcomes visitors for a few hours or several months. Eschewing any formal doctrines or creeds, the Foundation recognises that "all the major world religions share the same underlying principles" and seeks to put these principles into practice.

### Sailing

Stoneywood Outdoor Activity Centre organises sailing classes on the Loch of Skene (near Aberdeen) during the months of April, May and June. Moray Water Sports run sailing and windsurfing courses in Findhorn Bay from April–October. Aberdeen and Stonehaven Yacht Club sails in Stonehaven harbour.

### Shooting

There is a great deal of high-quality shooting available in Grampian, whether rough shooting, roe deer or stalking, driven pheasant or grouse. Most rural hotels can arrange shooting for their guests. Otherwise, contact one of Grampian's sporting agencies like MacSport or Meadowhead.

### Skiing

There is fine downhill skiing, in a good winter, at the Lecht , Glenshee and Cairngorm. There is a dry ski slope in Alford, open Tues 9.30 a.m.–11.30 a.m.,

Friday 6.30 p.m.–8.30 p.m., Sat and Sun 1 p.m.–5 p.m. Grampian's cross-country (nordic) skiing is outstanding: details from Ski Glenfiddich in Dufftown, Braemar Outdoor Centre, Highland Activity Holidays in Dufftown or Glenmulliach Nordic Ski Centre, Tomintoul.

### Tennis

Most of Grampian's larger towns and villages have public courts or clubs that are open to the public. Ask at your nearest Tourist Information Centre.

### Visitor Centres

Baxters of Speyside sell their quality Scottish foodstuffs throughout the world. Their factory by the A96 just W of Fochabers has a visitor centre, open 9.30 a.m.–5 p.m. Mon–Fri, March– December and from 16 May–13 Sept from 11 a.m.–6 p.m. on Sat and Sun. Another of Grampian's great industries, textiles, is well encountered at the Crombie Woolen Mill and Visitor Centre, Woodside, Aberdeen: open all year 9 a.m.–4.30 p.m. Mon–Sat and noon–4.30 p.m. on Sundays. For children, the Storybook Glen theme park at Maryculter, Aberdeen is fun: open daily 10 a.m.–6 p.m, March–October. For rose lovers, a visit to the renowned rose growers J Cocker & Sons on Aberdeen's Lang Stracht will prove rewarding. The Agricultural Heritage Centre at Aden near Mintlaw has something to interest everybody: open May–September daily 11 a.m.–5 p.m.

### Walking

An excellent booklet, *Hillwalking in Grampian Highlands*, is available for £1 from Tourist Information Centres and describes in detail 36 fine walks. Caution is the watchword: the weather on the higher hills and mountains of Grampian is notoriously fickle. Five relatively easy walks, however, give a comprehensive view of the endlessly varied beauty of Grampian: Clachnaben, Linn of Dee, Tap o' Noth, Bennachie and Glen Rinnes. Even for these, stout footwear and protective clothing are essential.

#### *Clachnaben*

*A* return walk of some 2.5 hours and 9.7km affords glorious views over Deeside and the Mearns. The ascent of 427km to the dramatic granite tor on the summit is best begun from the farm track 0.5km N of the Bridge of Dye on the B974 Cairn o' Mount road (NO 649 867): there are two cottages almost opposite the track. Follow the track through a wood and then downhill until a bridge crosses the Water of Dye. There, take the path to the right. This crosses Miller's Bog and comes in 1.6km to a wood. From the top corner of the wood the path follows the bottom of a ravine and leads to a col. From there, walk up the ridge to the summit. Only experienced climbers should attempt to climb the slippery and steep south side of the tor. During the grouse shooting season (12 August–30 September), you should only walk up Clachnaben on a Sunday.

### Linn o' Dee
This flat and easy walk of some 3 hours return takes in some breathtaking scenery and is very representative of the beauty of Deeside. In Braemar, take the minor road (signposted Inverey) that winds W along the river Dee's flood plain. From the public carpark at Linn of Dee, follow the track W along the N side of the Dee to White Bridge, where the blue waters of the Dee meet the greens of the Geldie. Keep to the path on the N side of the river which leads in 0.8km to the Chest of Dee, a series of deep pools. From here a path leads back to White Bridge and on back to Linn of Dee. When the Dee is in spate, the Linn, a narrow gorge 137m in length and in some places only 1.2m across, can be awesome. Here, as Al McConnochie put it, "the Dee hastens forward, seething, churning, and rushing with, as it were, the impetuosity of youth and the strength of maturity." The poet Byron had a great love for the place, despite almost losing his life here in a fall. Be warned!

### Tap O' Noth
The summit at 564m affords commanding views in every direction. The return walk takes some 3 hours up a straightforward path that is very steep towards the top. Take the A941 W from the village of Rhynie. There is a signpost to the public carpark 3.2km W of Rhynie. From there the path is unmistakable. Less arduously, one can follow the track that winds up and sadly scars Tap o' Noth. The summit contains one of Europe's finest examples of an iron-age hill fort.

### Bennachie
Rightly famed in poetry and song, Bennachie is an endlessly fascinating hill, dominating the fertile farmlands of Aberdeenshire. There are three recognised routes to the most prominent of Bennachie's three summits, the Mither Tap (518m): the shortest starts at the Forestry Commission's Esson's carpark, the longest from their carpark at the Back o' Bennachie. The most rewarding route takes 2 hours return and begins at the Rowantree carpark: follow the A96 N from Inverurie for 6.4km. Just before the A96/B9002 fork, turn sharp left and under a railway bridge, sign-posted for the Maiden Stone and Chapel of Garioch. The carpark is sign-posted to your right after 0.8km. From there a clear path leads up through trees to the "Maiden Causeway", a track leading gently up the shoulder of Bennachie. Ascending the actual Mither Tap, another fine iron-age hill fort, involves a steep scramble through the stones that formed the fort's formidable walls. An indicator on the summit identifies the distant hills.

### Ben Rinnes
The views are stupendous from this lonely hill of granite some 400 million years old. The eye reaches right across the Laich of Moray to the Moray Firth and the far hills of Ross. The main summit is Scurran of Lochterlandoch. The walk there is a straightforward 3 hours return on a clear path. Take the B9009 SW out of Dufftown. After 4km, turn right up minor road to Glack. Park after 0.8km and walk W from NJ 359 284 up a track which becomes a path after 366m. The path leads over Round Hill and Roy's Hill and through the Black Banks to the summit.

# SELECT BIBLIOGRAPHY

**GENERAL**
*Exploring Scotland's Heritage: Grampian*. Ian A G Shepherd, HMSO, 1986.
*The Grampian Book*, ed. Donald Omand. The Northern Times Ltd., 1987.
*The Moray Book*, ed. Donald Omand. Edinburgh, 1976.
*Discovering Aberdeenshire*, Robert Smith. John Donald, 1988.
*Aberdeen*, WA Brogden. Scottish Academic Press, 1986.
*Banff and Buchan*, Charles McKean. Mainstream, 1990.
*The District of Moray*, Charles McKean. Scottish Academic Press, 1987.
*Portrait of the Spey*, Francis Thompson. Robert Hale, 1979.
*Donside*, AI McConnochie. James G Bisset, 1985.
*Deeside*, AI McConnochie. James G Bisset, 1985.
*Portrait of Aberdeen and Deeside*, Cuthbert Graham. Robert Hale, 1984.
*What's In a Name?* Sheila Hamilton. Aberdeen Journals, 1986.
*Highways and Byways Round Stonehaven*, Archibald Watt. Gourdas House, 1984.
*Early Sources of Scottish History*, A O Anderson. Paul Watkins, 1990.
*The Statistical Account of Scotland*, 1791-99.
*The New Statistical Account of Scotland*, 1841-55.

**CHAPTER 1 - BARROWS, CAIRNS, STONES AND CIRCLES OF THE MOON**
*Sculptured Stones of Scotland* (2 vols), John Stuart. Aberdeen, 1856; Edinburgh, 1867.
*Proceedings of the Society of Antiquaries of Scotland*, FR Coles. Edinburgh, 1902-6.
*The Early Christian Monuments of Scotland*, Romilly Allen. Edinburgh, 1904.
*The Chambered Tombs of Scotland*, A S Henshall. Edinburgh, 1963.
*Megalithic Sites in Britain*, A Thom. Oxford, 1967.
*The Stone Circles of the British Isles*, Aubrey Burl. Yale, 1976.
*The Symbol Stones of Scotland*, Anthony Jackson. Orkney, 1984.

**CHAPTER 2 - BATTLES AND BLOODSHED**
*Grampian Battlefields*, Peter Marren. AUP, 1990.
*The Brus*, John Barbour. ed. W W Skeat, Edinburgh, 1894.

**CHAPTER 3 - CHURCHES, CLERICS AND CATECHISMS**
*Warlords and Holy Men*, Alfred P Smyth. EUP, 1984.
*The Faith of the Scots*, Gordon Donaldson. Batsford, 1990.
*The Pluscarden Story*, Ronald Hamilton. Pluscarden, 1988.
*St Columba of Iona*, Lucy Menzies. The Iona Community, 1970.

**CHAPTER 4 - FORTS, CASTLES AND CIVILIZATION**
*The Scottish Castle*, Stewart Cruden. Spurbooks, 1981.
*The Castles of Scotland*, Susan Ross. Letts Guides, 1973.
HMSO Guides to: *Kildrummy, Glenbuchat, Huntly*.
NTS Guides to Crathes: *Craigievar, Leith Hall, Fyvie, Brodie, Castle Fraser*.

**CHAPTER 5 - THE AGE OF IMPROVEMENT**
*The Shaping of 19th century Aberdeenshire*, Sydney Wood. SPA Books, 1985.
*The Age of Improvement*, Asa Briggs. Longman, 1959.

**CHAPTER 6 - FISHING: MORTAL MAN, IMMORTAL SEA**
*Fishing off the Knuckle*, David W Summers. AUP, 1988.
*Fishing Boats and Fisherfolk*, Peter F Anson. London, 1930.
*Scottish Fishing Craft*, Gloria Wilson. Edinburgh, 1965.
*The Fringe of Gold*, Charles MacLean. Canongate, 1985.

**CHAPTER 7 - WHISKY: WATERS OF LIFE**
*The Whisky Distilleries of the United Kingdom*, A Barnard. 1877. Reprinted by David and Charles, 1969.
*The Whiskies of Scotland*, RJS McDowall. Revised by William Waugh, John Murray, 1986.

**CHAPTER 8 - PARKS, GARDENS AND FLORA**
*North East Castles*, ed. John S Smith. AUP, 1990.
*The Country House Garden*, G Jackson-Stops and J Pipkin. National Trust/Pavilion, 1987.
NTS Guides to *Crathes* and *Pitmedden Gardens*.

**CHAPTER 9 - A CULTURED LAND**
*Scots, The Mither Tongue*, Billy Kay. Grafton, 1988.
*The Dictionary of Scottish Painters*, Paul Harris & Julian Halsby. Canongate/Phaidon, 1990.
*Scottish Fiddlers and their Music*, Mary Anne Alburger. Gollancz, 1983.
*Scottish Fiddle Music in the 18th Century*, David Johnson. John Donald, 1984.

# INDEX